Bronze Age Field System at Tower's Fen, Thorney, Peterborough

Excavations at 'Thorney Borrow Pit' 2004-2005

Andrew Mudd and Ben Pears

with contributions from

Maisie Taylor, Nick Branch, Barbara Silva, Christopher Green, Scott Elias, Alys Vaughan-Williams, Iñaki Valcarcel, Imogen Poole, Karen Deighton, Stuart Needham, Andy Chapman, Pat Chapman and Steve Critchley

Illustrations by

Jacqueline Harding and Pat Walsh
with Steven J. Allen

Edited by

Andy Richmond, Gary Coates, Andy Chapman and Pat Chapman

BAR British Series 471
2008

Published in 2016 by
BAR Publishing, Oxford

BAR British Series 471

Phoenix Consulting Archaeology Limited, Northamptonshire Archaeology
Bronze Age Field System at Tower's Fen, Thorney, Peterborough

ISBN 978 1 4073 0363 5

BAR Publishing is the trading name of British Archaeological Reports (Oxford) Ltd.
British Archaeological Reports was first incorporated in 1974 to publish the BAR
Series, International and British. In 1992 Hadrian Books Ltd became part of the BAR
group. This volume was originally published by Archaeopress in conjunction with
British Archaeological Reports (Oxford) Ltd / Hadrian Books Ltd, the Series principal
publisher, in 2008. This present volume is published by BAR Publishing, 2016.

Printed in England

BAR
PUBLISHING

BAR titles are available from:

BAR Publishing
122 Banbury Rd, Oxford, OX2 7BP, UK
EMAIL   info@barpublishing.com
PHONE   +44 (0)1865 310431
FAX   +44 (0)1865 316916
www.barpublishing.com

CONTENTS

Figures

Colour Plates

Plates

Tables

Appendices

Contributors

Project Management: Andrew Richmond and Gary Coates, *Phoenix Consulting Archaeology Ltd*

Andrew Mudd, *Senior Project Officer, Northamptonshire Archaeology*

Maisie Taylor, *Fenland Archaeological Trust, Flag Fen Centre, Peterborough*

Dr Nick Branch, *Director ArchaeoScape, Department of Geography, Royal Holloway University of London*

Dr Imogen Poole, *Environmental Archaeologist, G3, Eiteren 99, 3401 PS IJsselstein, Netherlands*

Dr Barbara Silva, *Research Assistant, Department of Geography, Royal Holloway University of London*

Dr Christopher Green, *Senior Geoarchaeologist, ArchaeoScape*

Prof. Scott Elias, *Lecturer in Physical Geography, Department of Geography, Royal Holloway University of London*

Alys Vaughan-Williams, *Environmental Archaeologist, ArchaeoScape*

Iñaki Valcarcel, *Laboratory Technician, Department of Geography, Royal Holloway University of London*

Andy Chapman, *Senior Archaeologist, Northamptonshire Archaeology*

Dr Stuart Needham, *Archaeological Consultant*

Karen Deighton, *Environmental Officer, Northamptonshire Archaeology*

Pat Chapman, *Post-excavation Supervisor, Northamptonshire Archaeology*

Steve Critchley, *Independent Archaeologist, Peterborough*

Acknowledgements

Phoenix Consulting and Northamptonshire Archaeology are particularly grateful to Aggregate Industries UK Ltd for funding the archaeological work, including the present publication. Staff who were particularly involved on the ground were John Penny (Aggregate Industries Area Estates Manager), Fred Dooris (Pode Hole Quarry Manager), Nigel Haynes (AI Croft) and Neil Gamble (Bardon Aggregates). Ben Robinson, of Peterborough City Council Archaeology Service, oversaw the fieldwork and offered valuable advice during the course of excavations. We are particularly grateful to Patrick Daniel of Network Archaeology for details ahead of the publication of their Pode Hole report.

Phoenix Consulting and Northamptonshire Archaeology also wish to thank the many members of staff who undertook the excavation in the winter of 2004. These include in particular Ben Pears and Tam Webster who supervised the work, along with Nathan Flavell, Andrew Ginns, Samantha Hepburn, Jennifer Jackson, Mo Jones, Adam Lodoën, Mark Patenall, Tom Phillips, Jackaline Robertson, Ben Savine, Carol Simmonds, Rob Smith, Steven Tamborello, Michael Tunnicliffe and LeeAnne Whitelaw. The publication was edited by Andy Richmond for Phoenix Consulting and Andy Chapman and Pat Chapman for Northamptonshire Archaeology. Typesetting is by Drew Smith.

Digital mapping is reproduced under licence from the Ordnance Survey (Northamptonshire County Council Licence No. 100019331).

Abstract

Archaeological excavation of about 11ha of land at Tower's Fen, Thorney, Peterborough, investigated part of an extensive pattern of ditched enclosures and fields associated with several waterholes and two ponds. One large pit, which may have been a waterhole, yielded Early Bronze Age pottery and is radiocarbon dated to the terminal 3rd millennium BC. Two other dates from the ponds came out at around 1500-1300 BC. The other features were probably also Middle to Late Bronze Age although the limited quantity of pottery was not datable precisely.

Waterlogged material recovered from the deeper features included most of an unusual wooden tub or bucket, as well as other pieces of worked wood. The palaeo-environmental evidence from pollen, plant macro-fossils, insects and charred plant remains indicated that the land supported a mosaic of woodland, scrub, arable fields, meadow and short grazed grassland. A wide variety of trees was present, particularly wet-loving species such as willow and alder, and there was abundant evidence for coppicing.

Nearby excavations at Pode Hole, and the wider picture provided by plotted cropmarks, indicate that the site formed part of an extensive prehistoric landscape. It is suggested that the Bronze Age agricultural landscape developed piecemeal and was based upon a mixed arable and pastoral economy. This contrasts with Fengate and other landscapes of this period where large-scale land divisions have been related to intensive livestock management. The sparse evidence for contemporaneous settlement is typical of many sites of this period.

Chapter 1: **Introduction**

Preamble

Phoenix Consulting Archaeology Ltd in association with Northamptonshire Archaeology were commissioned by Aggregate Industries UK Limited to undertake an archaeological excavation at Tower's Fen, Thorney (NGR TF 265 042) ahead of the extraction of aggregate for the construction of the Thorney by-pass. The site lay 1.2 km west of Thorney, bounded by the A47 and Pode Hole Farm and quarry to the south, with arable fields to the north, east and west (Fig 1). The excavation was carried out between October 2004 and January 2005.

The archaeological work was designed to comply with the policy and planning conditions of the Minerals Planning Authority (MPA) for the City of Peterborough. The background, objectives and procedures for the work were set out in a Specification prepared by Phoenix Consulting and subsequently approved by the Peterborough City Council Archaeology Service as archaeological adviser to the MPA (Coates and Richmond 2004b).

Previous Archaeological Work

Desk-Based Assessment

An archaeological desk-based assessment had previously been carried out as part of the Cultural Heritage input into the Environmental Statement for the borrow pit (Coates & Richmond 2004a). The desk-based study assessed the extent of known archaeology in and around the development area. The study concluded that the site was located within a landscape with a relatively dense pattern of archaeological evidence.

Aerial Photographic Assessment

To fully appraise the evidence, an aerial photographic assessment was undertaken to inform a trial trenching evaluation (Palmer 2004). The aerial photographic assessment mapped features, both archaeological and non-archaeological from air photographs held at the Cambridge University Collection of Air Photographs and at the National Monuments Record (Swindon). Part of this mapping has been reproduced as Figure 2.

The plot clearly shows a co-axial field pattern made up of ditches and droveways. Fields are of varying sizes and shapes and appear as mixed rectangular forms with larger enclosures. While undated, it was considered likely that these fields were of Bronze Age date, and essentially an extension of the Bronze Age fields known from Pode Hole Quarry south of the A47 (Phoenix Consulting forthcoming).

Trial Trenching

The trial trenching was undertaken by Phoenix Consulting in July 2004 and consisted of twenty-five 50m by 2m trenches positioned to investigate features identified from the aerial photographs (Coates & Cherrington 2004). The trenching identified a number of the cropmark features, although there was a shortage of artefacts and a lack of evidence to suggest that the prehistoric field ditches were associated with settlement. Overall, it was concluded that the site was occupied by agricultural fields and enclosures of probable Bronze Age date. The archaeology did not appear to be well preserved, probably because of the intensive arable farming of modern times.

Objectives

As a result of the preliminary work it was decided that the archaeology of the site was not of sufficient merit to warrant preservation in situ but would be preserved 'by record' using a strip, map and sample excavation methodology.

Sampling by excavation would be used to characterize key elements on the site and this would enable a chronological framework to be constructed alongside further investigation of possible nuclei of activity.

A number of key aims of the excavation were identified in the Specification and are re-iterated below.

- Expand current knowledge of patterns of fen edge exploitation and settlement at different periods
- Explore the transition from Late Neolithic and Early Bronze Age monument-dominated landscapes to the Later Bronze Age and Iron Age settlements and field landscapes
- Determine the main orientation and spatial pattern of the field system
- Elucidate the relationship between the borrow pit field system and the field system identified at Pode Hole Farm
- Investigate the relationship between the field system and its antecedents

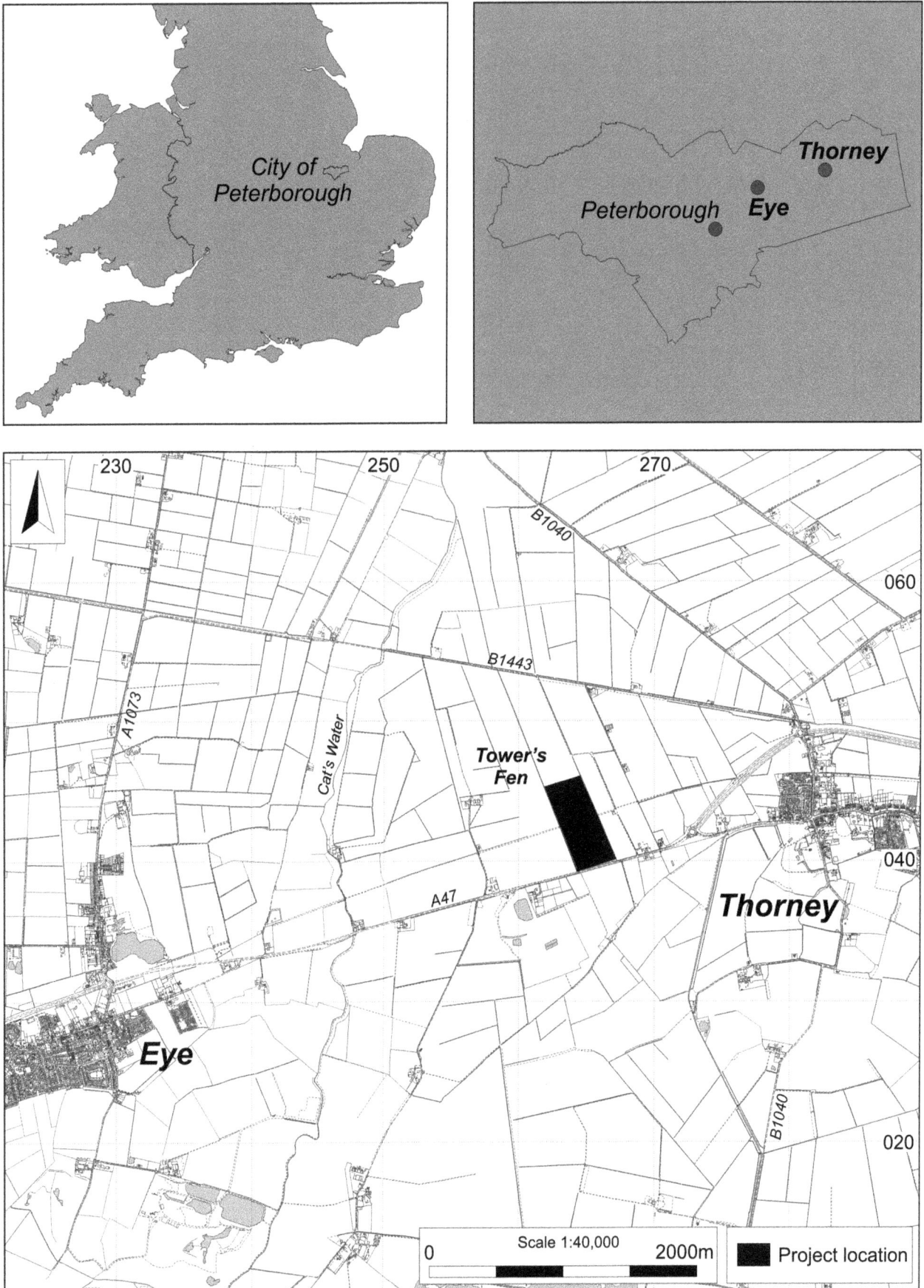

Fig 1. Project location
© Crown copyright. Licence No. 100019331. Published 2007

Methodology

The soils were removed down to the natural silts and gravels using suitable tracked excavators under continuous archaeological monitoring. Due to the need to clear areas of the site for mineral extraction at the earliest opportunity, the excavation strategy entailed planning and excavating several individual blocks of the site in sequence guided by the extraction programme (Fig 3).

All archaeological features were investigated. The excavation sampling strategy required a low level of excavation on lengths of ditch (2% by volume), but higher levels on discrete features of importance (100% by volume). All physical relationships were also examined. In practice most pits containing significant waterlogged remains were fully excavated while ditches were sometimes sampled only at terminals and intersections.

Archaeological Background

The excavation site covered about 11 ha of flat land north of the A47 1.2 km west of Thorney. The site lies on the March gravels of Thorney 'island' on a narrow ridge running westward to the Eye peninsula. The stripped surface lay at about 2.0 m OD. The palaeo-environmental context of the north-west Cambridgeshire fens has been examined in detail from a number of archaeological sites in the region and a general model of landscape and land use has been developed into which the present investigations can be fitted (Hall 1987, French 2003). The immediate archaeological context includes the extensive Bronze Age site at Pode Hole Quarry south of the A47 where a similar prehistoric 'landscape' has been investigated (Phoenix Consulting 2005). It is this site in particular which has overturned assumptions about the extent and date of the enclosed prehistoric landscapes in the area, which on previous cropmark evidence alone were thought likely to be of Roman date (*ibid*. 24; cf Hall 1987, fig. 33)

Mesolithic and Neolithic

There are few finds of Mesolithic and Neolithic date from Thorney and sites of these periods are generally rare in the region (French 2003, 145-6). It appears that the fen edge was used briefly or intermittently for hunting or foraging over this time. Soils buried beneath later peat incursions indicate lime-dominated woodland in the 4th-3rd millennium BC at Crowtree and Oakhunt Farm north of Eye, and also in the Maxey-Etton area of the lower Welland valley (French 2003). A few residual Mesolithic flints come from Pode Hole Quarry and Neolithic pits have been excavated here, perhaps suggesting seasonal activity (Coates & Richmond 2004a). It is likely that Thorney 'island' was only lightly occupied at this time. A Neolithic or Bronze Age wooden trackway was discovered at Guy's Fen to the south in 1984 but has since been lost, presumably through decay due to changes in groundwater levels (French 1991).

Bronze Age

A major marine incursion, responsible for the deposition of the 'fen clay' Barroway Drove Beds, took place in the earlier 2nd millennium BC. An embayment relating to this marine incursion has been mapped lying 200 m east of the Tower's Fen site, indicating that the site was in a fen-edge location in the Bronze Age with salt marsh not far to the east (Hall 1987, fig. 30).

Most of the Bronze Age sites recorded up until the 1990s and mapped by Hall (1987) were barrows (many ploughed over but surviving as earthworks at that time), or ring ditches. Seventeen were recorded in Thorney parish, showing a distribution along the fen skirtland. This is a pattern observed more widely from Deeping St James and Bourne in south Lincolnshire, to Borough Fen and the Eye Peninsula. It is likely that barrows were sited in marginal land used for pasture, although the concept of the interface between wet and dry land may have played a part in the choice of location for burials (French 2003). It should be noted that Tower's Fen lies to the east of most of the barrows and ring ditches mapped by Hall, and seems therefore to have been in more of a fen-edge location than the burial locations, although the burials are likely to be generally earlier.

The initiation of peat growth, caused by the marine disruption to the drainage system by the mid 2nd millennium BC, has been recorded in the low-lying Borough Fen and Flag Fen basins. There is ample evidence for late Bronze Age fen-edge fields being abandoned in the lower valleys of all the major rivers – Maxey and Welland Bank in the Welland, Fengate in the Nene, and Barleycroft Farm and Over in the Great Ouse. The pattern is the same at Pode Hole Quarry. In the early 1st millennium BC the fens around Thorney were subject to another marine incursion resulting in the deposition of the Upper Barroway Drove Beds under salt marsh conditions. It is probable that, generally, only 'islands' over 2.5 m OD would have been dry enough for settlement by this time (French 2003, 150).

Iron Age

By the Iron Age (from about 700 BC) settlement had retreated to higher ground. Evidence of settlements and fields is common in the region generally, but no sites have been recorded from Thorney 'island', probably due to its wetness. Extensive cropmarks on the gravels to the west include some probable Iron Age sites at about 3 m OD (Hall 1987, fig. 32). No Iron Age activity was found at Pode Hole Quarry and this slightly lower area appears to have become marginal. During the later Iron Age another marine incursion, mainly affecting south Lincolnshire to the north of Thorney 'island', led to the deposition of more marine silts (Terrington Beds).

Roman

Settlement locations appear to have been similar to those in the Iron Age, although there is an increase in the extent, density and visibility of sites. In addition, there was settlement on the Terrington Beds north-east of Thorney, suggesting drier conditions in the fens. The construction of the Fen Causeway in the late 1st century AD from Fengate across to Whittlesey and March 'islands' also suggests a drying out of the fen peat by this time. Very little Roman material has been found around Thorney 'island' and it is probable that the fen-edge below about 2.5 m OD was peat-covered, and perhaps used for seasonal grazing. There are the earthworks of a Scheduled Ancient Monument at Pode Hole which are detailed as Roman but are more likely to be medieval.

There is regional evidence for wetter conditions in the fenland in the 3rd century AD and many settlements show signs of flooding or were abandoned around this time. Sites include Stonea Grange and Fengate. Large areas of the lower river valleys became subject to freshwater flooding and alluviation, probably related to the ploughing and consequent runoff from slopes higher up the valleys.

Saxon and medieval

There are no Saxon finds from Thorney and it is probable that land suitable for settlement was very limited (Hall 1987, 52). The 'island' was called Ancarig as recorded by the Anglo-Saxon Chronicle in the year 656, referring to the presence of an anchorite or hermitage. The name Thornige ('thorn island') is first recorded in the 10th century. The monastery was founded there in 972 and reached the height of its prosperity in the 13th century.

It is likely that most of the fenland around the island, including Tower Fen, remained uncultivated in the medieval period, although there is the suggestion of a certain amount of reclamation and drainage in the area. Drainage works include perhaps Cat's Water (which is an artificial channel along the fen edge to the west) and Shire Drain, which forms the boundary with Lincolnshire to the north (Hall *op. cit.*). The fenlands around Thorney were relatively wet compared with other areas and may not have been ideal even for summer grazing (Hall *op. cit.*).

Post-medieval

Systematic plans to drain the Thorney fens were made by the earl of Bedford in 1626 and efforts to make the land agriculturally productive have continued until modern times. It is unclear when Tower's Fen and the surrounding area were brought into arable cultivation, but the widespread presence of claying trenches of probable 19th-century date indicate this episode of land use is likely to date from the agricultural improvements from the late 18th century onward.

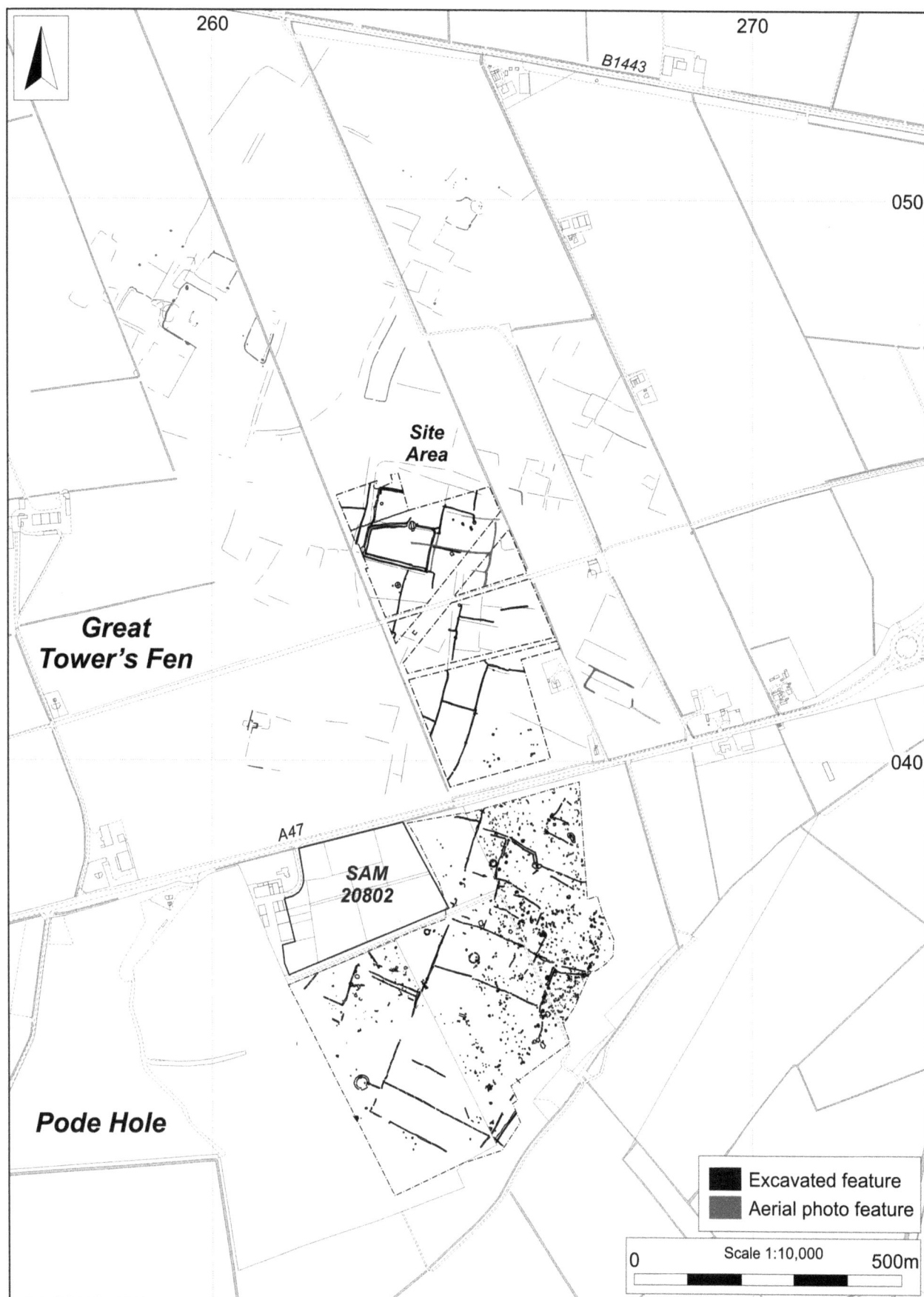

Fig 2. Overall site plan with excavated features from
Pode Hole Quarry and surrounding cropmarks
© *Crown copyright. Licence No. 100019331*
Published 2007

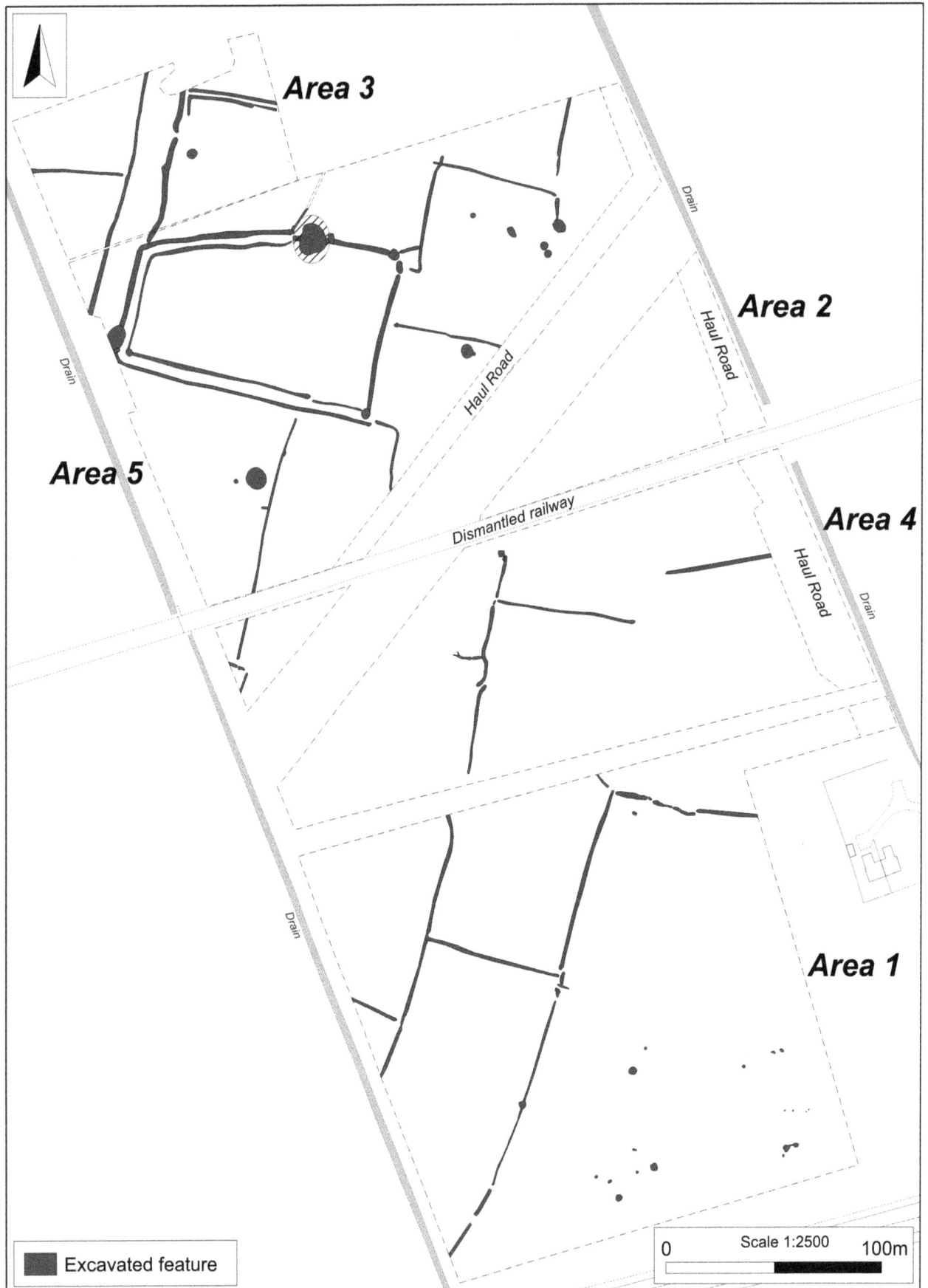

Fig 3. Great Tower's Fen site plan
© Crown copyright. Licence No. 100019331.
Published 2007

Chapter 2: **The Excavations**

General Site Description

The excavated area was approximately rectangular and covered about 11 ha, its size being determined by the amount of mineral needed from the borrow pit. The major constraint to extraction was the presence of high voltage overhead cables crossing north-east to south-west more or less centrally. Other soil baulks were left for access. The site was therefore divided into five areas (Fig 3) which were stripped of topsoil in sequence and formed convenient units for archaeological excavation and recording. The sterile geological substrate, directly under the modern soils, consisted of mixed silts and gravels.

The site layout consisted of a roughly rectangular arrangement of linear ditches and a scatter of large and small pits. Two exceptionally large pits on the boundaries of a double ditched enclosure were interpreted as ponds. The site shows a pattern of fields or other enclosures whose limits were not reached in any direction. The ponds, and the larger pits, and occasionally but not usually the bases of the deeper ditches, contained preserved organic matter within a metre or so of the stripped surface due to the high watertable.

There were numerous pit-like features showing various degrees of surface irregularity which were interpreted as tree throw-holes or other amorphous natural features. A number of the more regular ones were sample excavated, particularly in the early stages (Area 1) but not recorded unless they appeared to be man-made. Tree root holes and other natural features are not shown on the site plans as their investigation and mapping was not systematic. Where their interpretation was uncontroversial they were ignored.

There were occasionally small pits which might have been postholes, but there was no clear evidence of structures of any sort. Finds were sparse throughout. The pottery amounted to just 70 sherds and, where it was found, was Bronze Age. Some of it was Early Bronze Age but most of it was undiagnostic of specific date. Radiocarbon dates from the ponds gave consistent dates around 1500-1300 BC in the Middle Bronze Age and there is no reason to doubt that the pattern of fields and associated pits and waterholes are broadly of this date. Perhaps more surprisingly just five worked flints were recovered from the entire excavation. A small bronze palstave-adze was also found, stylistically of the Middle to Late Bronze Age. The most common type of artefact were cut and trimmed pieces of roundwood and split timber from the pits and ponds, many of which were probably originally used as stakes. Other pieces of wood and twigs were probably coppicing debris. The more unusual wooden artefacts are described (Chapter 3).

The excavated features are described by 'phase' where possible. The 'phasing' is more correctly defined as the construction sequence since it seems likely that a feature

(pit or ditch) did not become redundant when the next in the sequence was dug, but remained operative as part of the overall structure of land use.

The construction sequence was possible to determine where the relationship between the features (mainly the ditches) was physically present, or where it could be inferred from the layout. There were a number of features, mainly isolated pits, which could not be put into this sequence. The construction sequence shown must be qualified by the assumption that the developments in the southern and northern parts of the site were more or less synchronous, although since the two parts of the site were not physically joined this cannot be demonstrated and must remain a working hypothesis. The sequence of ditches and related pits are shown in nine 'phases' (Figs 4a – g). These features divide the site into Plots, numbered 1-11, which are convenient units for description and analysis (below).

The earliest feature on the site was Pit 160, Plot 11 (Fig 8). This was isolated and outside the phasing sequence developed for most of the features, but it was confirmed to be Early Bronze Age by two radiocarbon determinations (Chapter 7). It is possible that some of the unphased pits are also of this date. The construction sequence for the field system started with Phase 1 on the eastern side of the site and developed in a westward direction.

After the Bronze Age features had gone out of use and silted up, the area appears to have been covered by peat. Many of the larger features had dark humic upper fills indicating an anaerobic, organic deposition environment. These were cut by a pattern of widely spaced, sharply rectangular, claying trenches probably of 19th century date, and were directly overlain by the modern peaty agricultural soils.

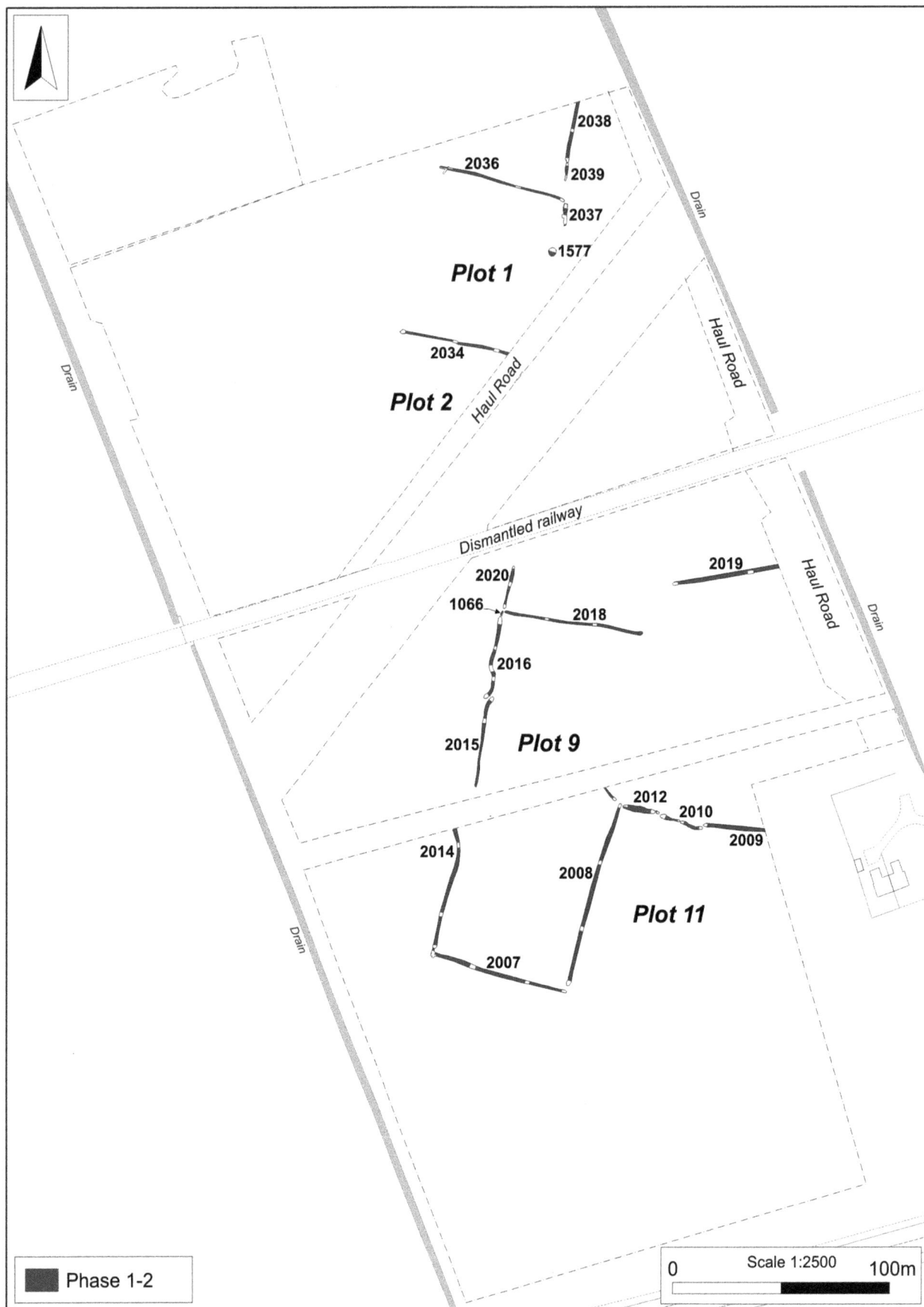

Fig 4a. Construction sequence; Phase 1-2
© Crown copyright. Licence No. 100019331.
Published 2007

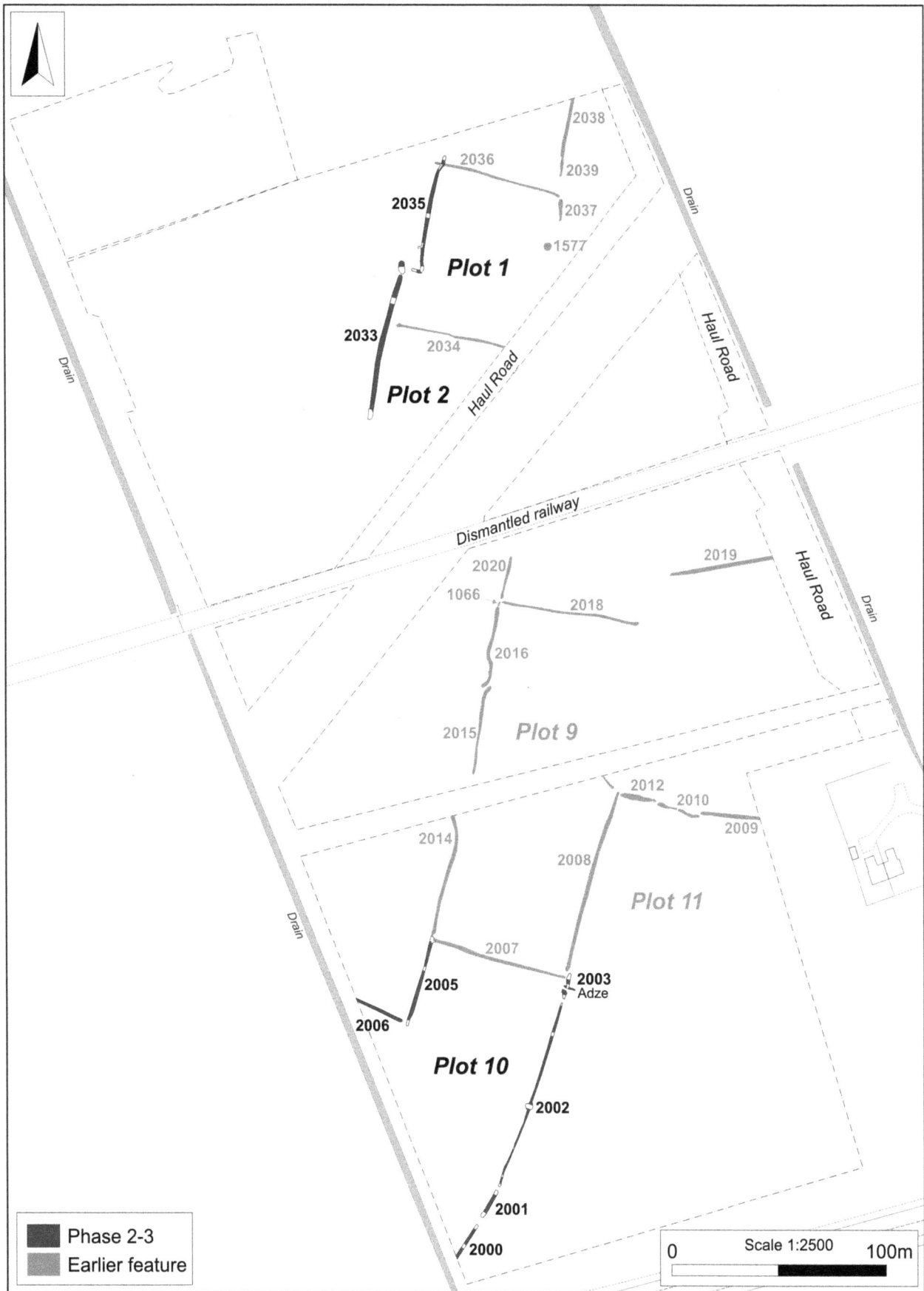

Fig 4b. Construction sequence; Phase 2-3
© Crown copyright. Licence No. 100019331.
Published 2007

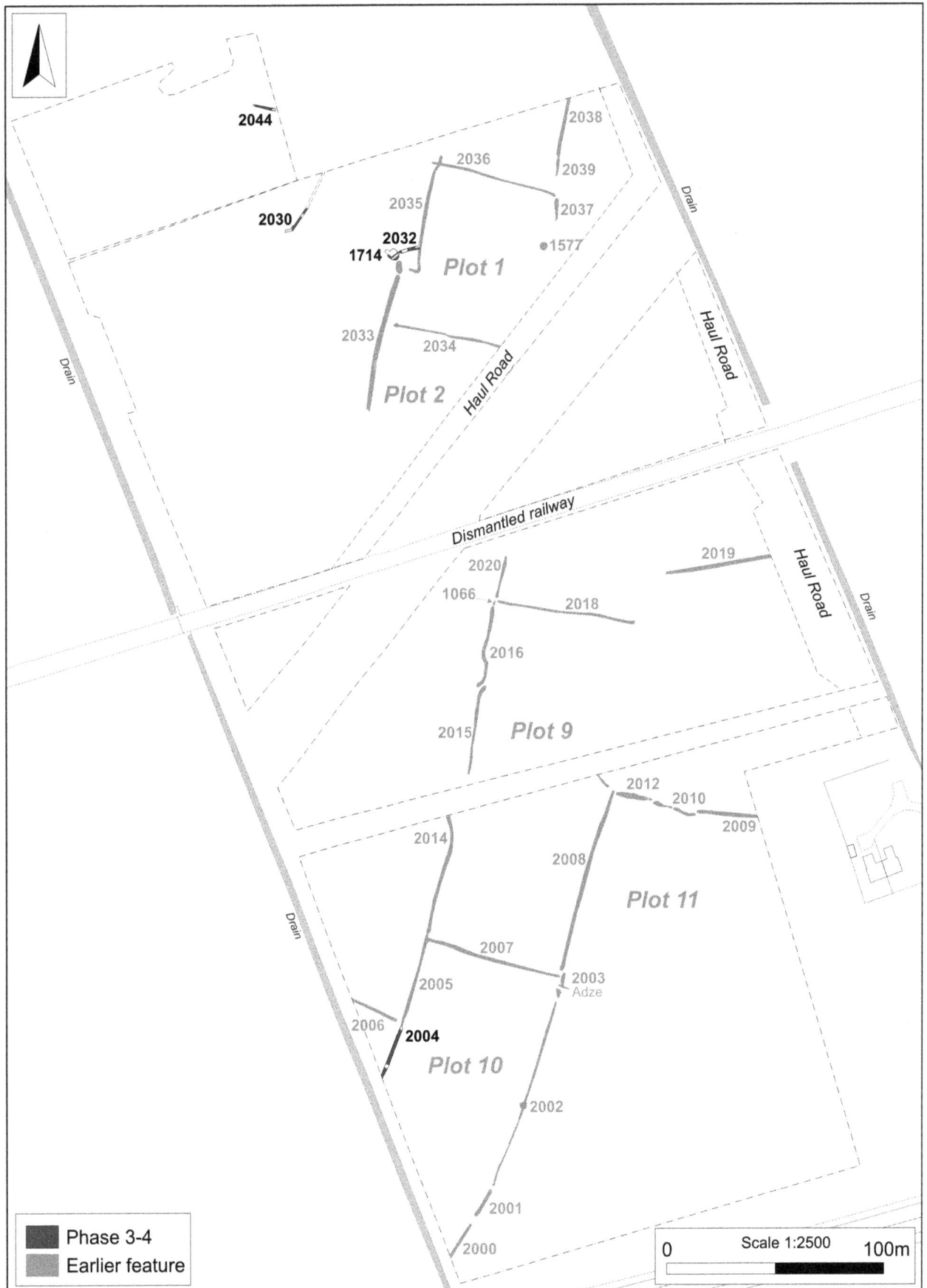

Fig 4c. Construction sequence; Phase 3-4
© *Crown copyright. Licence No. 100019331.*
Published 2007

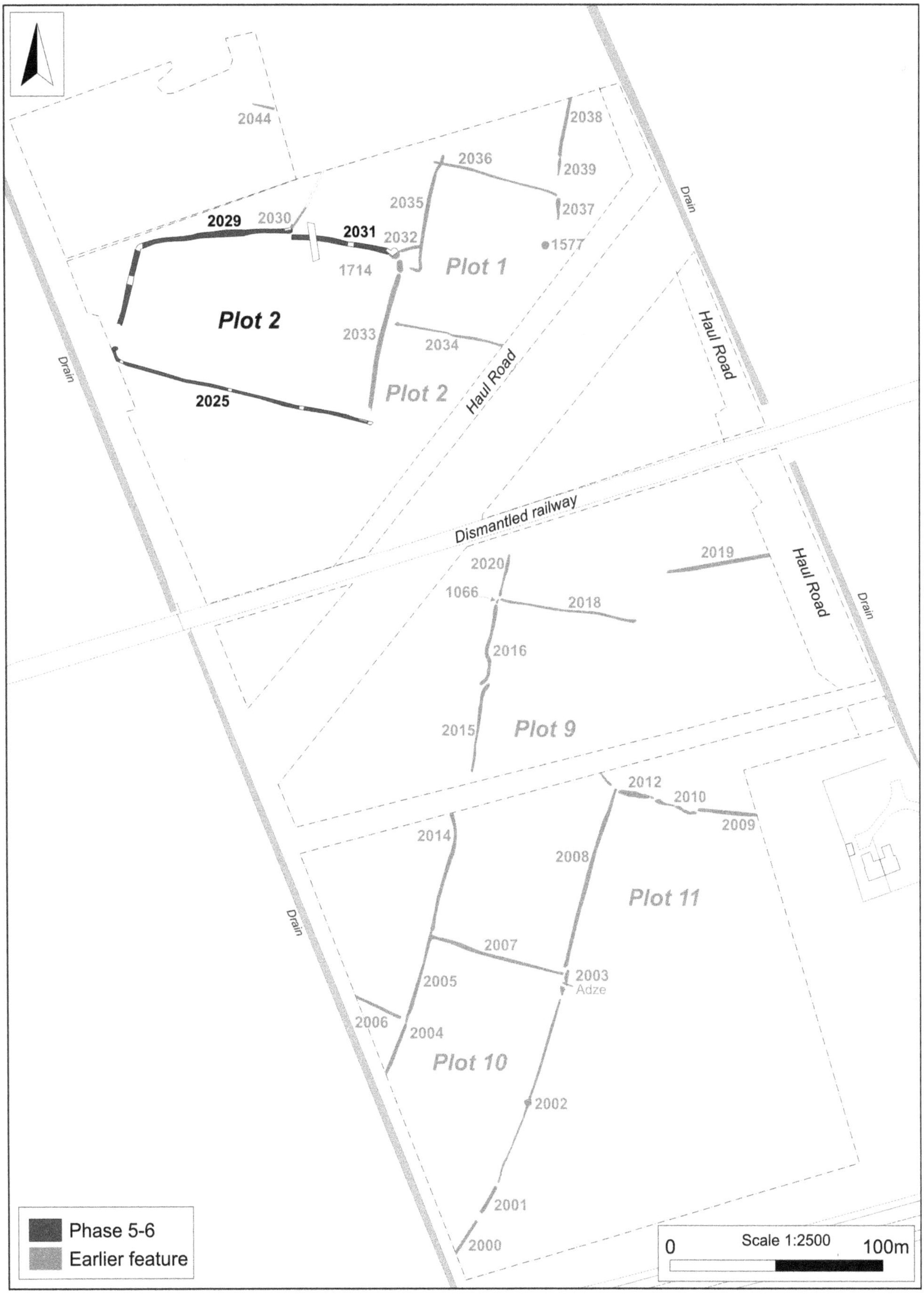

Fig 4d. Construction sequence; Phase 5-6
© Crown copyright. Licence No. 100019331.
Published 2007

11

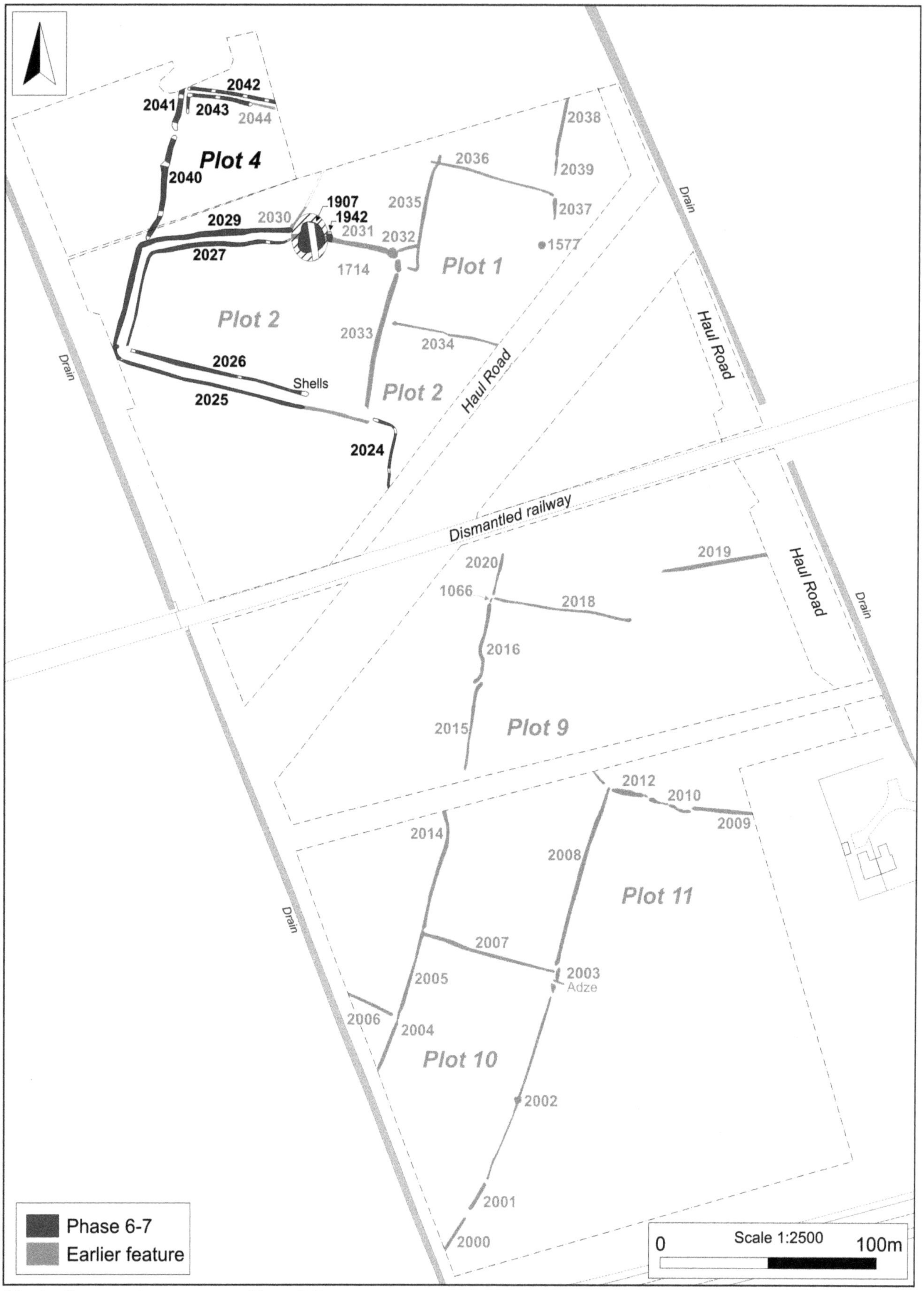

Fig 4e. Construction sequence; Phase 6-7
© *Crown copyright. Licence No. 100019331.*
Published 2007

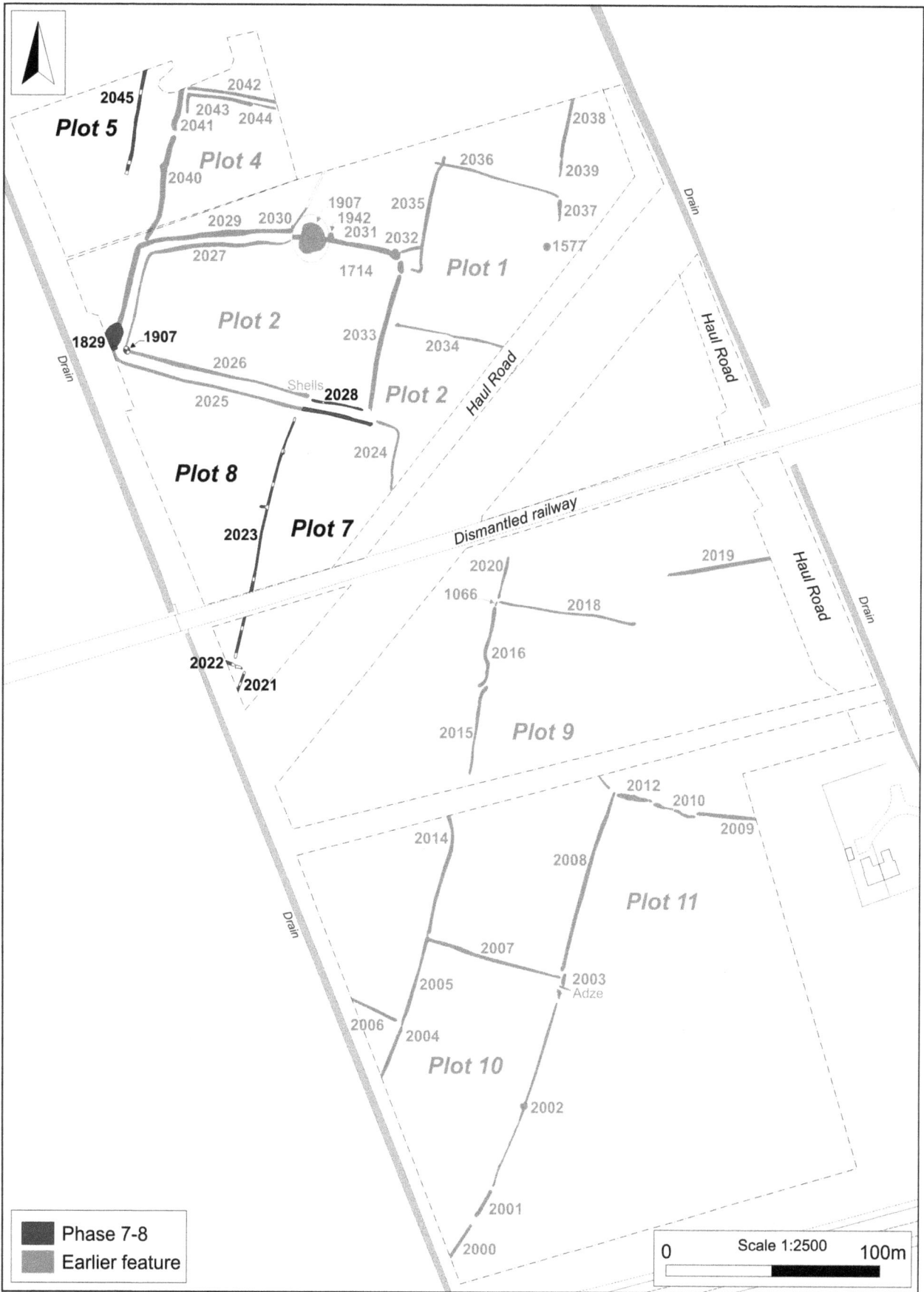

Fig 4f. Construction sequence; Phase 7-8
© *Crown copyright. Licence No. 100019331.*
Published 2007

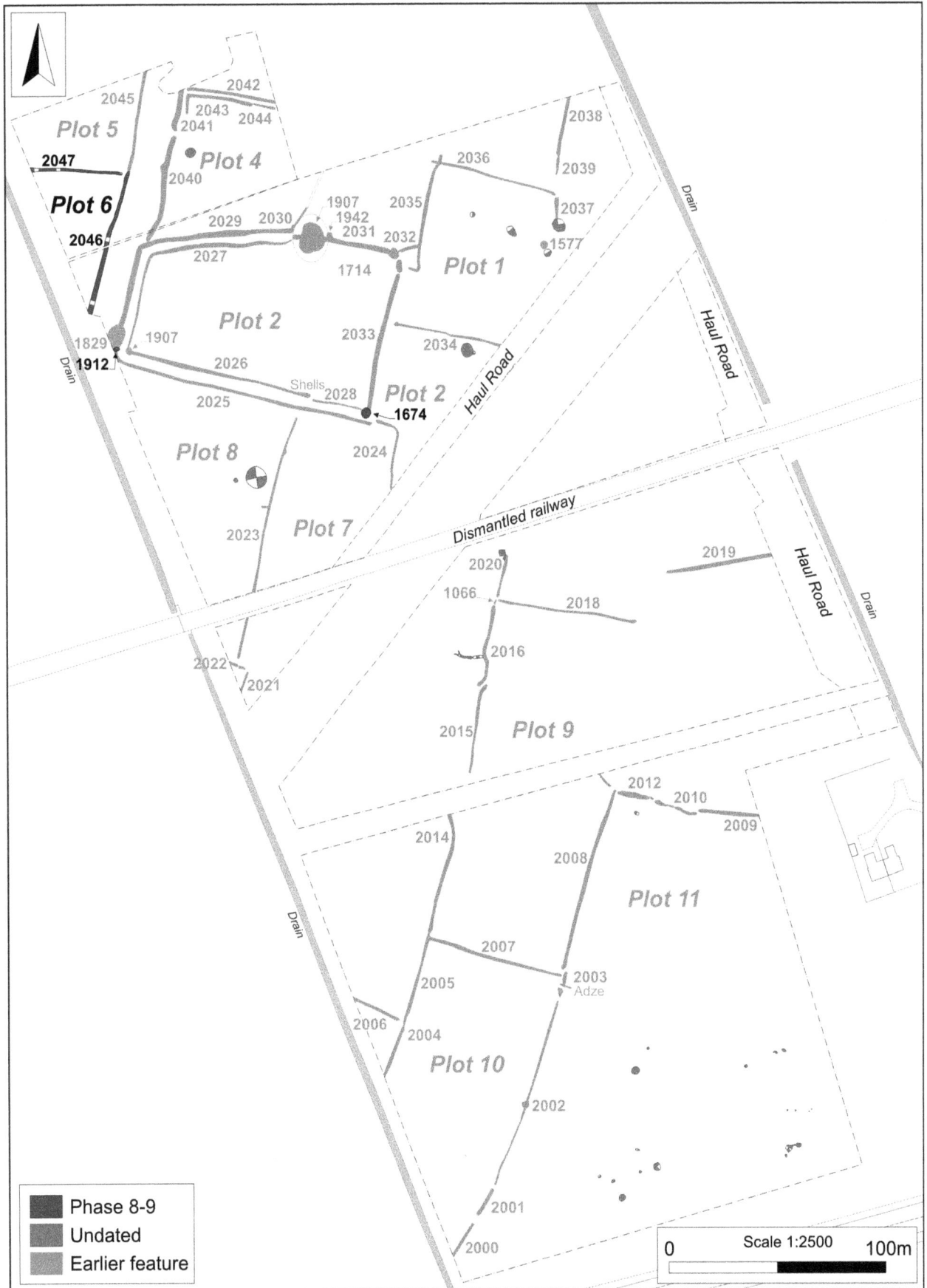

Fig 4g. Construction sequence; Phase 8-9
© Crown copyright. Licence No. 100019331.
Published 2007

Early Bronze Age

Pit 160: Plot 11

Pit 160 located toward the southern boundary of the site was 3.2 m in diameter and 1.0 m deep with steep, concave sides and a flattish base (Fig 5, S.56 – Plate 1; Fig 8).

The pit was mainly filled with greyish silty clays with lenses of gravel (197 and 196) which appears to indicate silting and edge erosion over a long period. This was succeeded by 175, a brown sandier silt which contained some cultural debris, including pottery of probable Food Vessel type. These deposits contained waterlogged organic material, particularly near the base, although 175 also contained roundwood with felling scars – at first thought to be a stake (see also Table 4.12, Sample 12). Gravel lens 197 contained much small material including twigs, coppiced roundwood, woodchips and gnarled bark – apparently detrius from woodworking, land clearance or maintenance (Chapter 3).

Nearer the top of the pit was a layer of gravel (195) which appears to have been a deliberate levelling deposit, the steepness of the north and south edges suggesting that it filled a shallow recut in the top of the pit. The upper fill was an orange-grey sandy silt (194).

Later another small but relatively deep pit (193) was cut into the western side of Pit 160. This was 0.7 m in diameter and 800 mm deep with a narrow, rounded base. It had a single fill (176) which was relatively soft and dark silt with some animal bones.

Interpretation

Although this pit was relatively shallow and the waterlogged material highly degraded, this is an important pit. The pottery from the lower and middle fills is radiocarbon dated through two determinations on associated wood to 2290-2040 calBC and 2120-1910 calBC (95% probability, 3765 +/- 35, SUERC-13970 and 3640 +/- 35, SUERC 13969). It is possible that that this is one of the earliest features. There is no indication that the pit was lined and the wood and other remains, such as they are, suggest some sort of wood clearance or maintenance.

It is not known whether this pit was the only Early Bronze Age feature or whether some of the undated pits were also of this date. It is interesting to note that the pit was later cut by a steep-sided shallower pit which has the form of a large posthole, so it is possible that the position of the pit was later marked. One of the main boundary ditches of the Pode Hole Quarry field system to the south is approximately aligned on this pit (Fig 2).

Plate 1. Pit 160, north-east quadrant, looking south

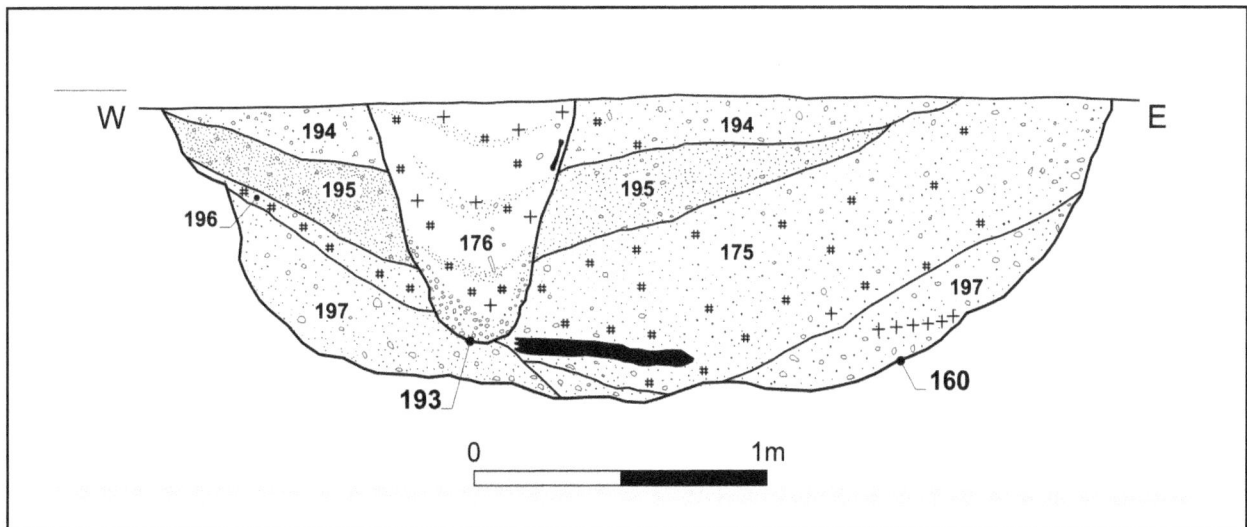

Fig 5. Pit 160, Section 56

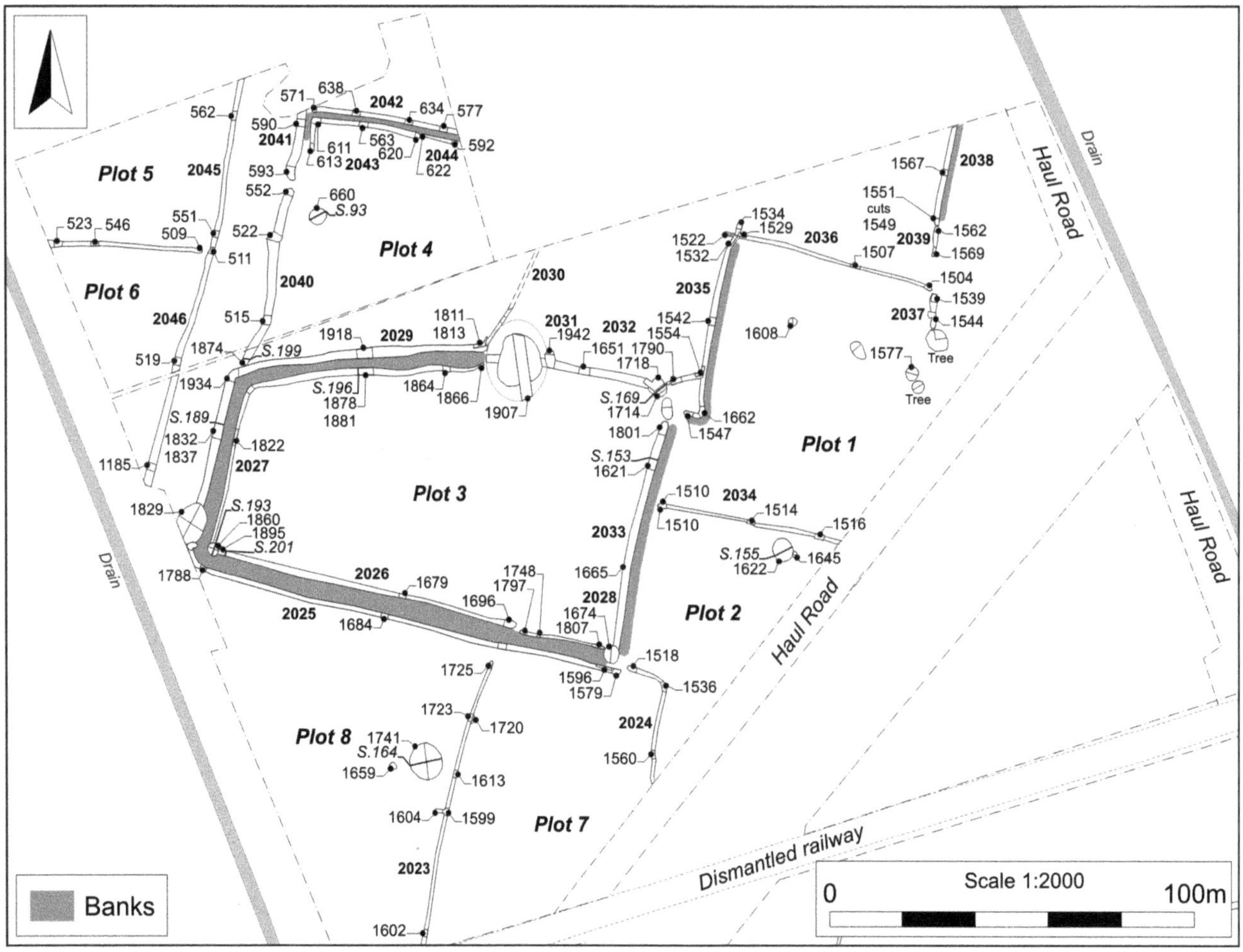

Fig 6. Site Plan, Plots 1-8
© Crown copyright. Licence No. 100019331.
Published 2007

Middle Bronze Age Boundary Ditches

Phases 1-2 (Fig 4a)

Ditches 2036, 2034, 2038, 2037, 2039

The precise sequence of ditch digging is not possible to determine, but because of the chain of observed stratigraphic relationships, it is clear that Ditch 2036 (cut by Ditch 2035) in the northern part of the site, is one of the earliest features in this area. Whether its eastern terminal was respected by the NE-SW aligned segmented system 2038, 2039 and 2037, or it was inserted into a gap in this group of ditches (and is therefore later) is difficult to resolve, but the logic of the site layout indicates that, as a whole, this group of ditches predates those to the west (Fig 6).

The neatest explanation of development would see the major NE-SW interrupted ditch (starting with Ditch 2038 in the north and ending with Ditch 2004 in the south – Fig 4c, Fig 8) as the primary feature, forming the principal axis of the field and enclosure patterns. There is, however, no compelling reason to see the layout as a unified undertaking. The fragmented nature of this pattern perhaps

indicated an accreted system, but one whose alignments were determined by still earlier land patterns to the east.

As a working hypothesis it is therefore suggested that there was an early NE-SW alignment in the NE corner of this area (Ditches 2038, 2039, 2037) together with Pit 1577.

Ditch 2038

The terminal showed two phases, a shallow early cut (1549) on the eastern side which had been recut to 0.36 m further west, suggesting the presence of a bank on the eastern side (Fig 6). To the north Cut 1567 was presumably the recut and was 1.4 m wide and 0.6 m deep with a round-based profile (S.138). A sequence of four fills were identified (from the base 1566 – 1563) which appeared to be natural accumulations of sandy silt, becoming greyer toward the top. Animal bone came from 1566. A few sherds of shelly pottery came from the middle fills 1565 and 1564. This

16

is not diagnostic of date. A soil sample from 1564 (Table 4.6, Sample 52) yielded some charred barley grains.

Ditch 2039

This short length of ditch was aligned on the earlier cut of 2038 and may therefore be an early feature added to restrict access here but not redug. It was examined with two cuts (1562 and 1569) and shown to reach a maximum of 0.5 m wide and 0.3 m deep with a steep-sided profile.

Ditch 2037

This short section of ditch was not precisely aligned on 2038 and 2039 and potentially lay with respect to the terminal of 2036 instead. At its southern end was a large tree root hole, but it is not clear whether this was a contemporaneous feature. The ditch was examined with two cuts (1539 and 1544) and shown to be 0.6-0.7 m wide and 0.2-0.3 m deep with a single fill (1538/1543). A few sherds of plain shelly pottery came from 1543 and Sample 46 (Table 4.7a) yielded poor quality waterlogged remains which included chickweed and orache. Both 1543 and 1538 yielded some animal bone.

It can be noted that Pit 1577, a possible posthole, aligns on 2038 and 2039 and may have been a boundary marker. The sequence could therefore be 1577 – 2038 – 2039 – 2036 – 2037, but it is possible that 2037 was added later.

Ditch 2036

This ditch may have been aligned with respect to Ditches 2038 and 2039. It was about 1 m wide and reached a depth of 0.56 m in the central section (Cut 1507) although the ends were shallower (0.3 m). It is possible that the central section, which had steep sides, had been recut, but there was no physical evidence of this. The fills were unremarkable, but 1505 yielded a few sherds of plain shelly pottery and scraps of animal bone. Bone also came from 1502.

Ditch 2036 was cut by 2035 after a considerable amount of infilling. It is possible that the ditch itself had gone out of use, although as elsewhere, it is assumed that it would have been marked by a hedgerow and still functioned as a boundary. There was no indication of a bank.

Ditch 2034

Seventy metres to the south and parallel to Ditch 2036, Ditch 2034 may have been laid out at the same time, although it is possible that it was laid out with respect to Ditches 2033 & 2035 instead, and therefore slightly later.

Its western terminal showed two possible cuts (1512 recut by 1510) but this was not apparent elsewhere. The ditch was 0.6-0.7 m wide and 0.3-0.4 m deep with steep sides and a single fill which contained some animal bones (1515). There was no indication of a bank.

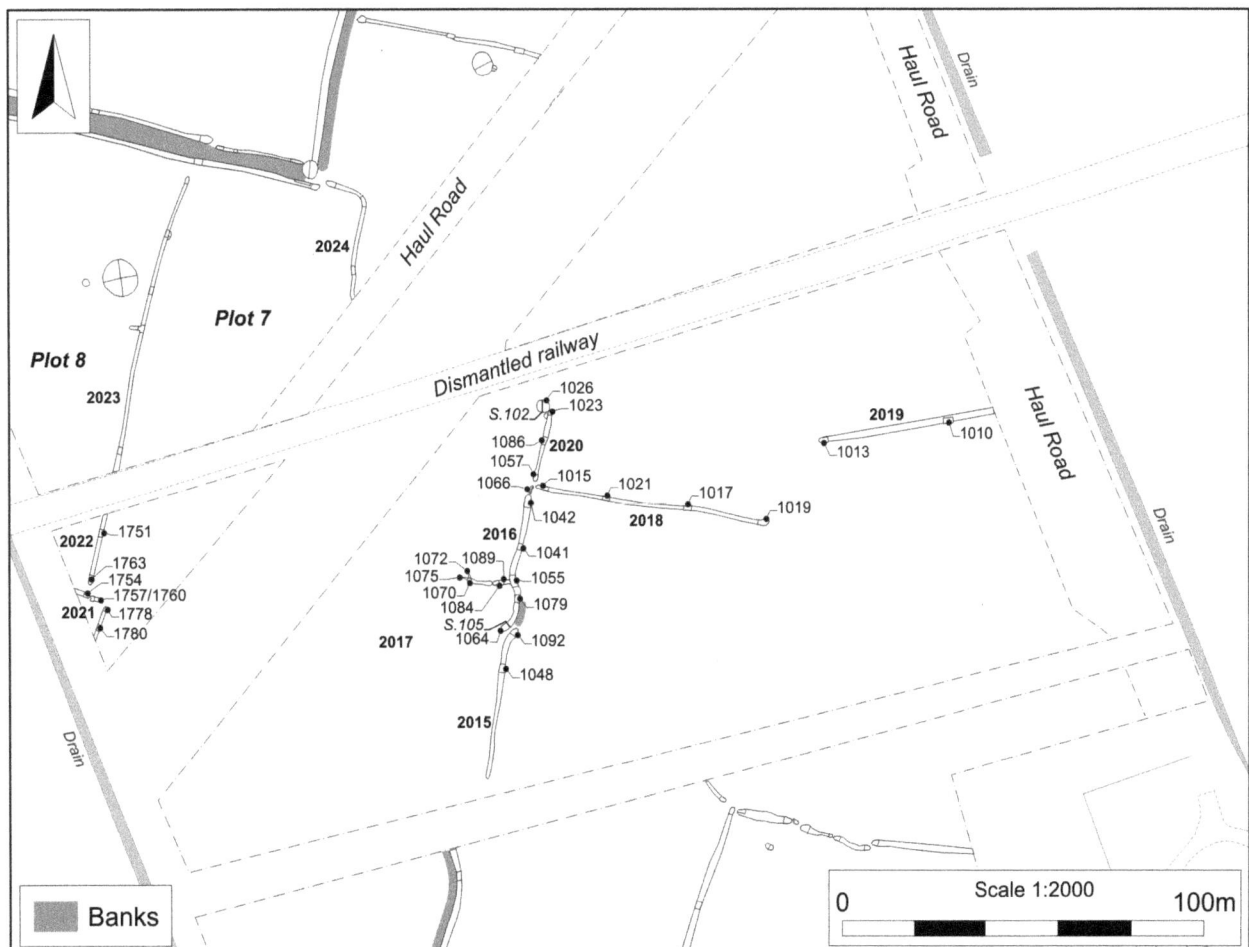

Fig 7. Site Plan, Plots 7-8
© *Crown copyright. Licence No. 100019331. Published 2007*

17

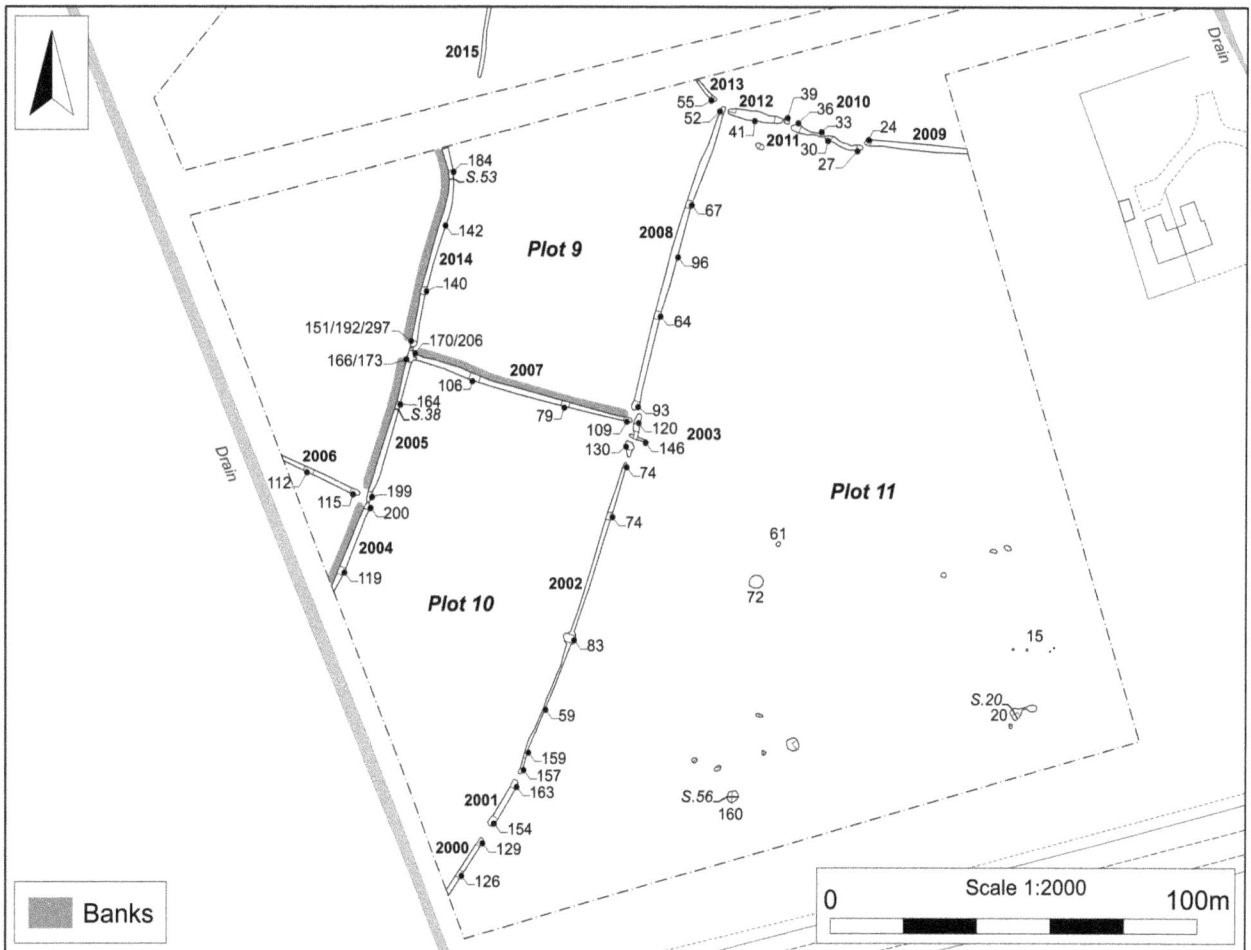

Fig 8. Site Plan, Plots 9-11
© Crown copyright. Licence No. 100019331.
Published 2007

Ditches 2020, 2018, 2016, 2015 and ?2019

The discontinuous NE-SW ditches in the central area of the site are part of the major axis of land division on the site, but they do not seem to be part of a single scheme. The ditches appear to have been dug on an ad hoc basis, but whether this reflected the subdivision of a pre-existing land division, or the accretion on similar alignments to existing fields, is difficult to judge.

Ditch 2020 was 0.8 m wide and 0.4 m deep with a steep profile, except the northern terminal (Cut 1023) which was shallower. It was aligned with respect to Ditch 2018 at right angles (it is not possible to say which came first), rather than with 2016 to the SW which is offset and taken to be later (although it could logically equally be the primary feature). The main point is that 2020 and 2018 form a unit (Fig 9). The NW-SE ditch was not added to an existing NE-SW ditched boundary. Ditch 2018 was similar to 2020, being 0.7-0.8 m wide and 0.4-0.5 m deep with steep sides.

Near the junction of 2020, 2018 and 2016 was a shallow, oval pit, 1066. It is not known what this was for. The pit was without finds.

Ditch 2016 (Fig 7) followed an irregular course in plan, possibly curving to avoid an existing feature or tree (whose root may have caused the 'gully' 2017, cut by

2016). The ditch was examined with five sections (Cuts 1042, 1041, 1055, 1079, 1064). It was generally about 1.2 m wide and 0.4-0.5 m deep although more substantial at the southern terminal (1064 – Fig 10, Section 105) where two, progressively shallower recuts (1080, 1060) were identified. Here the original cut was 1.7 m wide and 0.7 m deep with a flat base. This may have been deliberately infilled by 1062 – a sediment which appeared to be redeposited gravel and silt – recorded on the southern side. The later recuts were toward the northern side. The upper dark fill (1058) of the latest recut (1060) yielded low quality waterlogged remains, which included, in particular, bramble (Table 4.7a, Sample 41). Charcoal fragments included oak and plum/cherry as well as bedstraw seeds. Although shallower, Cut 1079 to the north had probable redeposited natural gravel on its southern side (1077) and a recut to the north containing a dark fill (1076). Cuts 1055 and 1041 also had upper dark deposits (1051, 1039).

Ditch 2015 continued the alignment of 2016 with a gap of 1.2 m between the terminals. This seems too narrow to have intended as an entrance, and it appears instead that the slight overlap between the terminals was intended to close any gap here. It seems probable that 2015 was dug as a separate event and was cut up against an existing bank on the eastern side of 2016. Ditch 2015 was 1.4 m

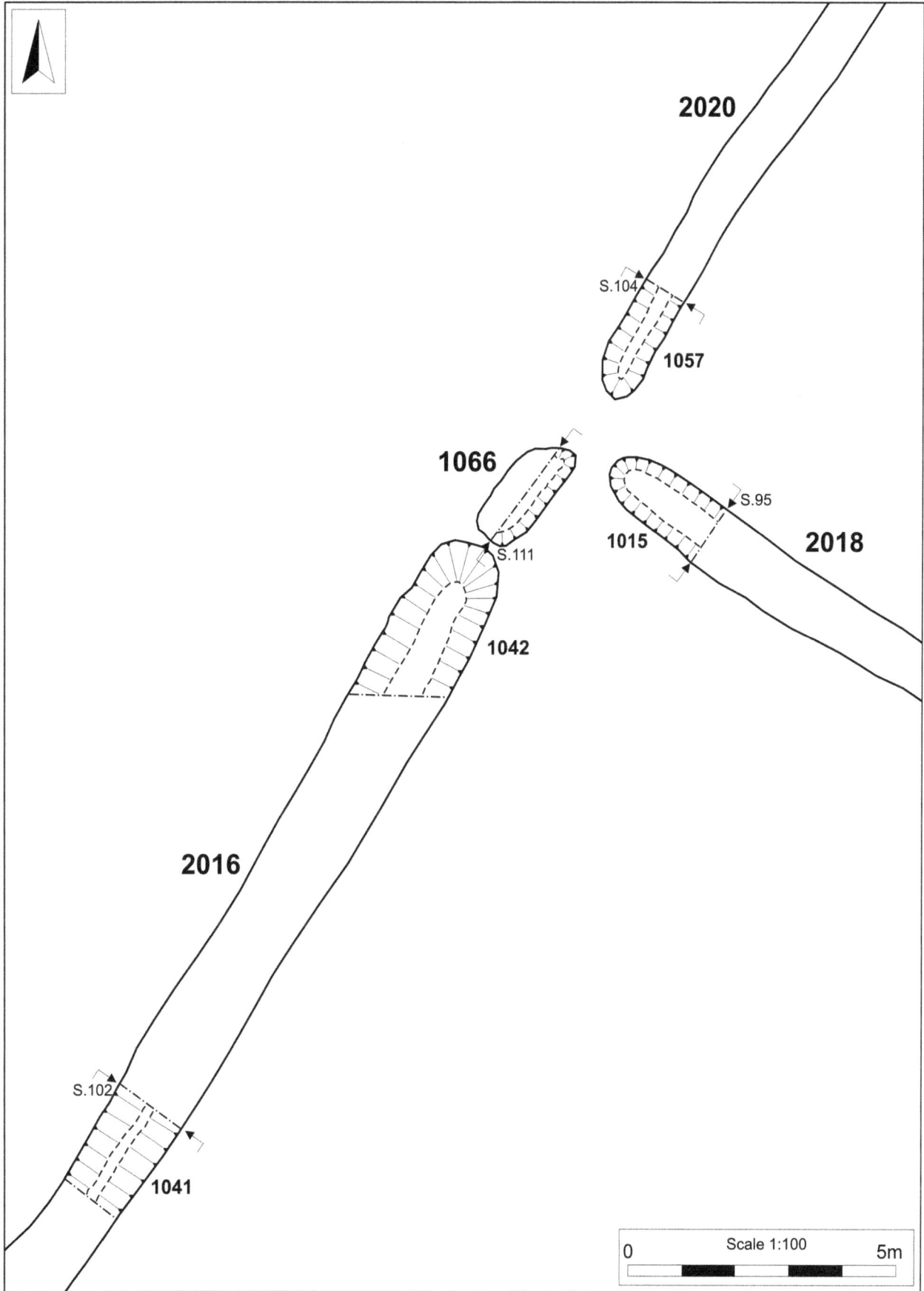

Fig 9. Plan showing junction of ditches 2016, 2018 and 2020

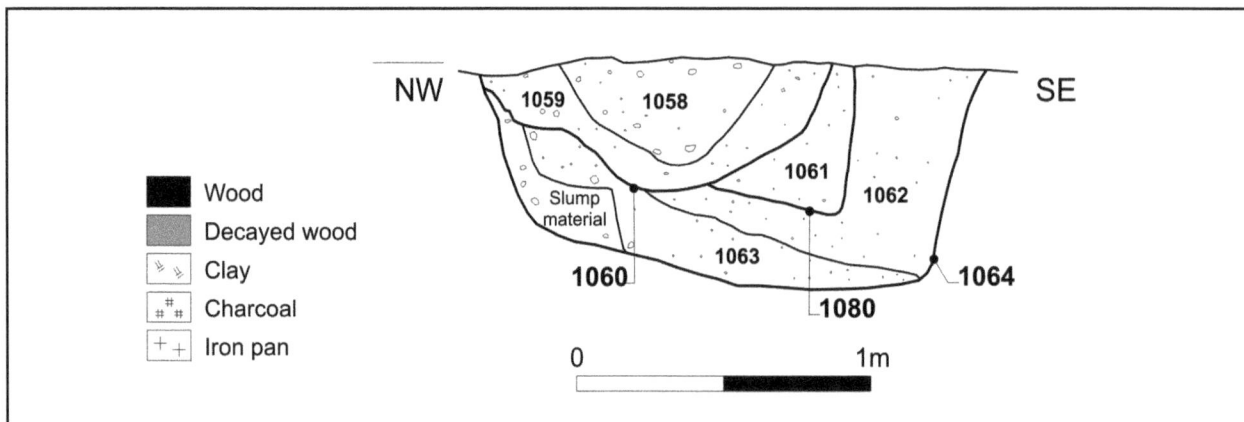

Fig 10. Ditch 2016, Section 105

wide and 0.5 m deep at the terminal (1092), becoming shallower further south. Cut 1092 shows a probable recut on its eastern side. (This seems to imply that 2015 was dug from the eastern side, whereas 2016 was dug from the western.) A soil sample (Table 4.6, Sample 42) from the upper fill (1090) yielded some low quality waterlogged bramble seeds.

Ditch 2019 was 1.4-1.5 m wide and 0.50-0.65 m deep with moderately steep sides. It was unphased and on a slightly different alignment to the other ditches. It had possibly been recut on the southern side. A sherd of plain pottery came from 1011 (possible recut terminal 1013).

Ditches 2012, 2011, 2010, 2009, 2008

The east-west group of segmented ditches (2012 including Pit 39, 2011, 2010 – Fig 8) were relatively shallow and irregular features – 1.0-1.5 m wide and 0.3-0.5 m deep. The section through Ditch 2009 at its terminal was deeper (0.56 m) with plunging sides. It is not clear whether this was typical of the feature as a whole (which it was not possible to examine further because it was crossed by a haul road).

The western terminal of 2012 was aligned with respect to Ditch 2008 which was of a different character. It was rectilinear, generally 0.8-1.1 m wide and 0.5-0.7 m deep with steep sides. The southern terminal (93) was broader (1.6 m wide and 0.55 m deep) with shallow sides. All four sections excavated showed an upper dark peaty fill. The complete skeleton of a sheep (95) was found in the base of the upper peaty fill of Cut 96 (Plate 2). This may have been laid in a grave cut through the peat (although no grave cut was found) or it might have sunk through the peaty deposit. In either case it would have been late in the sequence of deposits, but clearly interred when the ditch was visible.

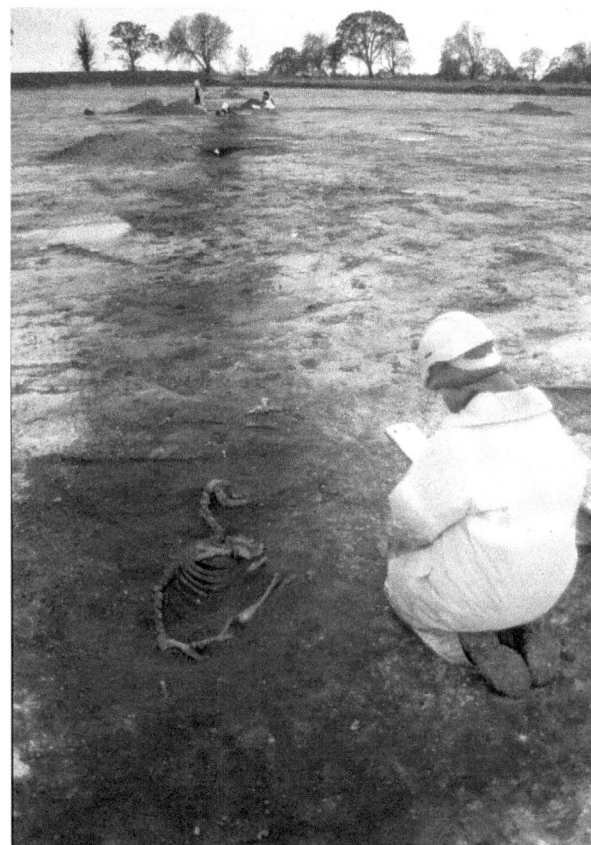

Plate 2. Sheep skeleton in top of Ditch 2008, looking south

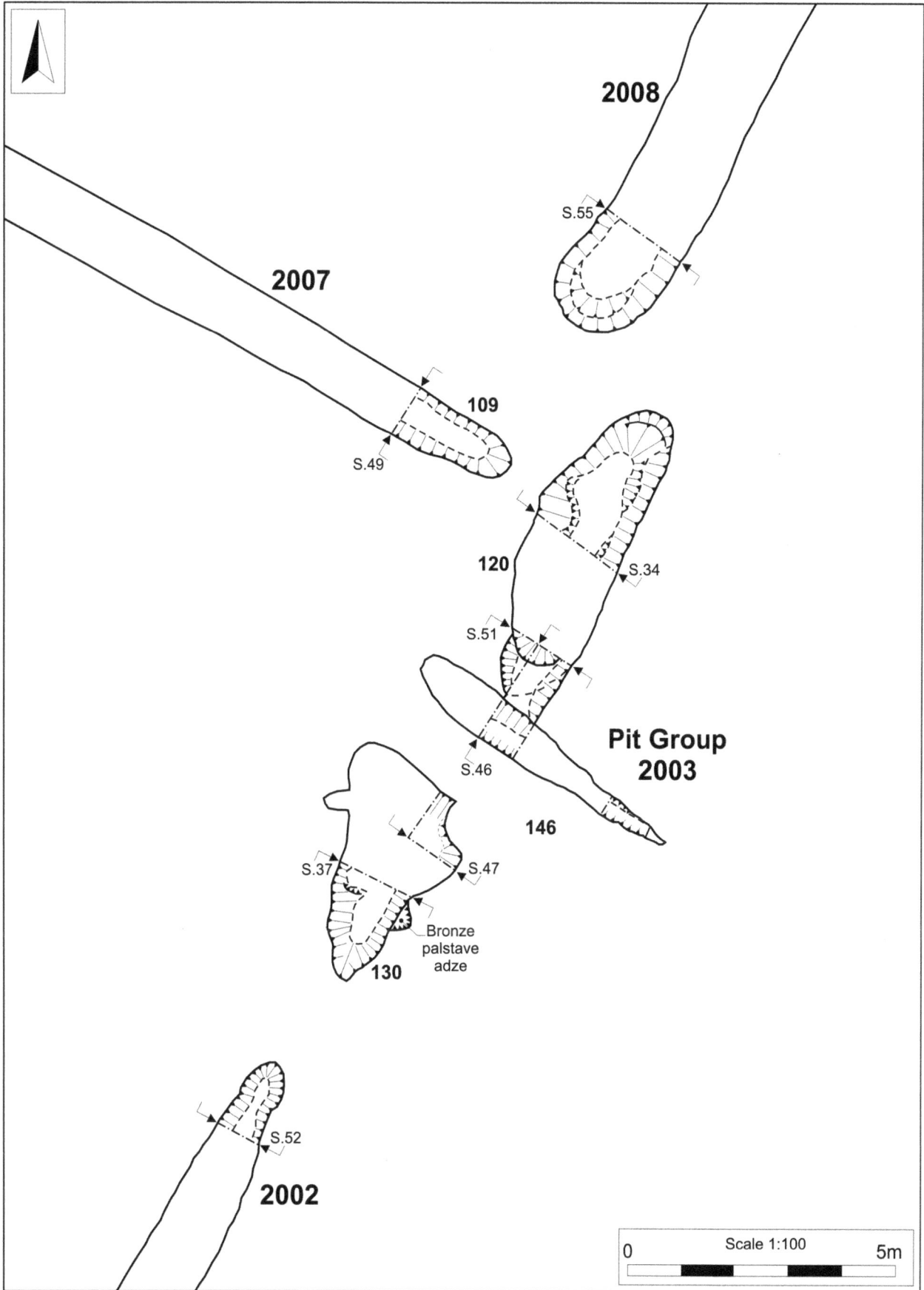

2008

2007

S.55

109

S.49

120

S.34

S.51

Pit Group
2003

S.46

146

S.37

S.47

Bronze
palstave
adze

130

S.52

2002

Scale 1:100

0   5m

*Fig 11. Plan showing junction of ditches 2002, 2007
and 2008*

Ditch 2007

The terminal of Ditch 2008 was aligned on the terminal of Ditch 2007, rather than Pit Group 2003 and the extended ditches to the south, so it appears that 2007 and 2008 formed a unit, with the southern ditches of a different phase (Fig 11).

Ditch 2007 was of varying size, being much shallower at the eastern end (Cut 109, 0.15 m deep), deepening to 0.54 m (Cut 79), 0.64 m (Cut 106) and 0.96 m (Cut 206) (Fig 8). The western cuts 106 and 206 showed two clear phases, with later recuts 102 and 170 at a shallower depth (Figs 12a & 12b). The offsetting of recut 102 to the south of 106 perhaps suggests that there was a bank/hedge on the northern side of the ditch.

The intersections of the western terminal cuts (206 replaced by 170) show complex relationships with the north-south ditches (Figs 12a-c), but it appears that in Phase 1 (Fig 12a) 206 respected a north-south ditch 192 (part of 2014) which may not have extended south of 2007 (if it did it had been lost to later cuts). In Phase 2 (Fig 12b) 206 was replaced by 170 and the ?terminal of

192 was replaced by a large pit 188, with 192 replaced by 207, now terminating short of the pit. It is still unclear whether 2005 to the south was in existence at this time. In the latest phase (Fig 12c), Pit 188 went out of use and was cut by Cut 166 (Ditch 2005), while the terminal of 2014 (Cut 151) was repositioned further north to leave a corner 'entrance' (or just a gap?) 2.0 m wide.

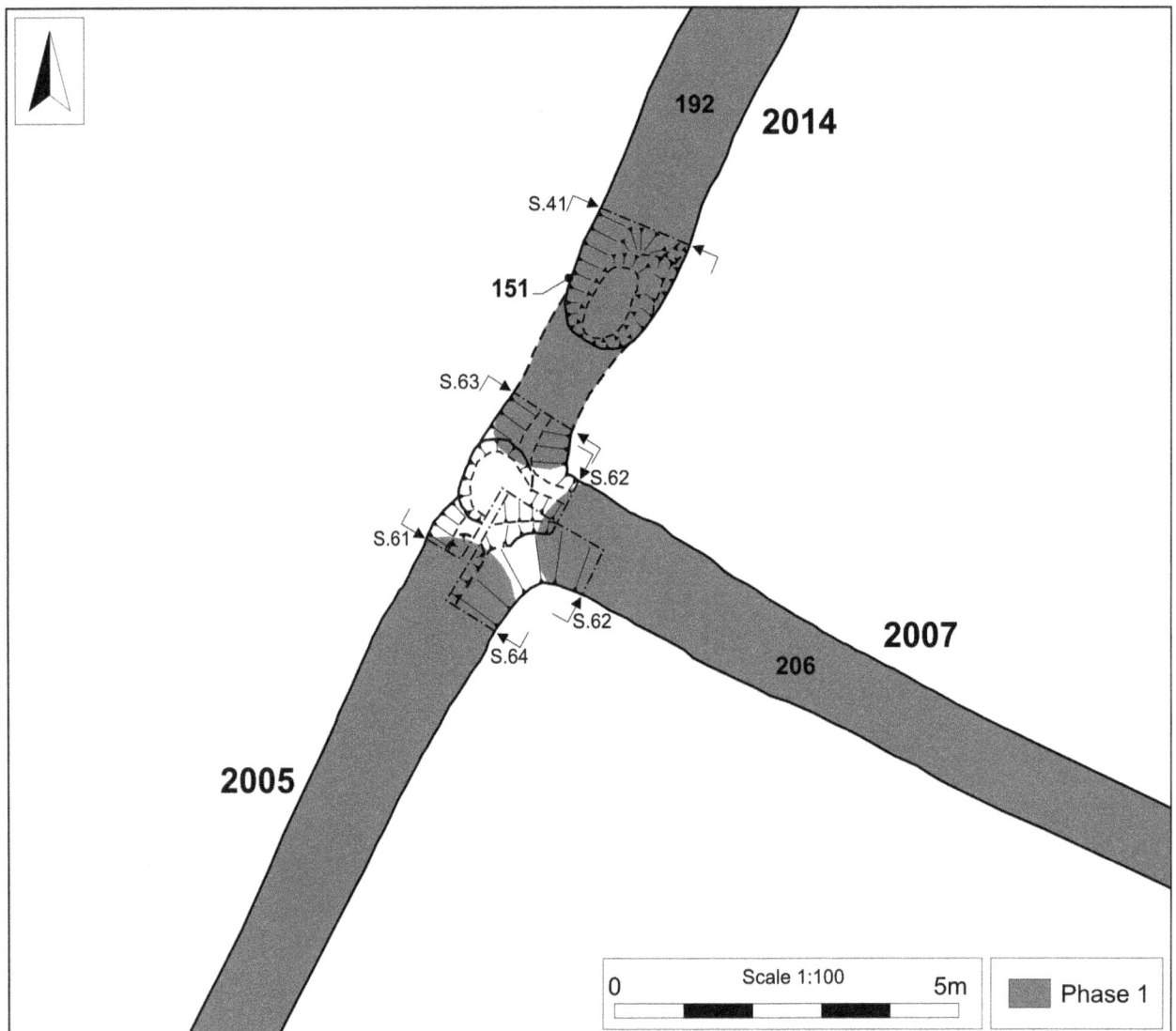

Fig 12a. Plan showing junction of ditches 2007, 2005 and 2014: Phase 1

Ditch 2014

Ditch 2014 showed a complex series of fills and it seems, from the southern terminal that there were three phases of ditch digging (Cuts 192, 207, 151) (Figs 12a-c). In the two other excavated sections two cuts can be identified in each.

The first phase was probably contemporary with the first phase of Ditch 2007, but it is not known whether Ditch 2005 was in existence at this time since the cuts of this ditch were deeper and would have removed a shallower earlier phase, had it existed. The first phase of 2014 was Cut 192 whose base survived at a depth of 0.5m below the stripped surface. It would have been about 1.2m wide. This is probably equivalent to Cuts 140/142 (Fig 13, S.38) and 184 (Fig 14, S.53) although 184 was deeper, at 0.7m. Cut 184 was also asymmetrical in profile with a very steep northern edge. Both this cut and 140/142 redeposited sand and gravel on the northern side above a greyish basal filling, suggesting the presence of a bank on this side (Fig 8). This suggestion is supported by the position of the recut on the southern side.

In the second phase the southern end of the ditch was redug to a shallower, squarer profile (Fig 12b, Cut 207). A soil sample from the main fill (Table 4.6, Sample 18, Fill 190) yielded occasional charcoal fragments but little of interest.

Later, in the third phase, the southern terminal was re-positioned further north to leave a narrow corner field entrance (Fig 12c). Cut 151 was 1.4m wide and 0.4m deep with a similar, squarish profile to the earlier cut, although it also had a deeper 'sump' in the terminal itself (to 0.76m deep). The recut ditches 137/145 (Fig 13, S.38) are probably the equivalents further north, although they were under 1m wide. There is a probable recut to Ditch 184 which maintained the steep northern edge (Fig 14, S.53).

With the exception of the terminal 151 (where the fill only became grey towards the top) the recuts were filled with dark silts containing charcoal. Sample 11 contained abundant charcoal, with oak the only identifiable species (Table 4.6, Fill 136, Cut 137). Sample 14 contained only occasional remains (Table 4.6, Fill 179, Cut 184). There was a thin peaty deposit in the top of this ditch.

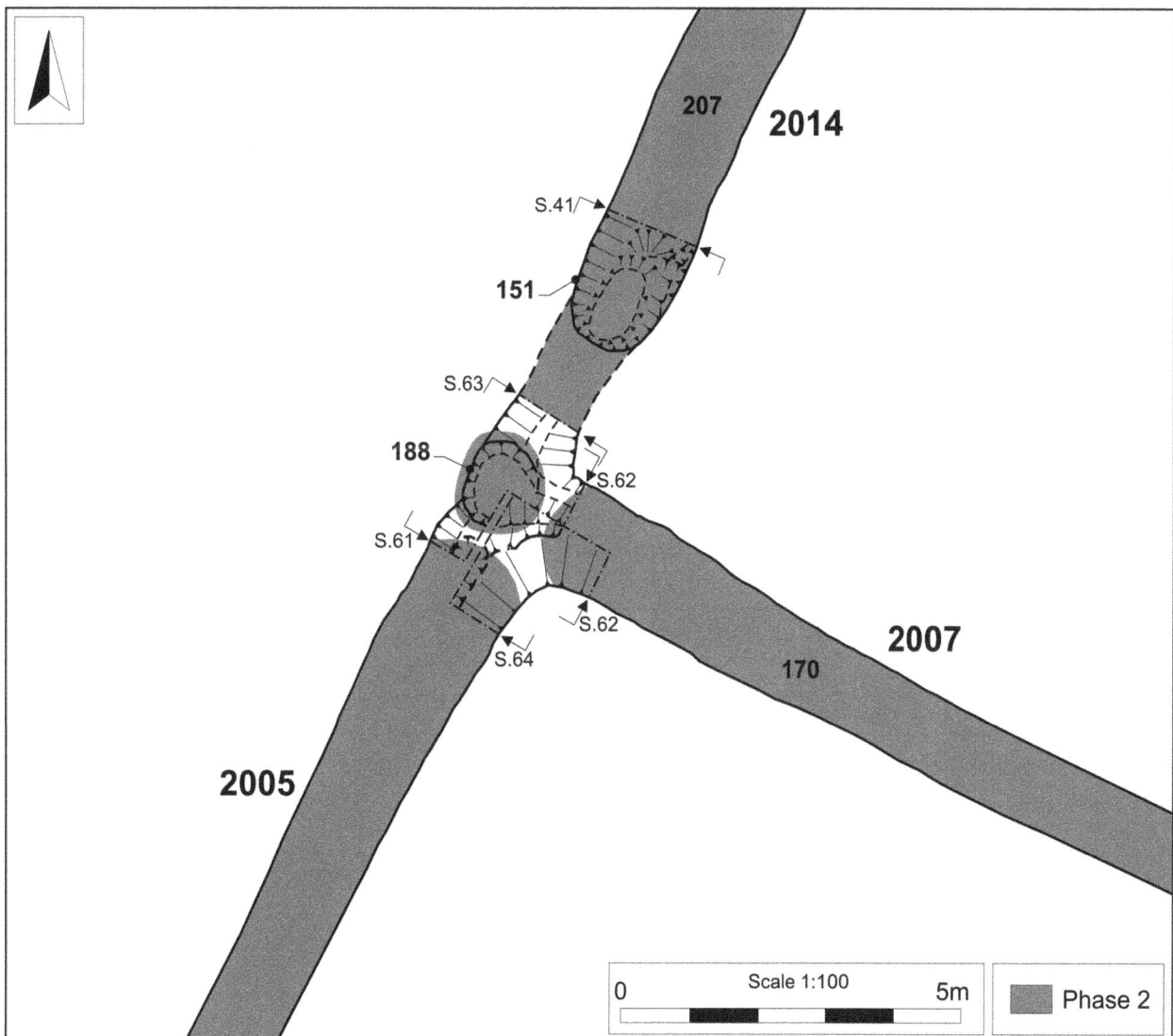

Fig 12b. Plan showing junction of ditches 2007, 2005 and 2014: Phase 2

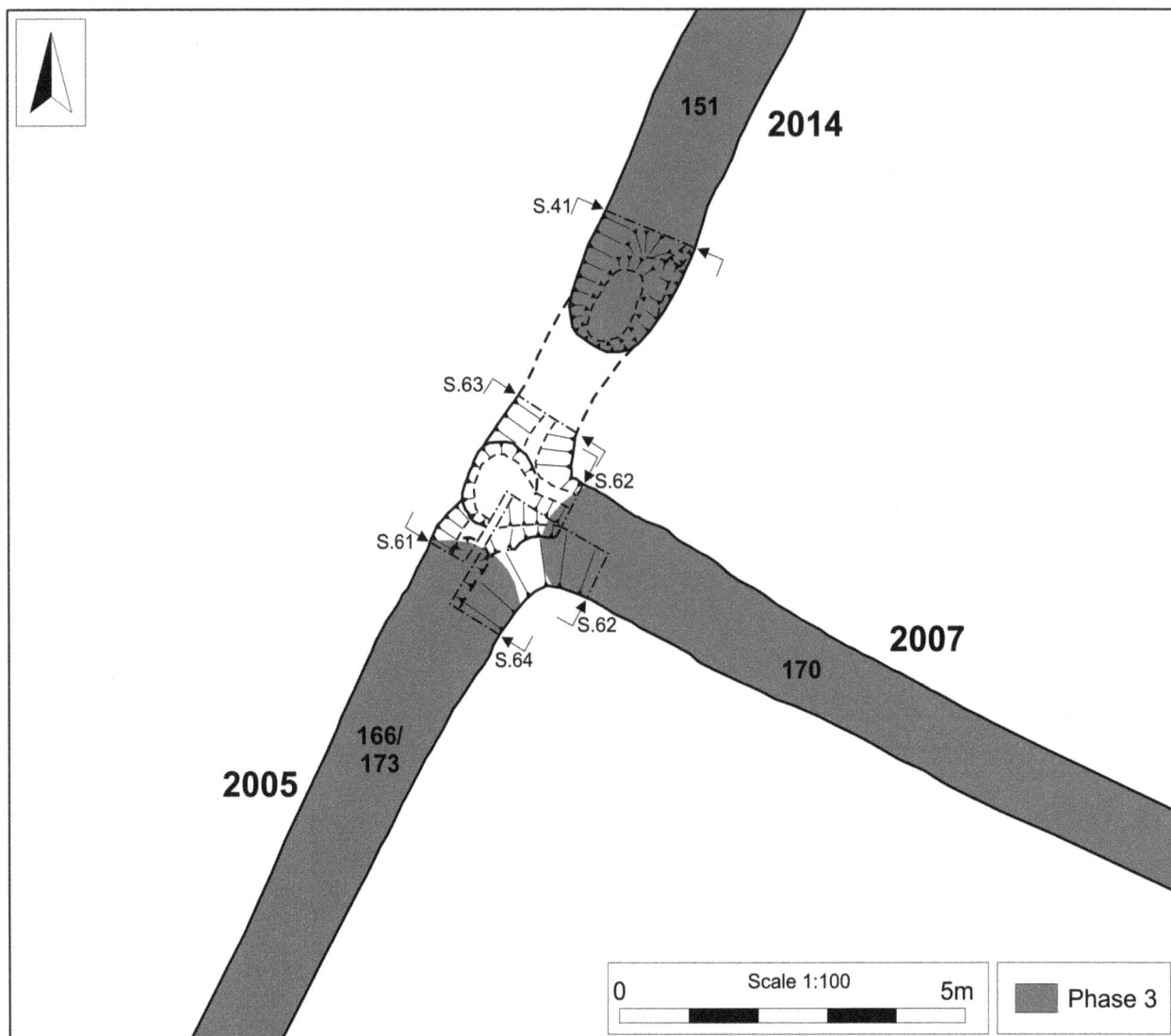

Fig 12c. Plan showing junction of ditches 2007, 2005 and 2014: Phase 3

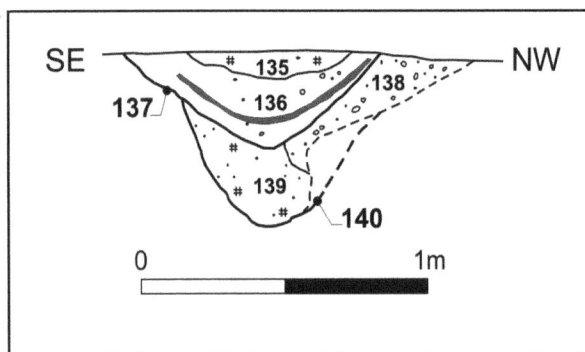

Fig 13. Ditch 2014, Section 38

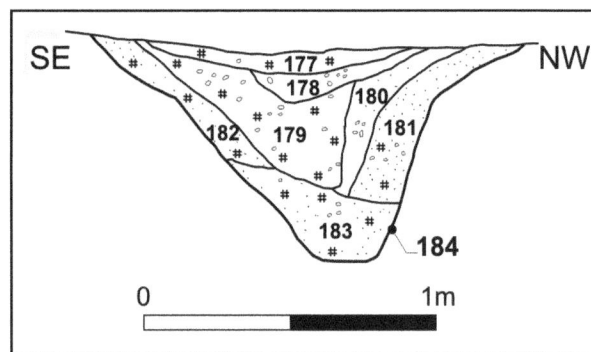

Fig 14. Ditch 2014, Section 53

Phases 2-3 (Fig 4b)

Ditch 2035

The ditch was generally about 1.1 m wide and 0.4-0.5 m deep but its profile was inconsistent. It is possible that there were two cuts, the earlier showing as a steeper lower section. Certainly, Cut 1662 (S159) seems to have had a wide recut (1.7 m) containing a darker, more charcoal-rich upper fill (1660). If this is the case, the recut would have been from the northern side (implying a bank on the southern and eastern sides?). This may have related to the re-definition of the southern terminal which curves sharply. The northern terminal also kinks inexplicably, perhaps because of an obstacle, and ignores the largely silted terminal of Ditch 2036.

The southern terminal (Cut 1547) contained a stony and charcoal-rich dump of material (1546) half way up yielding some undiagnostic pottery and animal bone. Most of the charcoal was identified as ash, but hazel, oak, elm and birch were also present (Table 4.6, Sample 51). The charred remains included barley and blackberry. Charred orache and cereal were identified from the upper fill 1545 (Table 4.6, Sample 53).

Ditch 2033

The ditch formed the eastern side of the double-ditched enclosure and appears to have been a primary element in its design. It was a large feature with a clear recut (Fig 15, S.153) and although its initial construction can be ascribed to Phase 2, it undoubtedly had a long existence and there is no reason to suppose that it was not maintained for as long as the other ditches of this enclosure (Phases 5-7).

The ditch was 2.0-2.2m wide and 0.5-0.6m deep with moderately sloping sides and a broad, flat base. The earliest fills were redeposited silts and gravels (1620, 1619, 1618) which may have built up over a considerable time. These were sharply recut, the section indicating that this was probably from the NW side (indicating a bank on the SE side? – Fig 15, S.153: Fig 6). The main basal fill consisted of laminated grey and dark grey silts (1617) which contained some animal bone and fired clay. There were no other slumping deposits in the recut and it is possible that the feature was kept clean. Later grey and brown fills 1616 & 1615 filled a weathered-back edge and the final fill was a dark peaty loam (1614) like others across the site.

The suggestion of a bank on the SE side may mean that there was no access between this ditch and 2034 or 2035, or the gap may have been a very narrow one (less than 2 m). This assumes that the bank was as wide as the ditch (ie generally 1-2 m wide).

Pit Group 2003

In the southern part of the site this group comprised three small, irregular pit/gully features (120, 146 & 130) with 120 and 130 on the alignment of Ditch 2002, but slightly offset from the line of Ditch 2008 (Fig 11). They may have been positioned with respect to Ditch 2007.

Their forms suggest that they may have been tree root holes, and this is particularly the case with Feature 146 which was cut by 120. They were of varying depth, up to *c* 0.5 m. The upper fill was peaty. Three soil samples from successive fills (131, 132, 133 – Samples 85, 86, 87) in Pit 130 yield no charred remains. It is possible that they represent the grubbing out of a tree at the meeting point of these field boundaries.

The only find of interest was a small bronze adze-head (Fig 40), found by metal detector on the edge of Pit 130.

Ditches 2002, 2001 and 2000

These ditches continued southward from 2003 on a slight curve. The ditches were of varying dimensions along their lengths, up to 1.5 m wide and 0.5 m deep (Fig 8, Cuts 74, 83), but the southern end of 2002 (Cuts 157, 159) were barely perceptible. It is possible that these ditch segments were once continuous with some parts dug deeper, although the 4 m gap between 2001 (Cut 154, 0.5 m deep) and 2000 (Cut 129, 0.2 m deep) may well have been a field entrance.

The ditch profiles were broadly bowl-shaped and although there was no complexity to the fills (generally a single main fill with a peaty upper fill) it is possible that they had been cleaned out from time to time – a factor which may have caused the varying depth.

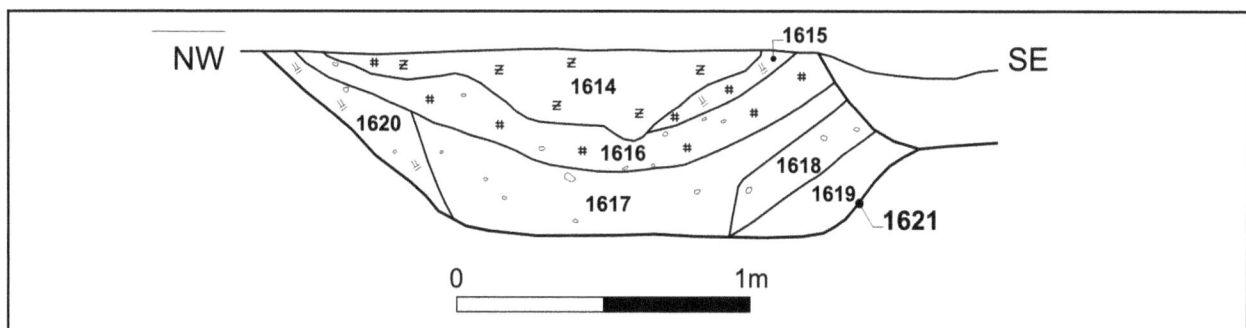

Fig 15. Ditch 2033, Section 153

Ditches 2005 and 2006

The NE-SW boundary was dug in two sections (2005 and 2004). The ditches virtually touched, but the fact that they were dug as separate events (with perhaps a very slight change in direction) suggests that one represents an addition to the other. It is possible that Ditches 2005 and 2006 formed a unit (the terminal of 2006 aligns on that of 2005) with 2004 the boundary of a later field to the south (Fig 4c, Phase 4).

Ditch 2005 showed two phases at its northern terminal (Cut 166, replaced by 173 to a slightly shallower depth - Fig 12c), but elsewhere only one cut was evident. These cuts belonged to Phase 3 of the ditch intersection here and the ditch would seem to have been an addition to the system to the north.

Ditch 2005 was also much deeper at its northern end (up to 0.7 m deep), whereas Cut 164 was 0.5 m and the southern terminal, 199, 0.4 m deep. Cuts 164 and 199 showed a markedly asymmetrical cross-profile with a much steeper western edge, perhaps an indication that the ditch had been dug from the eastern side (with a bank to the west, like 2014? – Fig 8). The southern terminal, 199, had a peaty upper fill (202).

Ditch 2006 (Fig 8, Cuts 112, 115) was *c* 0.8 m wide and 0.25-0.30 m deep.

Phases 3-4 (Fig 4c)

Ditch 2004

Ditch 2004 (Cuts 200, 119) was 1.2 m wide and 0.3-0.4 m deep. Cut 119 (S.32) had redeposited gravel on its NW side, perhaps indicating a bank on this side (Fig 8). Like 2005, the upper fill was peaty in both sections.

Ditch 2032 and Pit 1714

Ditch 2032 was a small feature, about 1.0 m wide and 0.35-0.5 m deep with steep sides. A steep interface between the upper and lower fills suggests a possible recut on the SW side, and there was a later small pit (or possible gully terminal) – 1588 – on this side. It is possible that this indicates a bank/hedge to the north.

The ditch cut Ditch 2035, perhaps an indication that any bank associated with this feature would have lain on the other, eastern, side (Fig 6).

The ditch was cut by Pit 1714 (Phase 4, see Pits), although had the irregular and shallow feature recorded as Pit 1588 been a terminal to a later cut, this would have respected Pit 1714, indicating that in the later phase the features were contemporary with each other.

Two soil samples were taken from Cut 1557 (Table 4.6, Samples 49, 50). The upper, darker fill (1555) yielded some wheat grains.

Ditches 2030 and 2044

Ditch 2030 was an insubstantial feature, 0.3 m deep, cut by Ditch 2029 (Phase 5).

Ditch 2044 (0.6 m wide, 0.35 m deep) may have been the earliest of this group forming the northern boundary of Plot 4, since the irregular terminal of 2043 to the west seems to have been shaped around it (Fig 4e). It may have formed part of an enclosure with 2030 Area 5 which was a similar slight feature. In any event, it clearly became integrated with the layout of the other ditches in Area 3.

Phases 5-6 (Fig 4d)

Ditch 2031

Ditch 2031 (Cut 1718) was cut through the upper fills of Pit 1714 and the pit must have been largely infilled by this time. The pit therefore defined the layout of the double ditched enclosure rather than being sited in relation to it. At the west end, Pit 1942 was probably later (Fig 4e). There is some suggestion that 2031 terminated to the west of Pond 1907, having been cut by it, leaving a gap of *c* 2-3 m to the terminal of Ditch 2029.

The ditch was 2.3 m wide and 0.8 m deep with moderate sides. The successive fills were dark clays and silts. The lowest (1653) contained poorly preserved, compressed, roundwood with peat (Plate 3). An environmental sample (Table 4.7a, Sample 59) was dominated by chickweed. The succeeding fills were grey silts (1652, 1650), but the middle fill (1649) was black. The section (S.156) suggests it may have been within a shallow recut. The upper fills (1648, 1647) were also dark suggesting the accumulation of a lot of organic matter.

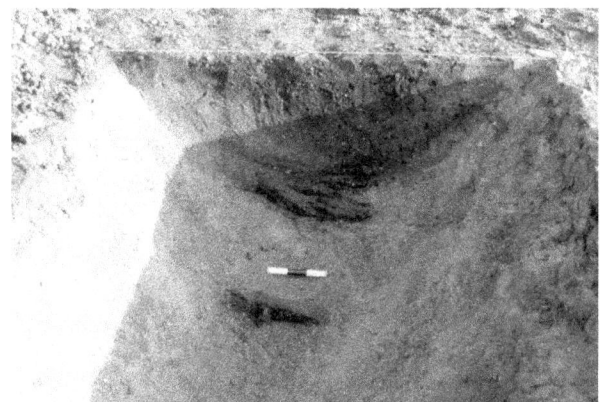

Plate 3. Ditch 2031 (Cut 1651) with degraded wood fragments in base, looking east

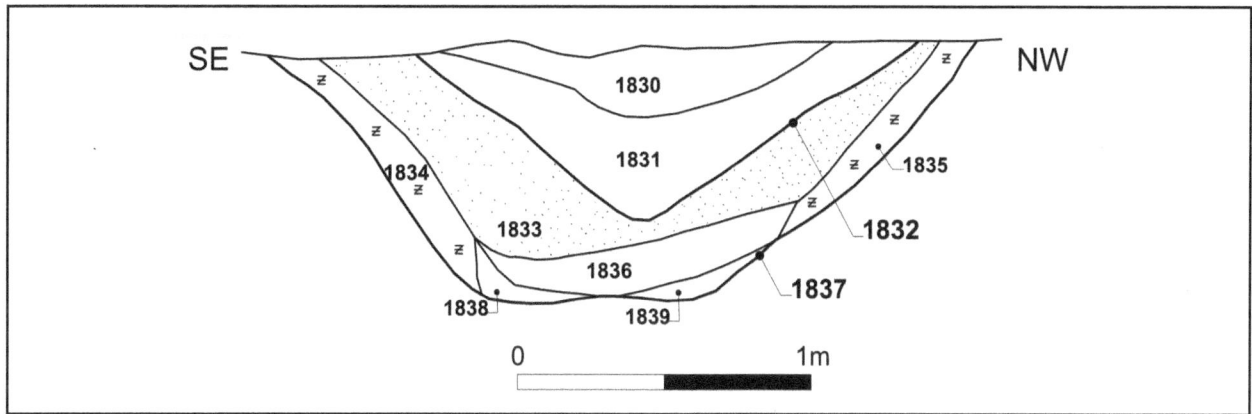

Fig 16. Ditch 2029, Section 189

First phase of Ditch 2029

Ditch 2029 was a substantial feature about 2.0 m wide and 0.8-0.9 m deep. The section on its western arm (1837) showed a shallower recut (1832) (S.189) and recuts can also be identified in the other sections (S.202, S.203, S.205).

No recuts were identified in the terminal (Fig 6 - 1811) but the terminal itself was shallower than the main body of the ditch (S.184) and it is possible that this was the later cut which extended further SE than the original. This later cut of 2029 was shown to cut Ditch 2030. Ditch 2029 may have been recut with respect to Pond 1907.

Cuts 1934, 1918 and 1837 showed comparable sequences of fills. Above greyish silty fills (1933, 1919, 1836) were substantial deposits of redeposited silty gravel (1932, 1917, 1833). These were mainly on the south and SE sides suggesting a bank on this side of the ditch and were steeply recut on the north and NW sides (Fig. 16, S.189). The fills of the later cut were light browns and greys, with an upper dark peaty fill present in Cuts 1918 (Fill 1913), 1837 (Fill 1830) and 1925 (Fill 1920). Cut 1925 was not typical of the ditch in its sequence of fills, although it did contain a basal deposit of sand and gravel (1924), again mostly on the south side, which may correspond to the redeposited gravels in the other cuts. An environmental sample from the silts above this gravel (Table 4.7b, Sample 77, Fill 1923) contained meagre remains but included mainly lentil and rose.

Plate 4. Ditch 2025 (Cut 1684), looking north-west

The evidence therefore suggests that this ditch was a long-lived feature, probably initially contemporary with Ditch 2031 in Phase 5, but continuing throughout the lifetime of the enclosure (Phase 7/8?).

First phase of Ditch 2025

Ditch 2025 was a continuation of 2029 although it was smaller, 1.5-2.0 m wide and becoming progressively shallower towards the east – from 0.75 m (Cut 1788) to 0.60 m deep (Cut 1657) (Fig 6). Cuts 1596 and 1579 at the eastern terminal were shallower still (0.44 m) and it appears that these relate to a later recut only, the earlier cut being absent. Shallower recuts are visible in the deeper sections to the west (S.157, S.180, S.162).

The early phase of ditch has a similar sequence of fills to Ditch 2029. Cut 1788 shows a substantial deposit of clean natural silt and gravel towards the top of the ditch on its NE side (Fill 1783). It is possible that this was deliberately deposited before the ditch was recut toward its SW side. There is similarly a deposit of clean silt and gravel on the NE side of Cut 1684 (Fill 1682) (Plate 4). This is not evident with Cut 1657 where the earlier cut was filled with a homogeneous light grey silt (1656).

The possible recut in these three sections contained darker fills. Its depth varied between about 0.30 and 0.44 m and its width between 0.7 and 1.5 m. These are similar dimensions to the terminal cuts 1596 and 1579. The upper fills of Cuts 1596 (Fill 1593) and 1684 (Fill 1680) had a peaty element which suggests that this recutting was quite late.

The evidence can be interpreted as indicating a gap of 25 m in the SE corner of this enclosure, later blocked by a re-digging and extension of the ditch. The gravel bank was on the NE side.

Phases 6-7

Ditch 2027

The ditch formed the inner boundary to the double-ditched enclosure and appears to have been laid out with respect to the outer boundary (2029), Pond 1907 and Pit 1942, which it may well have followed in the construction sequence, although all were in contemporaneous use.

Ditch 2027 was examined with four sections (Fig 6 - Cuts 1866, 1864, 1878/1881, 1822). The section on the northern arm (Fig 17, S.196) clearly showed two cuts, Cut 1881 lying to the north, recut by 1878 to the south when the earlier ditch had silted in and its line lost (or overgrown by a hedge?). The earlier cut was the larger (*c* 1.2 m wide and 0.72 m deep) while 1878 was 1.1 m wide and 0.6 m deep. Nearer the NE terminal, Cut 1864 can also be interpreted as two (S.195) with the original cut (0.4 m deep) recut to the north by a shallower cut. The ?earlier cut contained a few sherds of plain pottery (1863). The ?recut contained a substantial deposit of clean sand and gravel (1862) which may relate to a bank on this side. The latest fill (1861) was a dark silt which may have filled a second recut. The NE terminal (1866) itself was 0.35 m deep with a single fill.

In contrast the western arm of this ditch (1822) was a smaller feature (0.9 m wide, 0.26 m deep) with only a single cut evident. It is possible that the earlier ditch had terminated at the NW corner with just the later cut extending southward.

Ditch 2026

While this ditch would essentially appear to be an extension of Ditch 2027, forming the south side of the double-ditched enclosure, the excavated sections (Fig 6 - Cuts 1895, 1679, 1696) show complex series of fills suggesting several phases of cutting and infilling. Cut 1895 (Fig 18, S.201) shows three or four possible recuts to the original ditch (1.4 m wide and 0.63 m deep), each progressively shallower but tending to maintain an asymmetrical profile with a steep southern edge and a shallower northern edge. This probably indicates that the ditch was dug from the northern side. As elsewhere the upper fill (1889) was dark although not peaty.

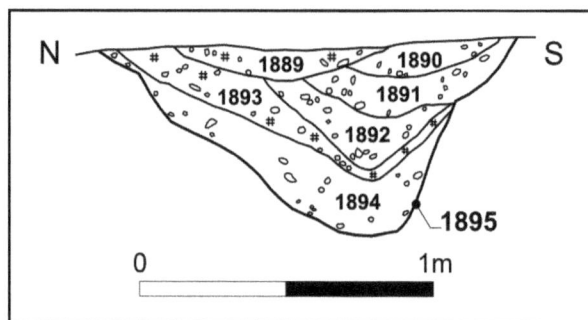

Fig 18. Ditch 2026, Section 201

Cut 1679 showed just three fills, the steepness of their interfaces perhaps indicating three separate cuts. The uppermost fill (1676) was a soft, mid to dark grey sediment.

The south-east terminal (Cut 1696) was 1.5 m wide and 0.88 m deep with steep sides and a flattish base. There were possibly two shallower recuts. The earlier recut contained a dark fill in its base (1693), overlain by a deposit of gravel (1692), edge silts (1695) which yielded a group of perforated shells (Chapter 5), and further grey silt deposits (1690). This appeared to have been recut to a depth of 0.4 m. The upper fills (1688, 1687) were dark grey, becoming black. This may relate to the onset of peat formation, although as elsewhere it is possible that concentrations of vegetation and leaf litter in the unmaintained ditch, which was becoming progressively inadequate for drainage purposes, resulted in the highly organic nature of these late sediments.

Ditch 2024

This ditch was a probable addition to the double-ditched enclosure on its SE side. Rather than continue the alignment of the enclosure boundary southward, it steps out to the east and appears to be aligned on 2035, so it forms part of the overall design of the eastern part of the site. The ditch was 0.7-1.0 m wide and about 0.4 m deep with unremarkable greyish brown silty fills (Cuts 1518, 1536, 1560).

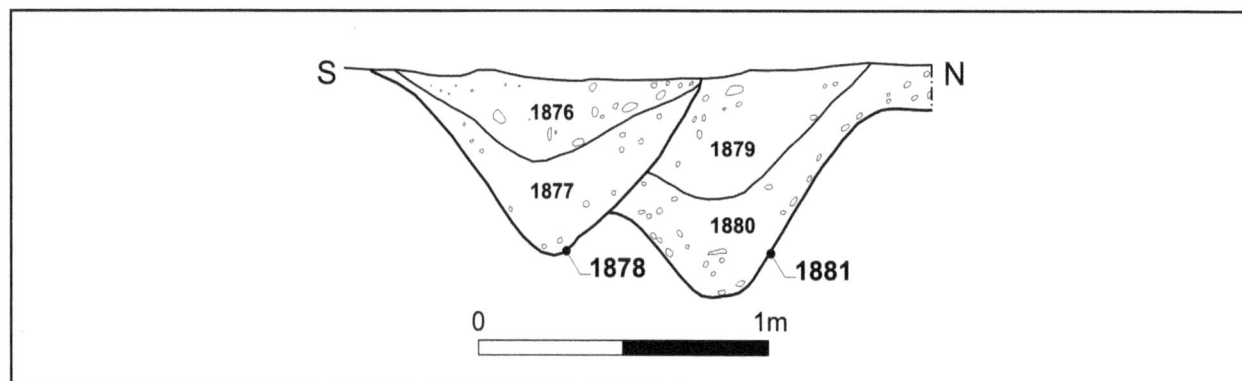

Fig 17. Ditch 2027, Section 196

Ditch 2040

Ditch 2040 was 1.8-2.0 m wide and 0.6-0.7 m deep, with a broad, flat or gently rounded base (Fig 4e). Its southern terminal (Cut 1874) was about 1 m from Ditch 2029 and it seems likely that it was positioned with respect to that ditch, although it is possible that Ditch 2029 was aligned on the terminal of 2040 (hence the non-rectangular shape of the double ditched enclosure?). The kink in the southern part of 2040 is not readily explicable, but there is an overall irregularity to the course of this ditch which suggests that it had to take account of existing features. There is a gap of 2.5 m between the northern terminal and Ditch 2041 which suggests a deliberate entrance.

There is a complexity to the fills in some of the sections which suggests recutting, but there is no consistent pattern. Generally the broad, flattish nature of the cross-profile suggests a long use of the ditch with periodic cleaning out. The southern terminal (1874; Fig 19, S.199) had an almost certain recut. The earlier cut contained a deposit of greyish gravelly silt (1872) on its SE side which appeared to be slumping or infilled ?bank material. The later central and narrower cut contained a series of light to dark grey silts, including a thin black lens (1869). The uppermost peaty fill (1867) filled a shallow depression.

To the north, Cut 515 had simple primary and secondary fills, again with a final peaty deposit in the top of the ditch, the earlier cut probably having been removed completely (Fig 6). In Cut 522 there were slumping deposits on both sides as well as the base of the ditch (526, 541, 530). Fill 526 yielded a plain sherd of pottery, but a soil sample (Table 4.6, Sample 26) contained little of note. These deposits were succeeded by varying brown and grey silts. The uppermost fill (536) was a dark, uncompacted peaty deposit. The section here was complicated by shallow features on either side which appeared to be root holes.

The northern terminal (Cut 552) contained a series of dark grey or grey-brown gravelly silts without substantial amounts of redeposited gravel or indication of recutting. A sherd of pottery came from a dark fill edge fill 557. The upper fill (553) was again peaty.

Ditch 2041

Ditch 2041 (Terminal 593, Cut 590) was very similar in form and size to 2040, with a similar character to its fills and can be considered to be essentially the same ditch. A lower dark silt in the terminal (Fill 600) proved to contain some waterlogged material (Table 4.7a, Sample 25) dominated by elder seeds. The charcoal was poorly preserved but included oak and hazel. A sample from the fill above (Table 4.6, Sample 24, 601) was less useful. Cut 590 contained a similar sequence of fills and both sections showed a peaty uppermost deposit. There was possible recuts in both sections but these were not clear.

Ditch 2043

Ditch 2043 was dug in 2 phases, the earlier only surviving as the short southern arm (Cuts 613 and 604) dug parallel to 2041, either at the same time or as a later addition. This was only 0.28-0.38m deep and would have been removed by the later cut (611, 563, 620) along the east-west arm. A soil sample from 613 (Sample 23) yielded little of interest.

The recut was about 1.2 m wide and 0.5 m or a little more deep and was shown to respect 2044 to the east. Its several fills were orange-brown and grey-brown silts without distinctiveness.

Ditch 2042

Ditch 2042 was laid out parallel to 2043 and 2044, and 1.5 m to the north. It was of similar dimensions to 2043 (0.75-1.20 m wide), and uniformly 0.5 m deep with steep sides. Cuts 634 and 571 showed narrower and shallower recuts offset to the north. Furthermore, deposits of redeposited sand and gravel on the southern sides of the earlier cuts of both sections are perhaps indications of a bank on this side. There were also redeposited sands predominantly on the southern side of Cuts 638 and 577, which presumably related to the recut.

There is therefore a good indication of a bank to the south which would have occupied the 1.5 m gap between 2042 and 2043/2044 (Fig 6). This probably extended down the eastern side of 2041 and 2040.

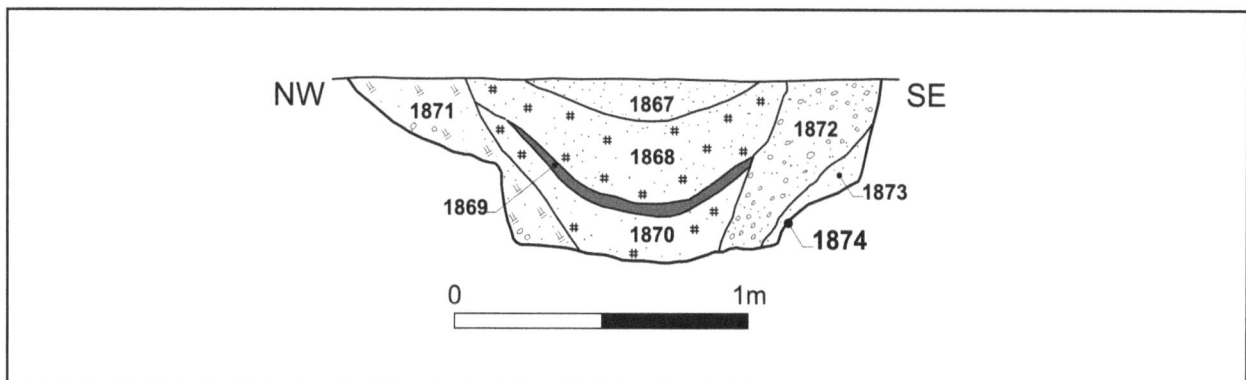

Fig 19. Ditch 2040, Section 199

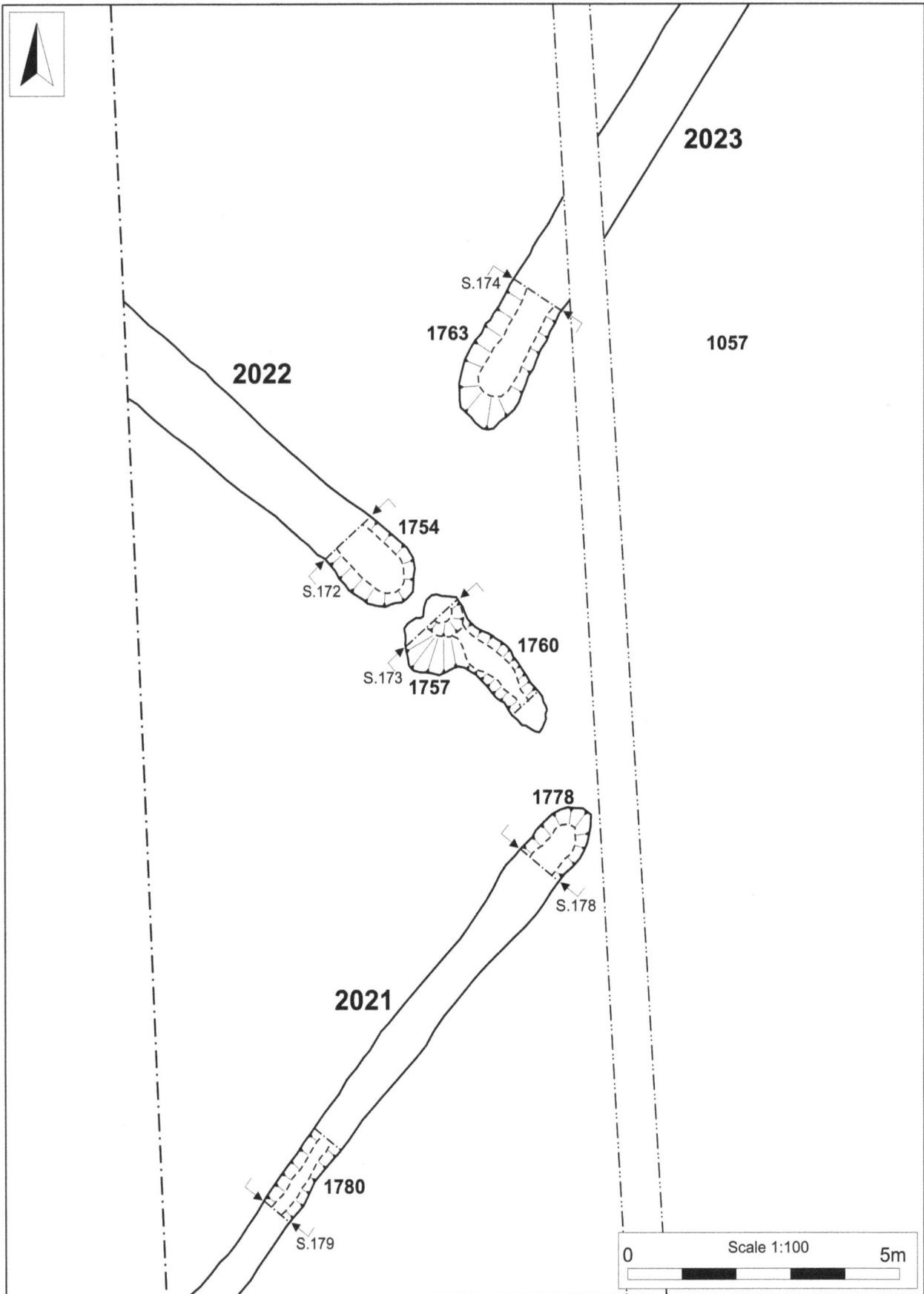

Fig 20. Plan showing junction of ditches 2021, 2022 and 2023

Phases 7-8 (Fig 4f)

Ditch 2023

Ditch 2023 was a rectilinear feature running SW from a northern terminal (Fig 6, Cut 1725) to a southern terminal (Fig 7, Cut 1763). Although it was clearly an addition to the double ditched enclosure, it was aligned on the terminal of 2026 and a possible terminal of the early phase of 2025, so it may have been contemporary with the earlier rather than later phase of this enclosure (ie. Phase 6). In Phase 7 the outer ditch (2025) was extended to block this 25 m gap.

The ditch was examined with seven sections (Cuts 1725, 1723, 1613, 1599, 1602, 1751, 1763). The ditch had a varying profile, about 0.7-1.1 m wide and generally 0.4-0.6 m deep, with a V-shaped profile, although the northern terminal 1725 and Cut 1599 were smaller. The fills were unremarkable with grey silts generally overlying browner silts.

Ditch 2028

In Phase 7 or 8 Ditch 2028 was added to the inner ditch 2026. This seems to have been undertaken to block a southern entrance to the double-ditched enclosure and presumably would have been contemporary with the extension of 2025.

Ditch 2022, Posthole 1760 and Ditch 2021

This arrangement of features formed the north-eastern corner of another enclosure at the southern end of 2023. Posthole 1760, at the terminal of 2022 and possibly cutting a small gully (S.173) may have been for a gatepost (Fig 20). The gap between it and the terminal of 2021 was 3-4 m. The pit was, however, quite substantial, 0.5 m in diameter and 0.6 m deep, and it may have been a free-standing marker post for Ditch 2023. There were hints of a possible post-pipe (1758) about 150 mm in diameter at the base.

An insubstantial ditch, 2022, aligned with respect to the terminal of 2023 and Posthole 1760, and a similar ditch, 2021 aligned with respect to 2022, indicating another sequence of construction of the sort found at other boundary corners.

Ditch 2045

Ditch 2045 was the first to be laid out parallel to 2040 to the west, 13-15 m away. It was about 1.0 m wide and 0.40-0.46 m deep. The fills were unremarkable and two soil samples from Cut 551 (Table 4.6, Sample 27, Fill 550; Sample 22, Fill 549) yielded little of note.

It is unclear how far south 2045 extended. It either terminated or was cut away by 2046 and extension or recut to 2045.

Phases 8 and 9 (Fig 4g)

Ditch 2046

Ditch 2046 was generally larger than 2045, 1.2-1.4 m wide, and deepening from 0.3 m (Cut 511) to 0.75 m (Cut 519) and 0.58 m (Cut 1885). (The shallowness of 511 actually suggests that 2045 never extended this far south since it should have been visible underneath 511). The deeper southerly sections showed a simple sequence of three fills, the upper of which was peaty.

The course of 2046 is not quite straight and appears to mirror the alignment of the ditches to the east, 2040 and 2029, although in a less pronounced fashion.

Ditch 2047 Phase 8-9

The westernmost ditch in this area was aligned either on the southern terminal of 2045 or the northern terminal of 2046. The terminal (Fig 6, 509) was disturbed by a later intrusion, but Cuts 546 and 523 showed similar broad, but relatively shallow profiles, about 1.3-1.4 m wide and 0.30-0.36 m deep. A soil sample (Table 4.6, Sample 29) from the main fill (525) of Cut 523 yielded meagre remains.

Middle Bronze Age Pits And Undated Pits

Pit 20: Plot 11

Pit 20 was irregular on the surface with the appearance of a tree root (Fig 8), but the main sub-circular pit proved to be quite regular in shape, about 3 m in diameter and 1.4 m deep (Fig 21, S.20). There were, however, large pieces of preserved rootwood in the base of the pit, extending beyond the pit itself. This would suggest that the pit had been dug to remove a tree.

The primary fill (97) was a thin deposit of dark, soft grey silt with preserved organic material (Table 4.7a, Table 4.10, Sample 8). Several pieces of preserved wood in this deposit were identified as alder and willow. (There was also charcoal.) There was no indication of worked wood.

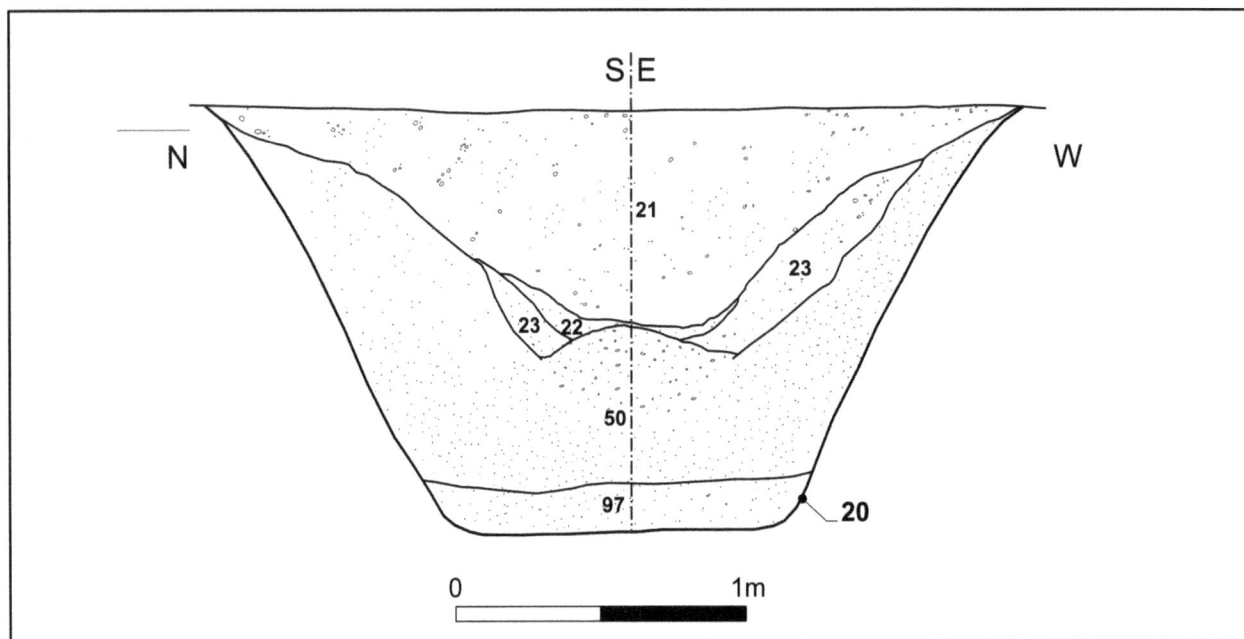

Fig 21. Pit 20, Section 20

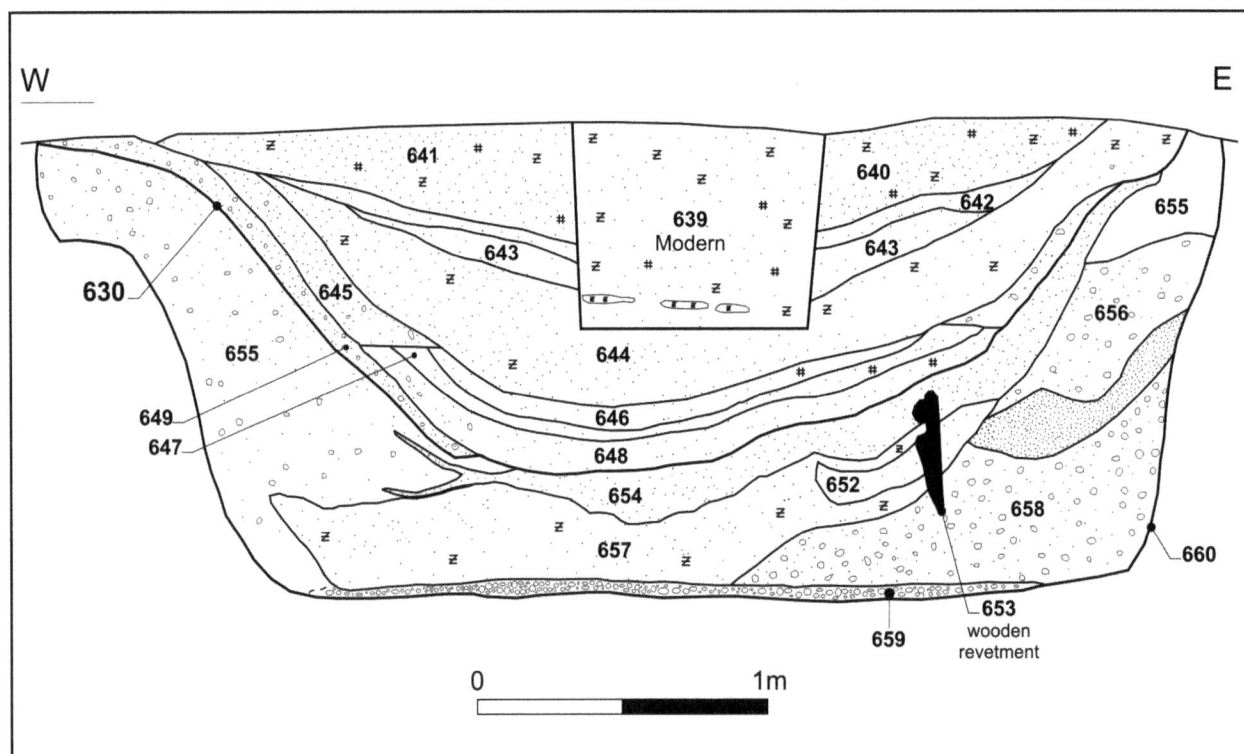

Fig 22. Pit 660, Section 93

This was succeeded a thick deposit of clean sand and gravel (50), up to 700 mm thick in the centre and extending up the sides, undoubtedly representing the collapsed pit walls. This deposit accounted for about half the volume of the pit, suggesting that original pit was much narrower. It may well have been more irregular as well, since the recorded sides should be interpreted as shear planes rather than the cut edges.

The upper fills, 23, 22, 21 were grey or dark grey silts with sorted gravel which probably represent natural accumulation over the long term. There were no finds other than a burnt flint from 21.

Pits 61 and 72: Plot 11

Pit 61

This was a small feature 1.2 m in diameter and 0.6 m deep with near-vertical sides and a flat base. The upper edges showed some weathering, but the pit largely had a single fill (60) which was a dark sandy silt containing some charcoal and ash lenses (Table 4.6, Sample 2). The charcoal was mainly of *Prunus* (plum or cherry), and there were smaller quantities of oak, alder and hazel. There were also some sherds of pottery and fragments of animal bone.

Pit 72

Pit 72 lay 10 m SW of Pit 61. It was of a different form to Pit 61, being about 3.5 m in diameter and 0.7 m deep with shallow sides. It had a sequence of four silty fills (71, 70, 69 and 68) becoming progressively greyer upwards. Sample 4 from Fill 70 contained charcoal from a variety of wood species including (in decreasing order) alder, willow, oak, beech, hazel and possibly hornbeam (Table 4.7a). Wheat and barley grains were also present. Small sherds of plain pottery and fired clay, together with some animal bone, came from this context, and pottery from the upper fill (68).

Interpretation

While it is difficult to determine the functions of these pits, the presence of charred material and small quantities of domestic refuse (including grain) suggest that they were near an area of domestic activity. The range of species of charred wood suggests a very varied local environment – perhaps scrub or managed hedgerows.

Pit 660: Plot 4

Pit 660 was about 4.3 m in diameter and 1.6 m deep with near-vertical sides and a flat base (Figs 6 and 22, S.93).

There was a thin primary fill of silty gravel (659) which was stained black with organic material. The only artefact from this fill was a split timber stake tip (40 mm long and 25x20 mm). Around the edges this was overlain by thick deposits of slumped sand and gravel (658 and deposits above, E side; and 655, W side). The main fill

in the centre of the pit was an organic bluish clayey silt (Table 4.7a, Sample 32, 657), partly interleaved with the slumping.

On the eastern side of the pit a group of four pieces of worked timber (653, i-iv), which had been used as closely spaced stakes, driven through 657 (at least partly) and into the gravel slumping below (658) (Plates 5 and 6). These were all roundwood and typically 500 mm long and 100-120 mm across, the tops of ii-iv having being broken or rotted away (Appendix 1, Wood Catalogue).

Artefact (i) was a ¼ split branch with a burr which appears to have been fashioned into a maul or mallet with a slender handle (30 mm in diameter). It seems too complete and does not seem to have been suitable for a stake, so it may just have been dropped with the other pieces (Fig 23).

Plate 5: Plate Pit: 660, looking south

Plate 6: Pit 660, group of stakes

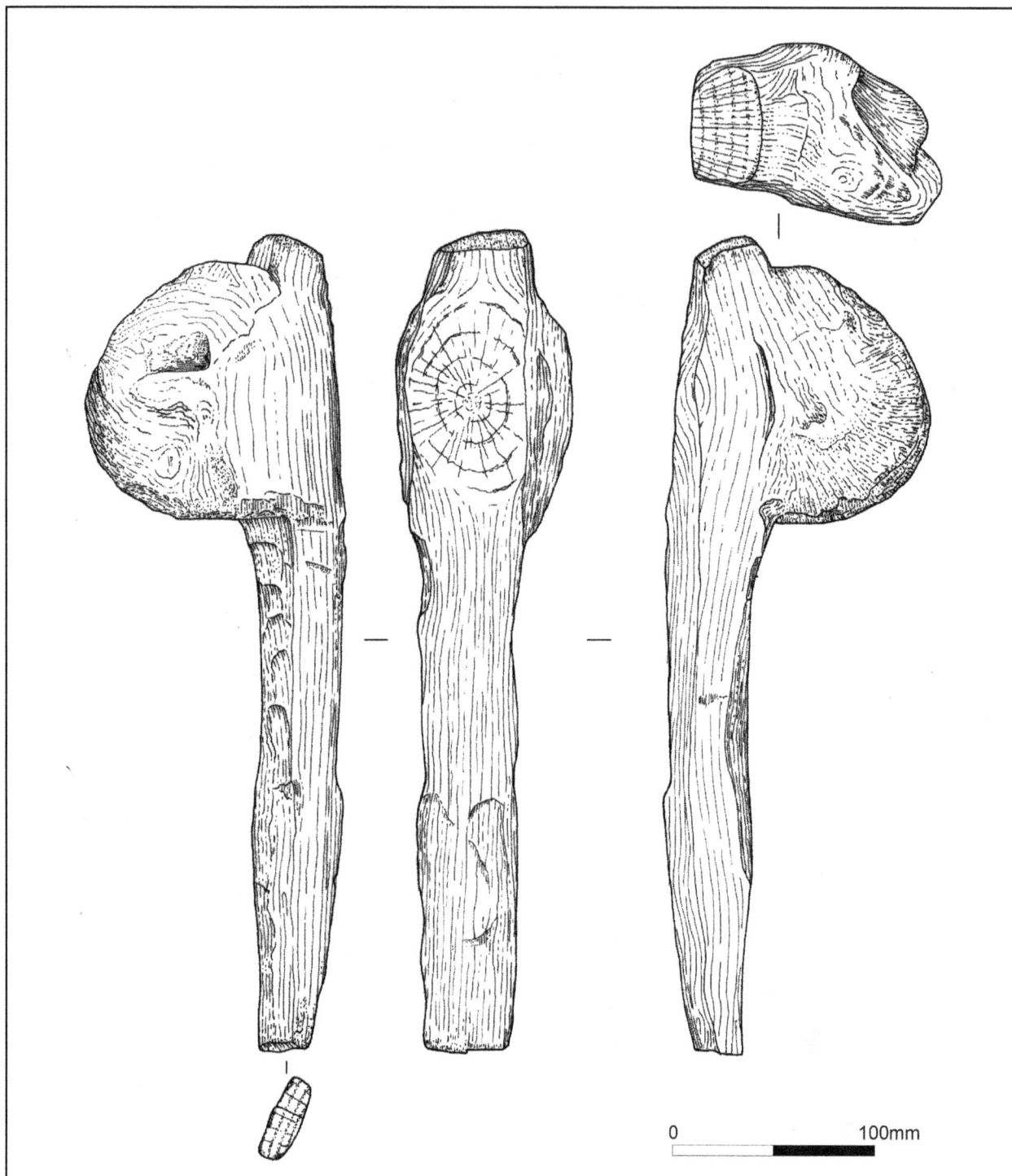

Fig 23. Wooden ?maul 563i from Pit 660 (drawn by S J Allen)

The fragmentary 'revetment' of stakes had an accumulation of grey silt behind it (652) but this was succeeded by laminated sandy silt which interleaved with a darker more clayey silt (654) in the centre of the pit. This seems to represent an accumulation following the demise of the revetment.

Above this were a series of dark bands of sediment, silty in the middle of the pit but sandier towards the edges (648, 647, 646, 645). Although this was originally interpreted as a filling a recut of the pit, it seems more likely to indicate a period of stability with a gradual accumulation in the centre which probably still retained

water. The bulk of the upper fill (644) also appears to be a minutely laminated accumulation which appears to be natural. The uppermost fill (641) had the dark loamy character of the 'peaty' fills elsewhere suggesting a very late infilling.

Interpretation

The amount of edge slumping would seem to indicate that the pit was originally rather smaller than it later became, the edges as defined representing the shear planes of later collapse. The lack of basal accumulation suggests that the feature was kept quite clean during its use, and the single stake point from the lowest fill (659) suggests that it was probably lined. This lining must have been largely removed before the sides of the pit collapsed since there was no evidence for it under the slumping.

The remains of stake revetment 653 must belong to a later attempt to shore up the sides since the stakes were driven into the slumping (658) and could not have penetrated the underlying gravel. After this was eventually removed or rotted, there was more inwash and some sort of stability achieved. Most, if not all, of the upper fills would seem to have derived from gradual silting, and it is possible that the development of peat started before the hollow was completely filled.

Pit 1026: Plot 2

Pit 1026 was located at the northern end of the long but discontinuous boundary ditch whose northern segment comprises Ditch Group 2020 (Fig 7).

The pit was 3.8m in diameter and 1.5m deep with an uneven profile of steep sides and a rounded base (Fig 24, S.102).

The central basal fill was a dark sandy silt with organic material (1036). A timber stake (1038) was found lying horizontally in the southern part, and recovered in seven fragments. It was split timber with a total length of about 1.38 m, 50-60 mm wide and just 20-30 mm thick. At the top of this fill, in the centre, was a jumble of wood, 1049, comprising (i) a ¼ split squared timber 875 mm long, and 124 x 98 mm thick, overlain by (ii) roundwood with a torn off limb, 560 mm long and 90/74 mm diameter. These overlay some highly decayed fragments.

Overlying 1036 at the edges of the pit were mixed slumped sediments 1034 and 1035. Fill 1035 contained a fragment of roundwood (1037), 320 mm long and 50 mm in diameter which had been cut diagonally at both ends. This does not seem to have been a stake.

The main fill above these slumping deposits was a dark greyish silt 1033, which was overlain by lighter sandier deposits 1032 and 1031. From the top of 1031 was cut a pit (1029) with a V-shaped profile. This was filled with a dark peaty sediment (1030), very similar to the upper layer of 1026 (1028) suggesting that it post-dated 1026 by a considerable time. Nevertheless, the position of 1029 centrally within 1026 suggests that the location was deliberate, possibly to hold a post or other marker (Plate 7).

Interpretation

The sequence of deposits suggests that the pit may originally have been lined with stake uprights, presumably holding shoring, and that the pit sides collapsed when this was removed. The length of Stake 1038 (the only evidence of the lining) suggest that the shoring could have been a metre or so high. Other wooden debris was deposited at abandonment, but any structural function of the fragments from 1049 is not known.

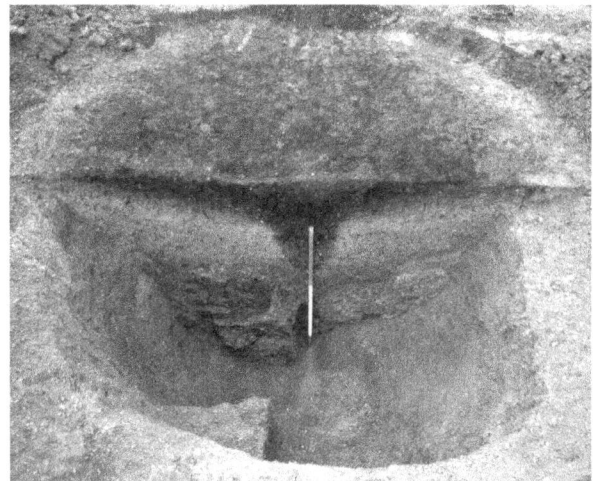

Plate 7: Pit 1026

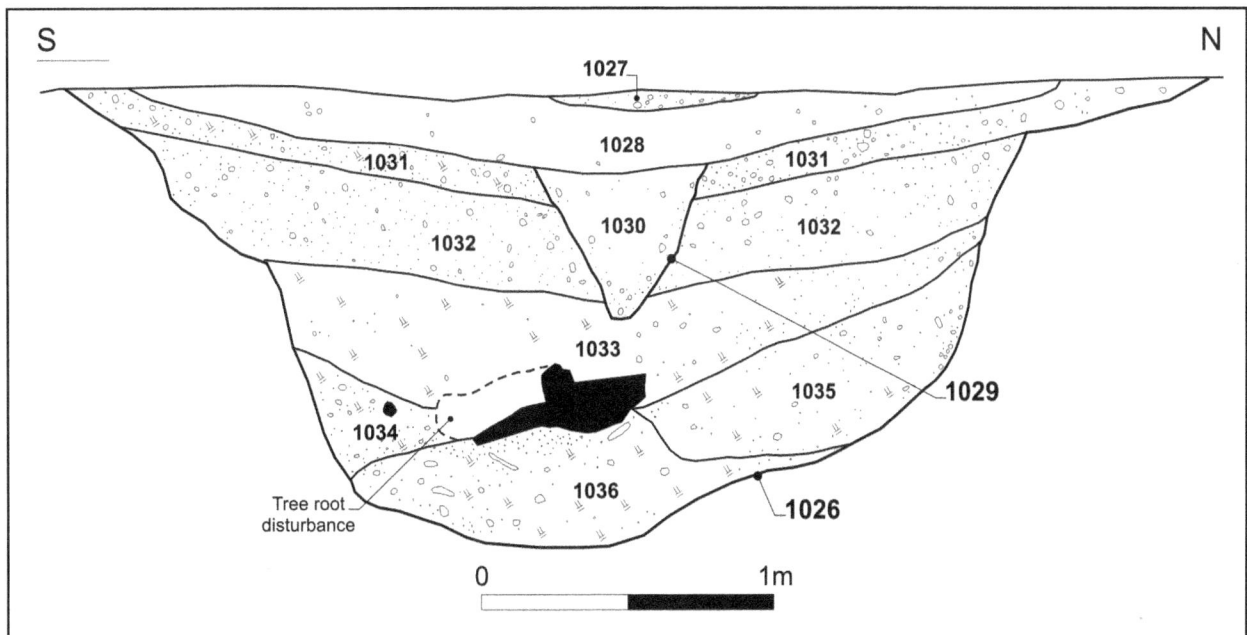

Fig 24. Pit 1026, Section 102

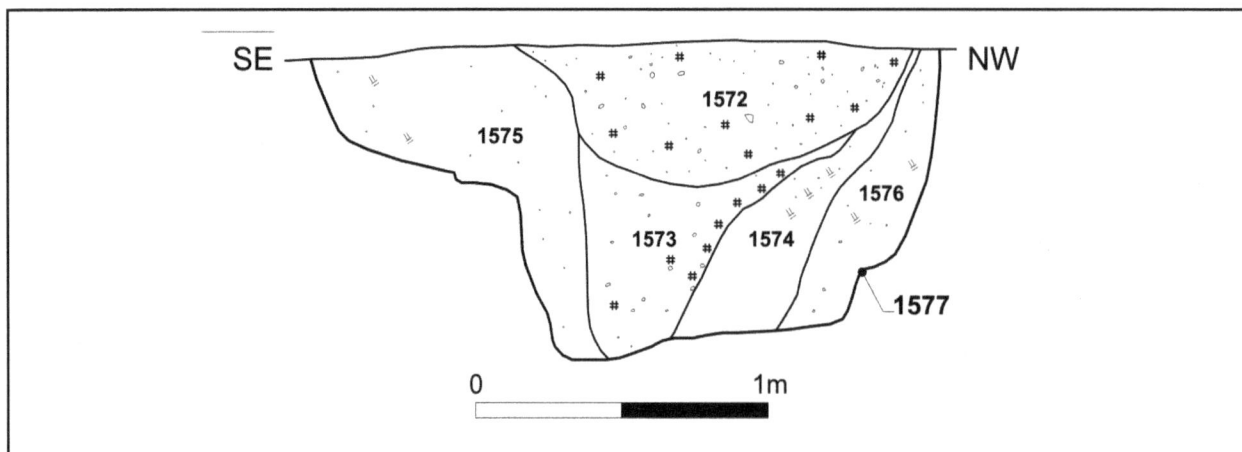

Fig 25. Pit 1577, Section 142

Pits 1577 and 1608: Plot 1

Pit 1577

Pit 1577 was located on the eastern side of the site in an area where some tree throw-holes were also partly examined (Fig 6). It is possible that it was in some way connected with the alignment of the NNE-SSW boundary ditches in this area. It may therefore have been of Phase 1.

The pit was roughly circular and up to 2.1 m in diameter, although this width includes a ledge on the SE side, and the diameter of the main pit was about 1.5 m (Fig 25, Section 142). The pit was nearly 1 m deep. Its pattern of fills was distinctive and unique on the site because of a steep to vertical edge between the redeposited natural sands on the sides (1575, 1576, 1574) and the darker main fill 1573. This suggests that the edges were held back by some means (such as a lining or a post) while the central part was filled.

The secondary slumped material (1574) contained occasion, steeply tipping, lenses of charcoal, which included some identifiable as wheat (Table 4.6, Sample 56). The main fill (1573) was a grey-brown silt containing little of note, although some plain body sherds of pottery were found in this and the upper fill 1572. Fill 1572, which also contained animal bones, occupied a bowl-like depression in the top of the pit and its final filling may have taken place over a longer term than the earlier filling.

Interpretation

The interpretation of this feature is somewhat conjectural, but it was unlike any of the other pits on the site. It was unlike the features interpreted as wells or waterholes on the site mainly because of its relatively small dimensions. It is possible, however, that it held water, because waterlogged material was found at depths of a metre, or less, in some of the other pits, although in this instance there were no dark organic silts in the base and no waterlogged material was found in Sample 55 (although this could be due to later drying out). It must be assumed that it had been lined throughout most of its depth to hold back the slumped material 1575 and 1576, and this

would have created a vertically sided 'well' about 0.7 m in diameter. The ledge on the SE side is without obvious explanation as it does not have the profile to have been caused entirely by slippage and seems rather to have been deliberately dug. Following the withdrawal of the lining the NW partly collapsed, but was sufficiently cohesive not to spread across the base of the pit. The pit must have been mostly infilled shortly afterwards.

Alternatively, the profile of the sediments suggests that the pit held a post. In this interpretation, the 'slumping' deposits would actually have been packed around the post and would have maintained their form for a while after the post had been withdrawn. The non-vertical edge between 1573 and 1574 on the NW side could perhaps have been cut to retrieve the post. The ledge on the SE side is still difficult to explain, but it may have been dug to help erect the post in the first place. The post would have had a diameter of about 300 mm, and, according to accepted thinking about the necessary depth to sink free-standing posts, it probably would have stood 2 metres high.

Pit 1608

Pit 1608 was a relatively isolated feature, 1.8 m in diameter and, as excavated, 0.46 m deep with a bowl-shaped profile. It was in an area of disturbance which was reduced by about 500 mm below the stripped surface, so its depth, in comparison with other features in this area would have been about 0.96 m.

It had a series of very gravelly lower fills (1611, 1610, 1609, 1607, 1606) which contained some organic material which was poorly preserved (Table 4.7a, Sample 58, 1610). The upper fill (1605) was a much darker peaty fill. This contained some waterlogged material including seeds of chickweed, fat hen, and orache, suggesting open ground.

The dark peaty fills are generally taken to indicate a late date, but it is not clear that at this depth, the peaty material would have been the same as that found in the upper fills of the larger ditches and pits. The purpose of this pit is not known. It seems to have been devoid of cultural material. Apart from the pits in Plot 11, which were scattered, the Bronze Age pits tend to cling to the edges of the enclosures. This pit is anomalous in this respect.

36

Pit 1622: Plot 2

The pit was located just south of Ditch Group 2034. It was circular, 4.2 m across and about 1.5 m deep (Fig 26). Its almost bowl-shaped profile appears to have resulted from the near total collapse of the sides which resulted in thick deposits of slumped sand and gravel (1640, 1632, 1639, 1635, 1633, 1630), interleaved with thinner silty lenses and overlying darker basal waterlogged silts (1631,1638).

At the base of the pit were several large timbers. Timber 1686 was a single piece, 1.24 m long and 80 mm in diameter, with a possible worked SE point. This was overlain by 1685, a forked and trimmed piece of roundwood, the main trunk/branch being 2.5 m long and 95 mm in diameter and the fork to the north being 900 mm long and 60 mm in diameter (Plate 8). This was overlain by 1663, a large piece of roundwood 1.55 m long and 92/81 mm in diameter with a pointed SW end.

Timbers 1686 and 1663 could have been used as stakes to line the pit. Their length indicates that they could have lined 2/3rds of the depth of the pit, assuming c 400 mm had been driven into the gravel. The forked piece had clearly been worked and showed a notch below the fork, but it is not known what it would have been for.

It seems that the dismantlement of the pit lining was followed by the collapse of the sides. The upper fills (1629, 1646, 1628, 1627, 1626, 1625, 1624, 1623) have the appearance of gradual accumulations in conditions of greater stability. Several pieces of animal bone were recovered from the higher fills. There was no peatiness to the uppermost sediment, 1623, perhaps suggesting that this was a feature of a relatively early phase which had completely filled in before the onset of wetter conditions in the later 2nd millennium BC.

Plate 8: Pit 1622, timber branch 1685 overlying timber 1686

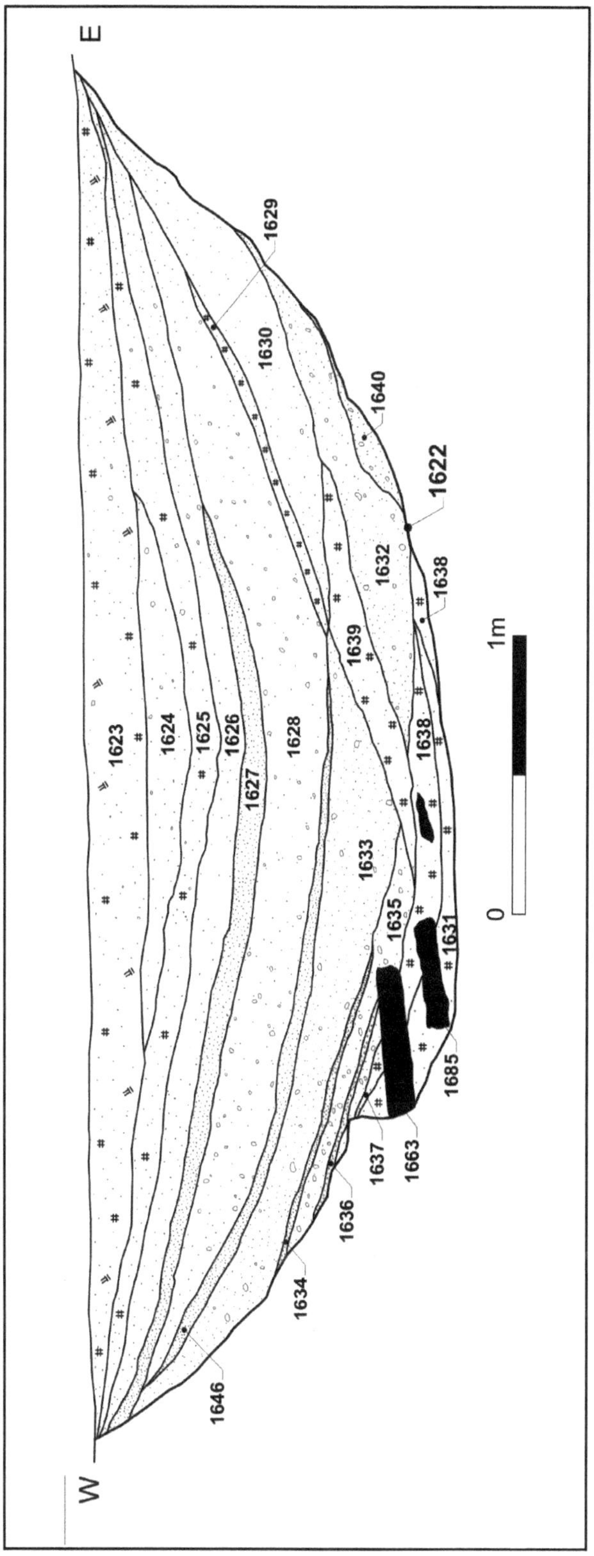

Fig 26. Pit 1622, Section 155

Pit 1942 and Pond 1907: Plot 3 (Phase 6-7)

Pit 1942

The pit was roughly oval and about 2 x 3 m in size. Its upper fills were the same as those in Pond 1907 and the pit was not distinctive until the level at which the timbers appeared (Fig 27). The pit appears to be later than Ditch Group 2031 and recorded in plan as such. The position of

Timber WW and Pegs BB and CC suggest that the pit is later, although it may be possible that the ditch was cut over the top of them since the levels show about 0.3 m between the top of the pegs and the base of the ditch.

Timbers WW and EE; pegs BB and CC
These two similar timbers were found horizontally, parallel, about 1 m apart. They were not at the base of the pit, but within fill 1940. The pegs were, however, driven well into the gravel.

WW was a ¼ split and squared plank (1.63 m long, 150-230 mm wide) with a square mortise hole at the western end 50 mm across, and a possible rectangular mortise hole at the eastern end 100 mm across the plank and 40 mm wide (Fig 28). Pegs CC and BB were set vertically underneath WW at the eastern and western ends respectively. CC was a ¼ split timber trimmed square, 900 mm long and 130 x 45 mm square. BB was roundwood, 650 mm long by 84 mm with a trimmed end.

Although the mortise holes in WW were the right shape to have received these pegs, the holes are too small. Both BB and CC must have been used as supports for WW only.

Timber EE was similar to WW, 1.74 m long, 210 mm wide and up to 55 mm thick, with a squared rebate (220 x 80 mm) at its E end. Toward its western end were two stakes set vertically. Stake DD touched EE on its south side (Plate 9 seems to show the peg broken out of a mortise hole in the plank). It was 580 mm long and 80 mm in diameter. Peg BC was a triangular-sectioned piece of trimmed timber found partly under EE. It was 330 mm long by 55-60 mm across. Also under EE were two horizontal pieces of wood (which may have been pegs). BD was a ½ split timber 360 mm long by 85 m wide and 35 mm thick. BA was squared, 530 mm long, 80 mm wide and 28 mm thick.

The positions of Timbers WW and EE in relation to the pit sides, the pegs, and to each other, suggests that they were more or less *in situ*, rather than discarded pieces, although the timbers themselves may have been re-used. It seems likely that they were some kind of staging to collect water from, although too far apart to use to straddle the water hole. Alternatively they may have been the remains of revetting on two sides (the pegs intended to hold the planks back) but their survival flat rather than on edge is puzzling. At its deepest the base of the pit cut was 1.5 m below the surface of plank WW and 1.25 m below surface of EE

Plate 9: Pit 1942, Timber EE and Peg DD

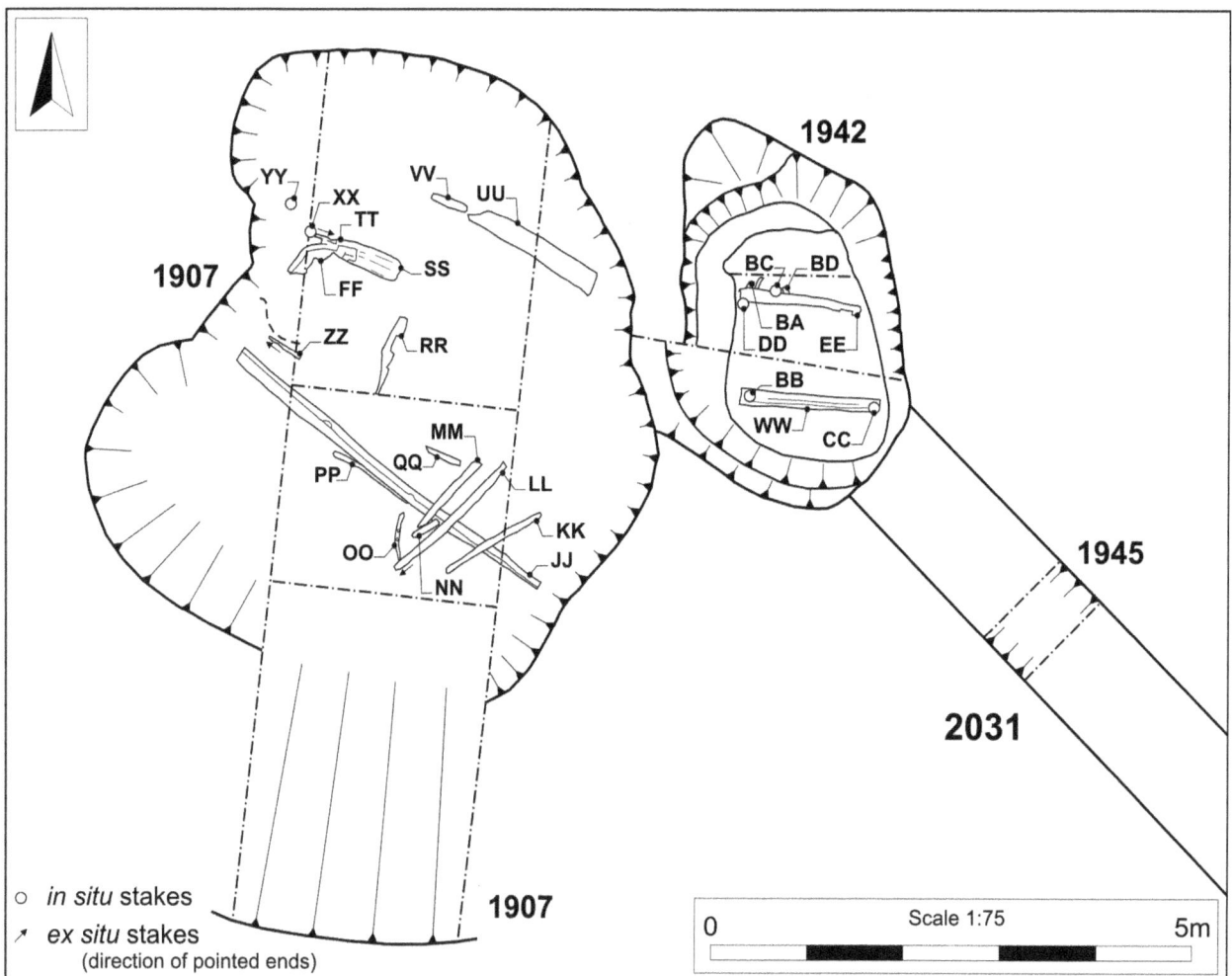

Fig 27. Plan showing pits 1907 and 1942 with wood remains

38

Pond 1907

Pond 1907 is recorded as cutting the lower fills of Pit 1942, but it is possible that it was in contemporary use (Fig 27). It does not seem to have been a direct replacement for 1942, being much larger and probably for a different purpose. The upper fills covered an area about 10 m in diameter, although the lower part of the pit was about 7 m by 5 m. The southern edge formed a shallow ramp suggesting access from this side. The pit had an overall depth of about 1.5 m (below the stripped surface). The lower 300 mm or consisted of dark, organic, olive-grey silts (1905, 1906, 1904) and above this lighter grey silts (1902, 1901) (Chapter 4 and Fig 35, pollen column 79). A cattle skull came from 1902. Fills 1900 and 1899 had a more orange-brown colour. These upper fills (1901, 1900, and 1899) contained several timbers and pegs.

Timber JJ

This was a horizontal ½ split trunk 3.7 m long, slightly thicker at the NW end (280 x 120-150 mm) than at the SE end (230 x 100 mm) where there was a possible tow hole. There were some miscellaneous lengths of wood nearby and under it (NN, OO, PP, QQ), and three almost parallel pieces overlying it at right angles (KK, LL, MM), (Plates 10 and 11).

Stakes KK, LL, MM

Stake LL was a radially split piece made into a stake with a triangular cross-section. It was 1.66 m long and 80 mm across. Its pointed end pointed SW and showed working.

KK, described as a possible stake, was 1.15 m long and 70 mm across. MM was 1.09 m long and 91 mm across. All these pieces were in an advanced state of decay, being the highest pieces encountered.

In situ stakes XX and YY

Stake XX was 450 mm x 70 mm, set almost vertically, and appeared to be holding the notch of Timber TT/SS although this may be just coincidence, 0.7 m to the south, Stake YY was 180 mm long with a triangular cross-section (73 x 60 x 43 mm). Stake XX was radiocarbon dated to *c* 1500-1290 cal BC (95% confidence, 3115 +/- 35, SUERC-13967 - Chapter 7).

Ex situ stake ZZ

This stake had been withdrawn and was lying with its point to the NW about 0.6 m S of XX. It was 330 mm long and 51 mm in diameter.

Worked wood TT/SS and RR

TT/SS appears to be the same piece comprising a halved timber *c* 900 mm long, 260 mm wide and 65 mm thick with a squared notch at the eastern end (TT). The sketch plan suggests that this end might have formed a lap joint, but this could be decay. The W end looks to have been cut.

RR is a notched piece of split and trimmed timber, about 800 mm long. These appear to be two lap joints while the end found pointing south is facetted like a stake. It is possible that this was a peg with rebates cut into it for holding planking on edge. (The gap between the rebates is 200 mm and the 'upper' rebate is about 80 mm deep). The northern end is broken.

Plate 10: Pond 1907, Timber JJ overlain by stakes

Plate 11: Pond 1907, Timber JJ

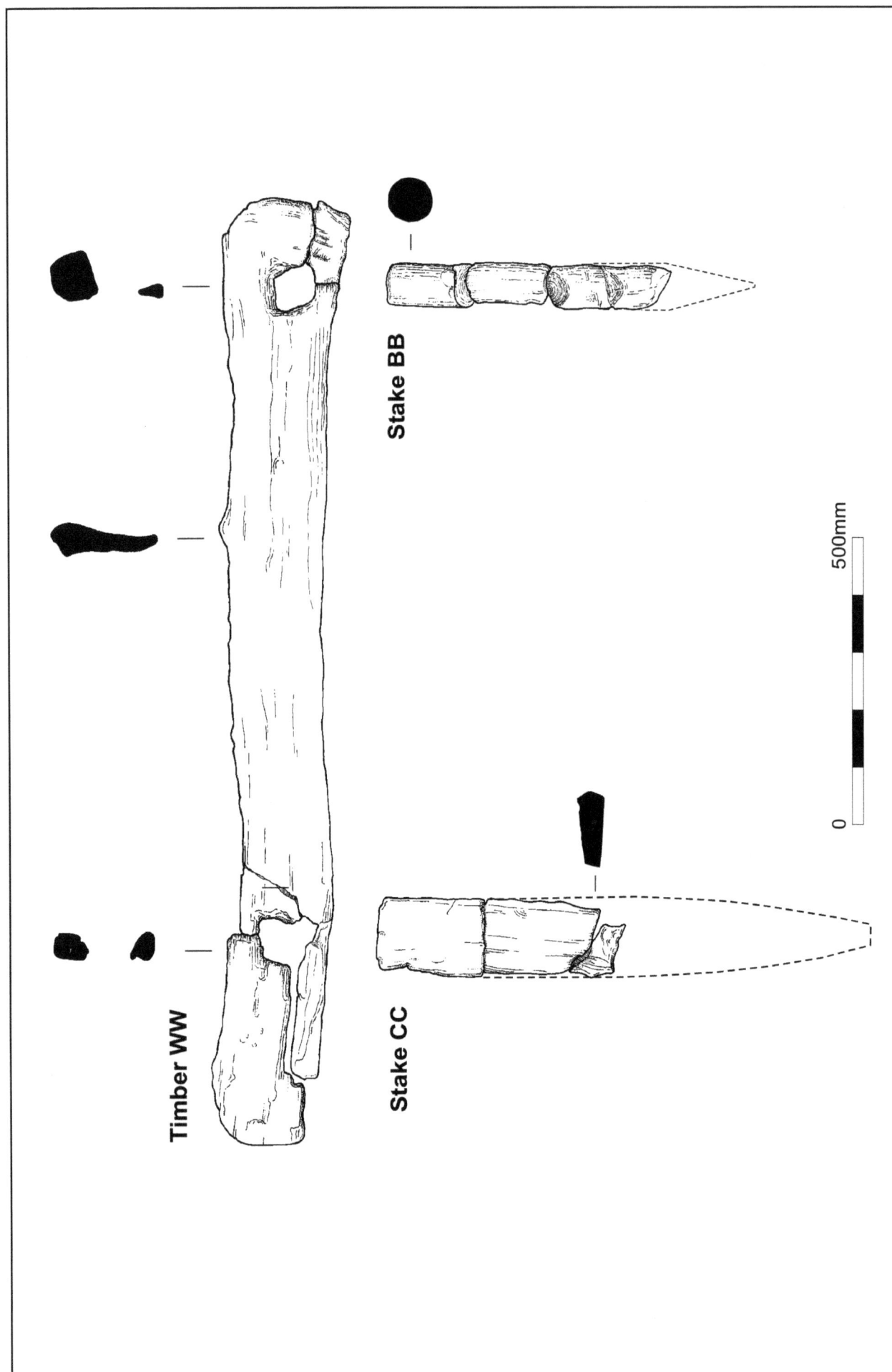

Fig 28. Timber WW and stakes BB and CC

Timbers UU and VV

UU was a large split timber 1.41 m long, 270 mm wide and 130 mm thick. About half the trunk is present, and appears to have sapwood, but no bark. Numerous shallow toolmarks along the trunk show where the bark was cut away.

VV is a smaller split log which seems to have been broken at both ends, the surviving dimensions are length 580 mm, width 150 mm and thickness 40 mm. There are two dished notches on one edge but they are too close together to have served as footholds on a log ladder and the piece is also too thin. It may have been debris from a construction.

Interpretation

There are only two stakes *in situ* to show that there was some form of construction within the pit. The other pegs must have been withdrawn before being discarded, presumably because a structure had been dismantled. If they were discarded quite close to their point of use, it is possible to suggest that there was some kind of revetment curving NW-SE. The long timber JJ seems likely to have been part of the structure since it seems unlikely to have taken to the pond to discard. It may have been too big to take away again. Its position suggests it may have one of the horizontal members of a revetment (the others having been taken out). It is less likely to have been a fence because it has no joints or other means of securing it.

The access to the pond appears to have been from the south and it seems likely that there was a revetment running from YY to KK to strengthen this edge. A possible interpretation is that the small pit 1942 was a waterhole for humans and the large one, 1907, one for their cattle.

Pits 1714, 1860, 1674 (at corners of Plot 3)

Pit 1714 (Phase 4)

Pit 1714, in the NE corner of the double-ditched enclosure, was recorded as cutting Ditch 2032 and cut by Ditch 2031, so it was a relatively early feature predating the enclosure itself (Fig 6). There is no suggestion that the pit had access restricted in any particular direction.

The pit was roughly circular in shape, about 4.6 m north-south by 4.2 m east-west, and reached a depth of 1.85 m (slightly deeper than the section shows – Fig 29, S.169). It was steep-sided with a bowl-shaped profile. It is probable that the sides were originally steeper because the fills showed evidence of side slippage throughout.

The lowest fill (1706) was a thick deposit of gravel stained black with decayed organic matter. Above this there were gravelly slumped deposits on the pit edges, passing through grey to orange-brown in colour (1709, 1708, 1707, 1712, 1711). The main fills consisted of a sequence of silty and gravelly deposits suggesting episodes of edge erosion and more stable silting. The fills were conspicuously dark, but there as little, identifiable

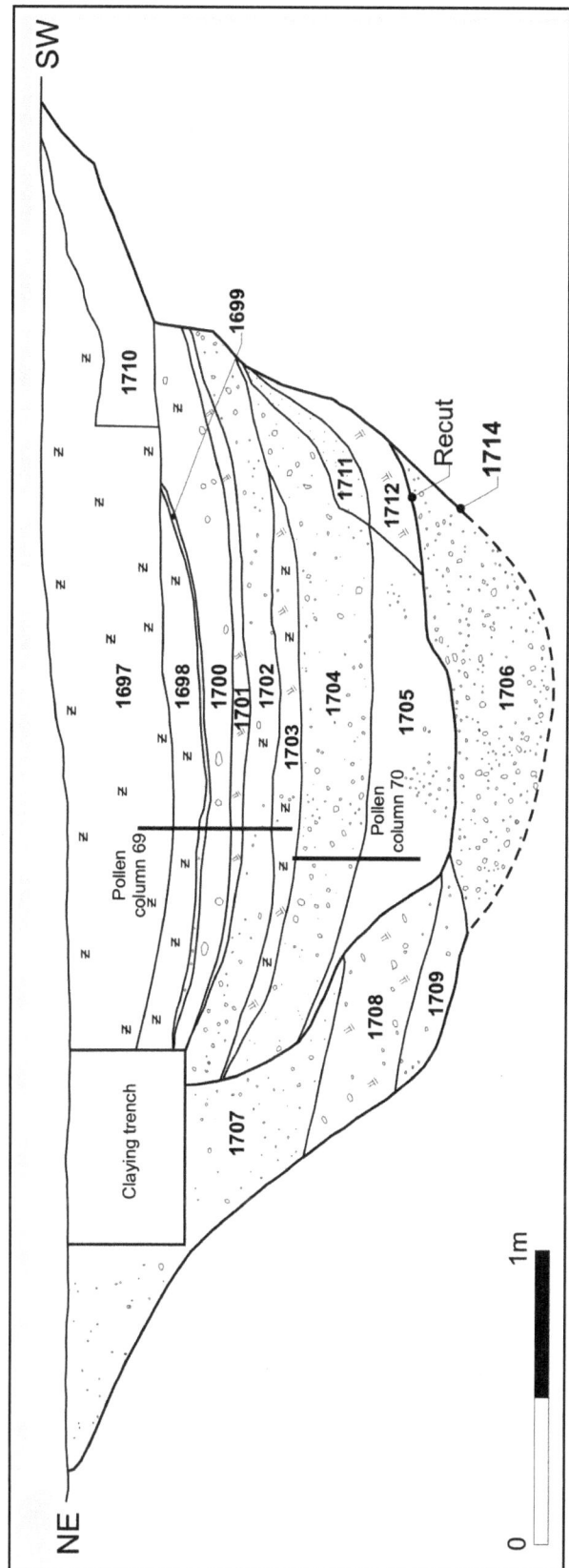

Fig 29. Pit 1714, Section 169

material within them. The lower main fill (1705) was a black, organic silt containing poorly preserved waterlogged remains (Table 4.7a, Sample 65). Above this was a series of grey gravelly silts (1704, 1702, 1700, 1698) interleaved with dark clayey silts (1703, 1701) with evidence of soil formation (Chapter 4, Column Samples 69, 70), and, near the top, a band of almost pure charcoal

(1699), identified as willow/poplar (Table 4.12, Sample 63). The uppermost fill was a dark 'peaty' silt (1697).

Despite the unusually dark fills in this feature, little material came from it, other than some animal bones from 1705 and 1704. It is possible that the remains comprised mainly vegetable matter which had completely decayed. The phosphate content was above background level, but not conspicuously so (Table 4.13; Fig. 44).

It is not clear what this pit was for. It seems likely to have been a waterhole as it certainly would have held water. There was no evidence that it had been lined, although it is possible that the lining had been removed without trace. The later filling, possibly just for refuse disposal would seem unrelated to the pit's original purpose.

Pit 1860 (Phase 8)

Pit 1860, in the SW corner of the double-ditched enclosure (Plot 3), cut Ditches 2027 and 2026 (Fig 6). It was 3 m in diameter and 1.26 m deep with a composite profile of 45° upper edges and steep lower edges (Fig 30, S.193).

Above a thin layer of redeposited gravel (1859) was a dark organic silt (1858) containing waterlogged remains which included chickweed, bramble and hazelnuts (Table 4.7a, Sample 76). This was sealed by clean redeposited sand and gravel (1857), probably derived from the pit edges. Above this were two further dark silty deposits (1856, 1855), probably waterlaid, followed by a thick brown sandy silt (1854) which appears to have derived from the SE side of the pit from edge erosion or collapse. This was succeeded by dark silty and sandy fills (1853, 1852, 1851, 1850) probably representing edge erosion with an input of organic material. The only finds from this pit were some animal bones from 1854 and 1850.

The pit was probably dug as a waterhole, although a drainage sump is another possibility.

The steep-sided lower section, with very little basal gravel suggests that the pit was lined and kept clean, although there was no trace of lining present and this was probably removed when the pit went out of use. The lower deposit of clean sand and gravel indicates edge slumping at this time, although the steep edge between this fill and 1854 suggests that there was a continuing revetment of this edge until later on (by which time the upper part at least may have rotted away). It may be pertinent that this NW side was between the inner and outer ditches of the enclosure, and may well have been occupied by a bank or hedge. This could explain the non-removal of the lining on this side which may have been difficult to reach.

Pit 1674 (Phase 9)

Pit 1674, in the SE corner, was oval in shape, about 4 m long (N-S) by 3 m wide. It cut Ditch 2033 and was respected by 2028 which therefore appears to have been a later addition. The pit was about 0.7 m deep, which is relatively shallow. The edges were gently sloping and somewhat irregular, with probable root disturbance on the SW side (1671).

The lower deposits (1673, 1672, 1671, 1669) were light clayey sediments which appear to represent deposits from edge erosion. The middle fills were darker brown or grey-brown silts (1670, 1668, 1667). There was no cultural material other than a few fragments of animal bone from 1667. None of the deposits were waterlogged although it is possible that the pit originally reached the watertable.

There is no indication as to the purpose of the pit and it may merely have served as a drainage sump for Ditch 2033. Its base was at a similar level to that of Cut 1621 of Ditch 2033, although it was cut after the ditch had partly silted up. It does not appear that the pit would have been lined.

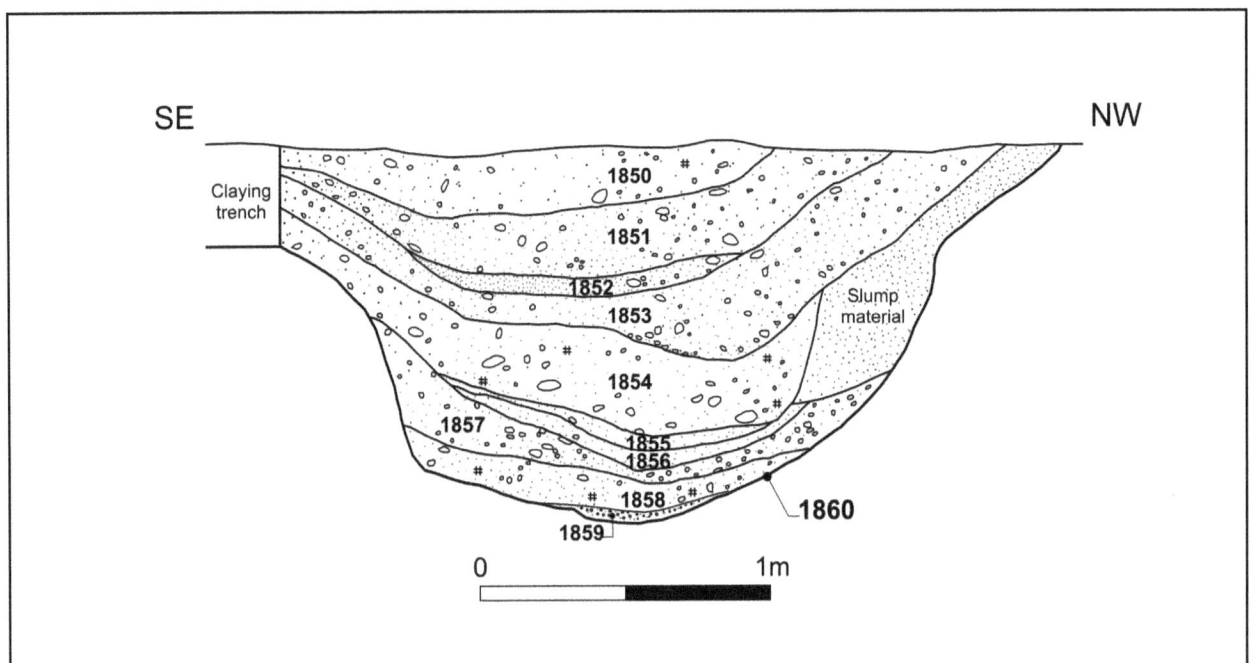

Fig 30. Pit 1860, Section 193

Pit 1741 Recut of 1744: Plot 8

The area covered by Cut 1744 extended some 9 m NE-SW by 8 m NE-SW (Figs 6, 31, S.164). This was recut by 1741 which had a diameter of *c* 5 m. The phasing of these features is uncertain since they had no relationship with the enclosure ditches or any other dated features.

Cut 1744

This cut, at least 8 m across, had very shallow edges and reached a maximum depth of 1.0 m before its base was truncated by the deeper pit 1741. Its overall depth is not known, but since it was probably intended to reach the watertable, it is likely to have been similar to 1741 (ie 1.6 m deep). This is similar in overall size to Ponds 1907 and 1829, and it is possible that 1744 was also used as a waterhole in the same way. There is no particular indication of an entrance ramp on one side or the other. If access was unrestricted, could it therefore have pre-dated the field boundary 2023? Its fills consisted almost exclusively of redeposited gravel suggesting that it had been deliberately infilled (or at least infilled around the edges) before 1741 was dug. There is too much material lying at too shallow an angle for this to have derived from edge slippage.

Recut 1741

Pit 1741 was less wide than its predecessor with a relatively shallow upper edge, which after 0.5-0.9 m depth plunged to a vertically sided central pit. Its overall depth reached about 1.6 m and it had a flat base 1.4 m across. It is possible that the upper slope was generated from weathering, but if so the central pit must have been cleaned out regularly since there was no indication of redeposited gravel within it. Alternatively, the upper slope may have been a deliberate design to provide stability or access, or both.

Above a thin sandy basal fill (1728) was a dark grey organic clayey silt (1729) and above this, but filling the SE quadrant at the base, a greyish brown, sandier silt (1730) showing some evidence of soil forming processes (Chapter 4, Table 4.5, Column Sample 72). This deposit contained a jumble of wood (Appendix 1, Wood Catalogue, pieces A-H).

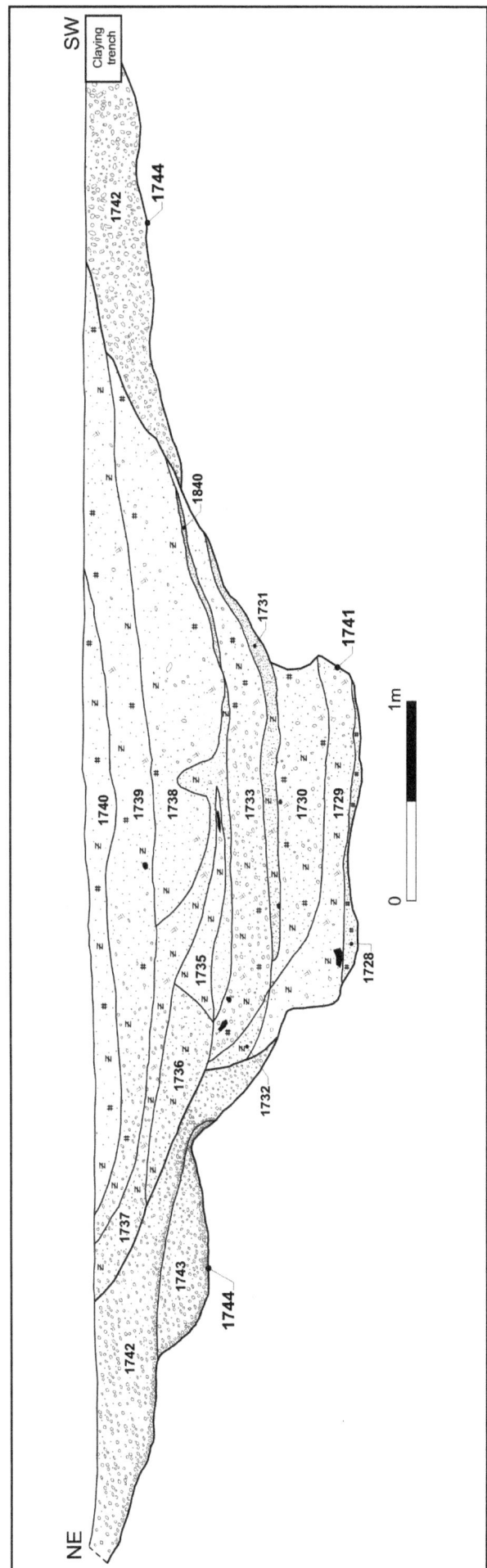

Fig 31. Pit 1741, Section 164

The most important among these was a two-piece tub or bucket with a carved rim handle, lying at the base of the pit (Figs 32 and 33; Colour Plates 4-8; Chapter 3). The bucket was made from a hollow trunk, oval in shape (perhaps because it was squashed?), and 270 mm high, 260 mm long and 140 mm wide (external dimensions). The base was a separate piece, but the handle was integral and had been carved from the trunk on one of the narrower ends. There was no sign that it had had an opposed handle.

The other pieces of wood comprised lengths of roundwood (A, E, F, G & H) 525-680 mm long and 34-130 mm in diameter. All had at least one end missing. There were also two thin radial split timbers also with ends missing. Piece C had been hewn into an oval dowel, 615 mm long by 59 x 16 mm.

It is possible that these pieces had been used as stakes in a lining for the pit, the vertically-sided part of which was about 0.5 m deep (as surviving). There were, however, no stakes found around the base of the pit.

A pollen column (Table 4.5, Sample 72) was taken through 1730 and part of the overlying fill 1816, a browner and more clayey peaty sand which may have filled a recut or stable hollow.

Above 1730, in the base of the weathering cone and apparently spilling in from the western side, was a sandier fill (1733). This contained a cow skull and other bones. A timber (H) is also recorded from this layer (but presumably much decayed). The siltier fill above (1734) contained a few sherds of plain pottery.

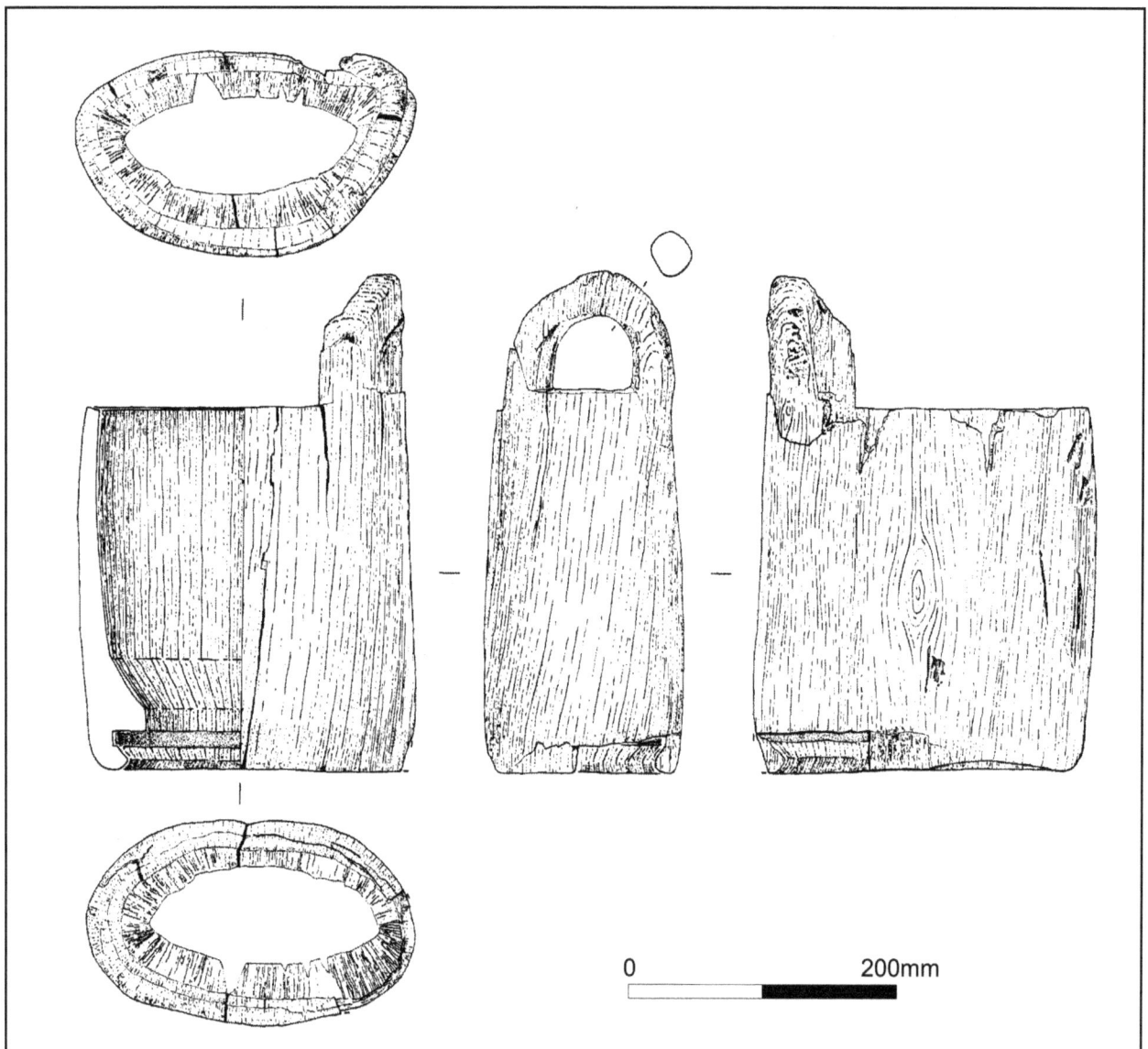

Fig 32. Wooden bucket (drawn by S J Allen and Lesley Collett)

44

Pits 1659, 1774, 1776: Plot 8

Pit 1659 (Fig 6)

Pit 1659, near Pit 1741, was a shallow circular scoop, 1.7 m across and 250 mm deep. The fill of the feature was a firm dark peaty silt (1658) which contained several fragments of pottery from a partially complete slack-shouldered bowl of probable late Bronze Age date. There were no charred remains or other finds.

Pit 1774 (not illustrated)

Pit 1774 cut the edge of Pit 1741 on the NW side. It was not recorded in plan, but the section shows it to have been 2.1 m across and 520 mm deep. The lower fills (1768, 1767, 1769, 1770, 1772, 1771) were mixed sandy silts. The main fill, however, was a loose very dark grey-brown silt (1773) similar to the peaty deposit 1658 (Pit 1659). There were no finds.

Pit 1776 (not illustrated)

Immediately to the NW Pit 1776 was another shallow scoop, 2.2 m across and 440 mm deep with a single dark grey-brown sandy fill (1775). It was without finds.

Interpretation

It is not known whether these shallow pits were contemporaneous, but there is some suggestion of a relatively late phase of activity in this area, apparently at the time of the formation of peat on the site.

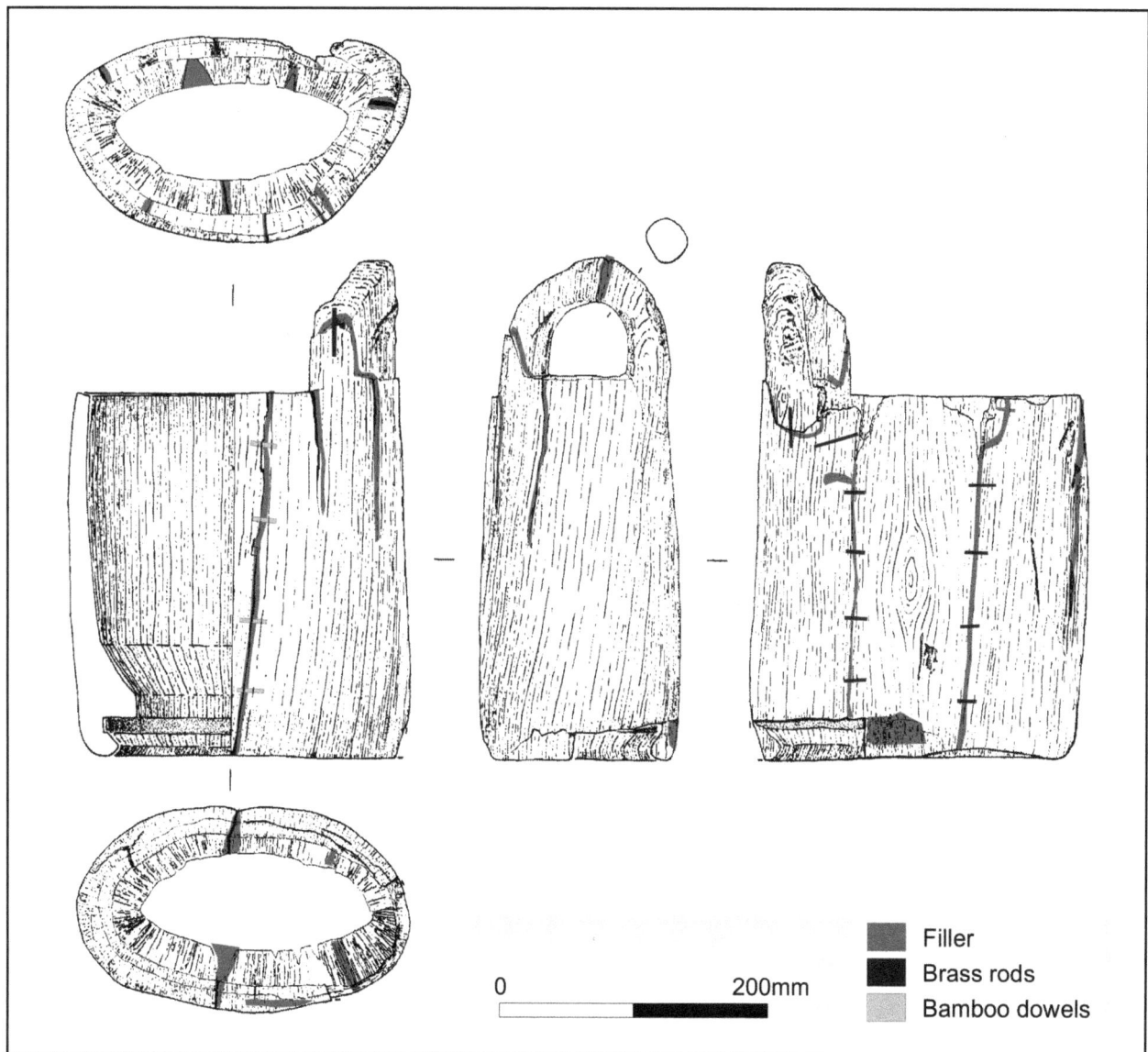

Fig 33. Wooden bucket showing conservation repairs (drawn by S J Allen and Lesley Collett)

Pond 1829 and Pit 1912: Plot 3 (Phase 8-9)

Pond 1829

Pond 1829 was roughly circular, about 7 m in diameter and 1.5 m deep (Fig 34). It had a steep eastern edge and a much shallower western edge indicating that access was from the west. Like Waterhole 1907 it was paired with a smaller pit. Pit 1912 lay to the south, but its upper fills were the same as those for 1829 and it was not visible as a separate feature until the upper metre or so of fill had been removed.

Pond 1829/Pit 1912 was recorded in plan as cutting the southern and western boundary ditches, 2025 and 2027, and therefore would have been a later insertion. It is possible, however, that the boundary ditches were partly open when the waterhole was dug, so that all features were in contemporary use. (It was not recorded whether some of the lower fills were shared).

Waterlogged wood was recorded towards the base of the feature. This included several *in situ* stakes, driven into the underlying gravel, indicting that a structure had once existed and that it is unlikely that all the wood was discarded from use elsewhere.

In situ stakes AH, AG, AE and AP

Four wooden stakes were discovered in the base of the pond. Their surviving lengths were between 450 and 600 mm (most of this length driven into the gravel) and they were about 110 m in diameter. It is possible that they were on an arc about 4 m in diameter which defined the edge of the deepest part of the pit. Stake AE was submitted for radiocarbon dating and yielded a date of 1430-1260 cal BC (95% confidence, 3080 +/- 35, SUERC-13967 - Chapter 7).

It is unclear whether the complete arrangement of stakes would have provided a revetment to the steep eastern edge (although this seems likely). It is possible that slumping layers 1887, 1875 and 1888 (S. 200 – not illustrated) built up behind the revetment, unless the revetment were right up against the vertical edge with the slumping coming after the withdrawal of the stakes.

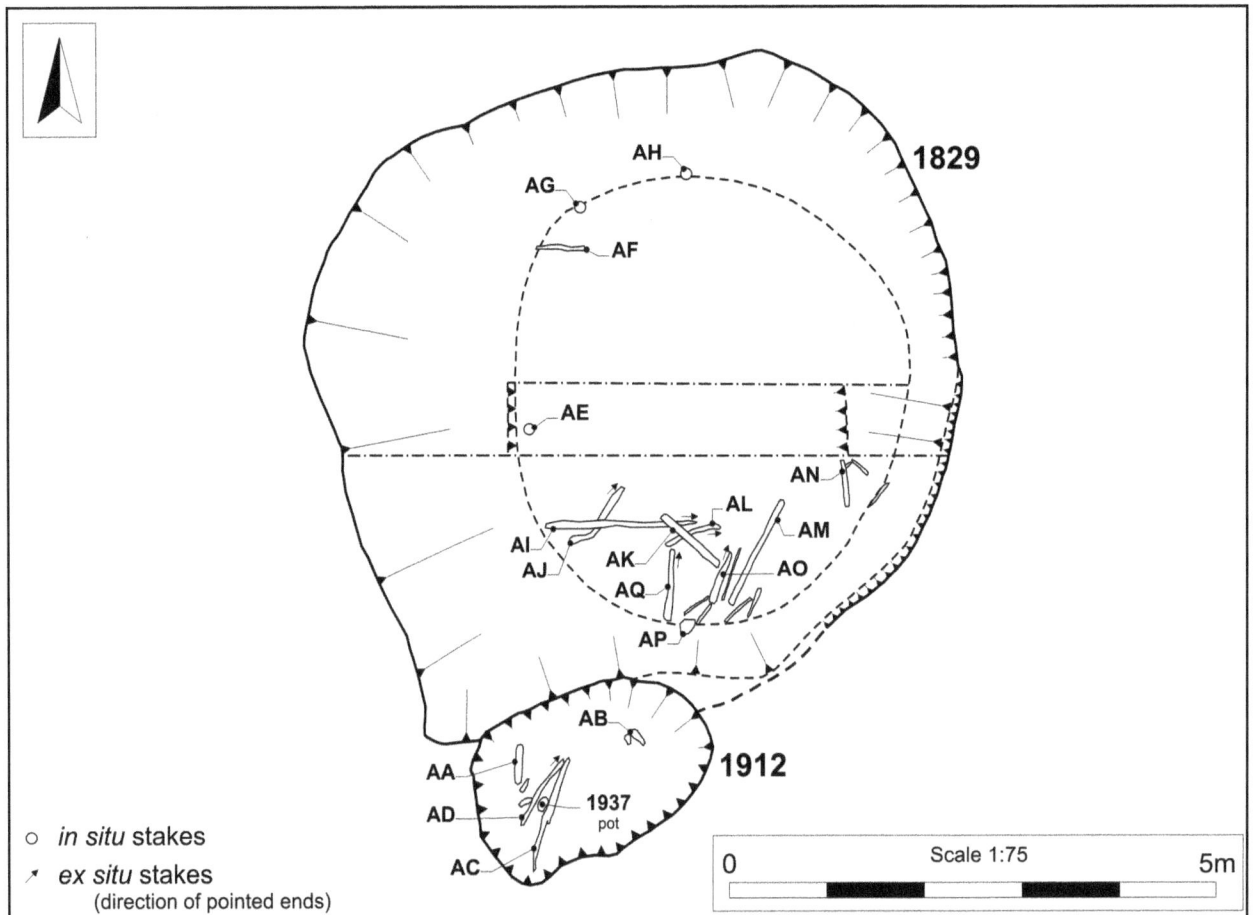

Fig 34. Plan showing pits 1829 and 1912 with wood remains

46

Ex situ stakes AI, AJ, AL, AO, AQ

Five stakes lay on the southern side of the pit. It seems likely that they had been withdrawn from this part of the waterhole and had been discarded with their pointed ends inwards. The longest was AI – 1.68 m surviving, but it was only 75 mm wide and 35 mm thick - made from a squared timber. To judge by the lengths of the *in situ* stakes (above), about 1.2 m of AI would have been standing clear of the ground, and there may have been some loss at the upper end as well. Since the total depth of the waterhole (from the modern ground surface) reached *c* 1.6 m, it seems that this stake must have been positioned as part of the revetment to the steep eastern side of the pit.

The other stakes were shorter – AQ and AL 740 mm, and AJ and AO about 600 mm.

Other timbers AK, AM, AN, AF

There were several other possible stakes without pointed ends. All were made from squared timber. AM, was 1.15 m long and 80 x 70 mm wide; AN was 480 mm by 90 x 50 (wider than some but not as wide as the roundwood stakes); AF was 720 mm by 45 x 35 mm; and AK was 820 mm by 65 x 25 mm.

Pit 1912

Pit 1912, on the south side of Waterhole 1829, was approximately oval in shape and about 2.5 m long by 1.5 m wide. It was not as deep as 1829 and it was cut from the top of fill 1848, so it is possible that 1829 had gone out of use when 1912 was dug. (According to the section this is logically the case, although all fills were similar and the sequence is not absolutely certain).

The pit contained a few surviving pieces of wood associated with a piece of shelly ware pottery (1937).

Stake AD

A roundwood? withdrawn stake, 780 mm by 68 mm, with the sharpened end pointing inwards (NE).

Timbers AA and AC

AA was found horizontal and may have been a piece of plank. It was a split timber 300 mm long 100 m wide and 45 mm thick.

AC was a longer narrower piece, 1.2 m long and up to 80 mm wide and 45 mm thick. This (and also AA) may have been stakes (they were both narrow for planks) but were without pointed ends.

Irregular wood AB

This irregular piece was interpreted as a probable root.

Interpretation

The pairing of Pond 1829 and Pit 1912 is a similar arrangement to the pairing of Pond 1907 with Pit 1942 and suggests similar purposes behind them. The stratigraphic sequence between 1829 and 1912 is, however, reversed, with the smaller, in this case, succeeding the larger. The phasing of these features, when compared with the earlier phasing of 1907/1942, indicates that there was not simply a reversal of functions between different areas of the site (1907 succeeding 1829 and 1912 succeeding 1942), but that the pairing of large and small features side by side was part of a design which was maintained in both phases. That being the case it seems that each had different functions (probably the large one for animals and the small one for humans) and that were probably in use at the same time for part of their durations.

There is evidence that 1829 contained a wooden structure made with upright stakes although only a few stakes had been left *in situ*. A number of others had been withdrawn and discarded in the waterhole. It is probable that the structure formed a lining to the waterhole, which can be estimated to have formed a rough circle about 4 m across. There is no evidence of plank lining and it seems likely that all this had been removed when the waterhole went out of use (wattle would surely have survived). With access to the waterhole via the shallow western side, the lining would not have been deep on this side, although the *in situ* stakes show that it existed here. It would have needed to have been deeper on the steep, near-vertical, eastern side and a discarded stake with a surviving length of 1.68 m is likely to have been from this side.

There is no evidence of a lining to Pit 1912 although a stake and two other timbers from this feature may have been from a dismantled one.

Chapter 3: # Waterlogged Wood

by Maisie Taylor

Introduction

Waterlogged wood came from six deep pits and two ponds associated with the Bronze Age field boundary ditches. Amongst the pieces were roundwood (some of which showed evidence for coppicing), timber and timber debris (or 'off-cuts'), a small amount of root, a possible artefact, a definite artefact (a tub/bucket), half a tree, and a few miscellaneous pieces. A catalogue of all the material is presented in Appendix 1.

Condition of material

The quality of the material is variable, depending on context, as some material came from deeper features than others, and some appears to have been exposed in the ground for some time. Using the scoring scale developed by the Humber Wetlands Project (Van de Noort *et al* 1995, table 15.1) most of the material could be seen to fall between 1 and 4. The bucket rates as 5.

The technology analysis was greatly hampered by the fact that many pieces had lost one or both ends, sometimes through decay. Most of the data on wood working in prehistoric contexts is usually derived from the ends of pieces (sharpening and shaping) and from wood working debris, such as woodchips. Surprisingly few woodchips were recovered.

Some of the material is very well preserved and there are three pieces which produced toolmarks. This is not enough for any statistical analysis. Much of the material is too broken or dried out for other sorts of detailed analysis.

Pits And Ponds

All the wood came from large pits and ponds which differed in shape, size and range of date. Wooden linings, particularly made of woven wattle have been a feature of excavated pits used as waterholes on the gravel terraces of the area, although no wattle came from the features on the present site.

Pit 160

Pit 160 was probably one of the earlier ones since it contained pottery of Early Bronze Age date and radiocarbon dating from associated wood gave two dates of broadly 2290-2040 BC and 2140-1910 BC (95% confidence, 3765 +/- 35, SUERC-13970 and 3640 +/- 35, SUERC-13969 - Chapter 7). It had no evidence for a lining (Fig 5). In the base of the pit was a great deal of very small twigs and general woody detritus. There were also fragments of bark and weathered coppice, weathered woodchips and other material which, although indicating ongoing wood working activity in the area, were too fragmentary for detailed analysis. Part of a small felled tree, approximately 92 mm in diameter came from slightly higher up in the feature (Context 175).

Pit 1622

Pit 1622, which is also likely to be fairly early, was larger than Pit 160 and more bowl-shaped (Fig 26). The interpretation in the field was that it had originally been lined, and when this was removed, the sides had collapsed. There are two fairly long pieces of roundwood from the pit. The piece of wood 1686 is over a metre long and approximately 58 mm diameter with a blunt end, which would make it unlikely that it was ever inserted vertically. Piece 1663 is nearly one and a half metres long and approximately 86 mm diameter, but both ends are missing making interpretation difficult. The forked roundwood from this context, 1685, was unmodified for any specific use. It is trimmed from two directions at the bottom from felling. One arm of the fork is trimmed in one direction, but the other is missing. There is no further modification or signs of wear. Forks of various shapes and sizes were used in a variety of activities, especially coppicing. The other wood in this pit is a quantity of roundwood, 20 fragments in all, mostly oak (*Quercus* sp.) and ash (*Fraxinus excelsior*) and all very weathered, probably having been in the pit for sometime before it was finally buried. There was obviously a certain amount of wood working activity in the area, but the fragments are too weathered and fragmentary for detailed analysis.

	Museum Conservation	Technology Analysis	Woodland Management	Dendro-Chronology	Species Identification
5	+	+	+	+	+
4	-	+	+	+	+
3	-	+/-	+	+	+
2	-	+/-	+/-	+/-	+
1	-	-	-	-	+/-
0	-	-	-	-	-

Table 3.1 Scoring system for wood condition assessment

Pit 1741

Another pit which produced considerable quantities of wood was 1741, a recut of 1744 (Fig 31). Most of the wood which survived was in the basal deposits. The most spectacular wooden find from the site was from here: Timber D, the body of a 2-piece vessel, carved from tree trunk of alder (*Alnus glutinosa*) with an integral, carved loop handle (Figs 32 & 33). The vessel has been conserved and is reported on in S J Allen 2006.

Most of the other wood from this feature is roundwood in variety, not particularly weathered, some showing signs of coppicing. All the pieces of roundwood have at least one end missing, making detailed discussion of the technology impossible. The diameters of most of the roundwood are between 32 and 54 mm. This is within the range of sizes recommended for modern wattle hurdles (Forestry Commission 1956). There is also a large piece of coppiced oak (*Quercus* sp.) with a diameter of approximately 140mm. There is no evidence that any of this material had been used, although most of it would have been suitable for wattle work. Other wood from this deposit included a well-made oval dowel, a thin, radially split piece of timber debris and a half split tree. The oval dowel is probably an artefact but as both ends are missing it is impossible to say more. The timber debris is similarly missing both ends making it impossible to discuss the technology in detail. It is probably derived from splitting a large timber which has not survived.

Pit 660

Pit 660 was a large pit with steep sides. A strange piece, which is possibly an artefact, is a quarter split stem of oak (*Quercus* sp.) with a large burr at one end. It has been suggested that it may be a maul or hammer but it is unlike any other found of a similar date. The remainder of the wood from this feature comprises three stakes set toward the bottom of the feature (Fig 22).

Pit 1942

Pit 1942 contained larger timbers and possibly a structure. Two timbers had been set parallel to each other in the base (EE and WW – Fig 27). EE is a fragmentary rough-hewn plank approximately 210 mm wide and between 35 and 55 mm thick. Although difficult to identify because of its condition it appears to be hazel (*Corylus avellana*) or alder (*Alnus glutinosa*). Because of its size and function it is more likely to be alder because alder is resistent to wet rot and is frequently chosen for functions where this quality is valuable. Timber WW (Fig 28) is very similar in size and likely species but differs in fabrication, being a quarter split tree trunk. There is a broken mortise at one end which may be the remnant of a tow hole but the joint was so badly shattered on excavation that further analysis is impossible. The width (190 mm) is only slightly narrower than that of EE, and the thickness similar at 55 mm. Two other pieces of wood were found under Timber EE (BA and BD). Both are half split pieces of ash (*Fraxinus excelsior*). BA is trimmed at one end from one direction but the other end is missing, and BD has both ends blunted by trimming. They may be bearers helping to hold EE in place, or to stop it sinking. Timbers WW was also pegged into place by BB and CC. Timber BB is ash (*Fraxinus excelsior*), possibly coppiced and trimmed to a point at one end from three directions. Timber CC is quite different. It is oak (*Quercus* sp.), which has been roughly quartered and trimmed tangentially (Fig 28).

Pond 1907

Pond 1907 was a larger waterhole containing a remarkable collection of large timbers, and complete trees (Fig 27; Plate 10). Timber JJ is a complete felled tree trunk, probably alder (*Alnus glutinosa*) with the felling notch preserved and a total trunk length of nearly 4 metres (Plate 11). Timber SS is a felled oak tree (*Quercus* sp.) but this time rotted in half. All the other pieces are worked and may represent the remains of a step or platform but are too badly damaged and decayed for detailed analysis. Timber LL is radially split with one end trimmed from two directions. Timber UU is a rough half split of what is probably an overgrown alder (*Alnus glutinosa*) coppice. Two other timbers, VV and XX, are ash (*Fraxinus excelsior*), half tree trunks. Timber RR is a quarter split alder (*Alnus glutinosa*) trunk, trimmed at one end from all directions with a broken mortise joint, a half lap joint, and several toolmarks, unfortunately only partial, so not adding a great deal to the statistical analysis.

Pond 1829

Pond 1829 is quite a large feature with a small amount of wood and a large amount of hazel nuts (Fig 34). There were four vertical oak (*Quercus* sp.) stakes in the base of the pond. Two of them are quite substantial, and the ones which retained their ends were sharpened to a point to aid insertion. Although there were other timbers which might have been more verticals, or the horizontal components of a structure, they were all missing their ends making interpretation impossible. Pit 1912 also contained a few timbers which may have been derived from a lining.

Pit 1026

Pit 1026 is located at the northern end of the discontinuous boundary ditch. It is not particularly large but with steep sides (Fig 24). The wood from this feature is unusual in that it is almost exclusively oak (*Quercus* sp.). It is also almost exclusively off-cuts from working timber, again, very unusual.

Roundwood

Much of the roundwood is broken or so badly decayed that detailed analysis is difficult. Many of the diameters are distorted, probably through drying out (Taylor 1998, 138). It was possible to identify several examples of felled trees, however. These trees vary in diameter from 250 mm (1906 SS), and 200 mm (1906 JJ), down to 100/85 mm on Timber 175 (Pit 160), and 90/80 mm on 1049 (Pit 1026). Piece 1829 has a diameter 100/90 mm but is not felled like a conventional tree, but more like a coppice, from three directions. There are other possible trees but they do not have the characteristic felled ends. These are 1049 (2), which has a diameter of 90/74 mm, and 1663 (i) with a diameter of 92/81mm. It may be that these too are derived from coppice stools.

There is evidence that quite a high proportion of the roundwood is derived from coppicing. This applies to some of the material in 197 (Pit 160), but it is all very dry and small, some oak and some other species. The clearest examples are 1733 H (Pit 1741) with a diameter of 32 mm, a piece from 1906 (Pond 1907) with a diameter of 37 mm, 1730 F (Pit 1741) with a diameter of 42/49 mm, and 653iv (Pit 660) with a diameter of 75/61mm. There is also material from the ponds which are coppiced wood, mostly with diameters between 31 and 40 mm. This is within the classic range of sizes for hurdle making (Forestry Commission 1956).

There are also a number of larger coppiced stems. The half split timber, Pit 1942 BA, is ash (*Fraxinus excelsior*) and derived from a coppice stem with a minimum diameter of 67 mm. BB and DD, from the same context, are also ash and both have one end trimmed from three directions, to compensate for the curve of the coppice. BB is 84 mm diameter and DD is 70 mm. A similar piece from 1942 (BD) is half-split and 80mm in diameter. 1829 has a diameter 100/90 mm and is another which is felled, not like a conventional tree, but more like a coppice, from three directions. Timber UU from Pond 1907, although technically a timber should be mentioned here as it is an important piece of coppicing. It is a piece of ash wood which has been split but which was clearly from a coppice stool. The original diameter would have been approximately 240 mm. The ring pattern of the piece shows slow growth early on but later the stem grew very quickly, suggesting that other trees or shrubs were cleared from around it when it was half grown.

Forked pieces of wood are quite a common find on waterlogged sites of all prehistoric dates. It is rarely possible to deduce the function of them and they come in all shapes and sizes. The forks here vary greatly in size. One from 1685 (Pit 1622) is well over 2 metres long with the 'handle' having a diameter of 95 mm, and so not likely to be a hand tool. Given the quantities of coppiced wood on the site, it is possible that they were used by the coppicers for bundling the cut stems, or simply cut by the coppicers for future use. They do not show any signs of utilization.

Timber And Timber Debris

Very little of the timber from the site is derived from mature trees, although there is some bark from large woodland trees amongst the background debris. Most of the timber is either oak or ash and derived from trunks between 100 and 250 mm. Many of these trunks seem to be derived from multiple stemmed overgrown coppices. The simple radial splitting of many pieces reflects the fact that they are derived from these relatively small trunks. From Pit 1026, the diameter of 1038i was originally approximately 125 mm, and that of 1049i closer to 225 mm, for example. Half split timbers show similar diameters: Pond 1829 had timbers AE and AP with diameters of 140 mm and 130 mm respectively. The half split, ash timber, 1907 UU, had a diameter 240 mm (but tapered) and 1907 VV, also ash, had a diameter of 145 mm.

Most of the timber debris appears to be radial, suggesting that it is debris from splitting, possibly the splitting of these smallish trunks. There is virtually no debris from any other woodworking activity which is strange given the number of sharpened stakes and other roundwood.

There is also a hewn plank, 1942 EE. This is quite rare but unfortunately not identifiable to species (it is, however, not oak) and too fragmentary for detailed analysis.

Toolmarks

The best preserved toolmarks come from the felling of 1907 UU. The original tree was felled by an axe 40 mm wide and 4 mm deep. There are also two partial marks on Timber R from Pond 1907: one in a joint (30:2.5) and one on the end (27:2). All of these are quite small and curved like socketed axes (either bronze or iron) rather than flatter and wider like the flat iron axes (Taylor 2001, table 7.28).

Artefacts

Bucket

The most important artefact is part of a two-piece vessel (1730 D from Pit 1741; Figs 32 & 33; Colour Plates 4-8) constructed from a carved cylinder of alder (*Alnus glutinosa*) tree-trunk (Allen 2006). These vessels were usually carved in two pieces, with a separate base which fitted into a carved slot. The base is missing but the vessel is otherwise complete, which is very rare. The cylinder of the vessel has been compressed giving external 'diameters' of 140 mm and 262 mm. This would suggest that the original diameter of the vessel was probably around 200 mm. The vessel is 269 mm high base to rim with an integral carved loop handle. The whole of the outside of the vessel shows signs of working, suggesting that the original tree was probably 250 mm or greater.

The working on the outside of the trunk shows up as 'fluting' of the surface. This is where the outer wood, the sapwood, has been systematically removed, probably with an axe. The sapwood is the newest wood on the tree and is richer in sap and cellulose. It is more susceptible to shrinkage and decay. A similar vessel was found in Pode Hole quarry, also in a waterhole (Phoenix Consulting forthcoming) but it was found still with rope through the loop. This suggests that they were indeed used for collecting water.

Maul or hammer

There is another object which is potentially an artefact (653i from Pit 660; Fig 23). The object is made from a quarter split branch of oak (*Quercus* sp.) with a burr at one end. It may have been utilised as a maul or hammer.

Species

One hundred and sixty-eight samples were taken for species identification. Initial sorting produced 18 examples of oak (*Quercus* sp.) and eight of ash (*Fraxinus excelsior*). The remaining 142 samples were all fine grained and diffuse porous. A 10% sub-sample was selected at random, thin sectioned and examined under transmitted light at high magnification. Everything examined was derived from wet loving plants which would be expected to be growing adjacent to water: alder (*Alnus glutinosa*), willow (*Salix* sp.) or poplar (*Populus* sp.).

There is, however, *Prunus* in the charcoal (Chapter 5), and this would be appropriate for the hedges which must have accompanied the field ditches in the area. Charcoal also produced evidence for alder (*Alnus glutinosa*), willow (*Salix* sp.), oak (*Quercus* sp.), beech (*Fagus sylvatica*), hazel (*Corylus avellana*) and possibly hornbeam (*Carpinus betulus*), all of which can be hedge species.

Discussion

Pits and ponds

The first large pits excavated in Fengate were found to be waterholes, often with wattle and timber linings (Pryor 1974, plate 6 and 7). Some of the large pits at Thorney have some evidence for wooden linings (eg Pit 1026) and some have no evidence at all (eg Pit 1741). Not all waterholes require linings, so the lack of evidence does not necessarily mean that some pits had a different function. There are several reasons why a waterhole may not be lined, some of them post-depositional. If a waterhole or well subsequently dries out totally, any evidence for the lining may disappear along with any other organic material. Linings to waterholes seem to have been added where the matrix is loose, and they were needed to keep the water clean and clear of collapsing sides. They vary in design, implying that they are often ad hoc and are often modified through time depending on need.

The wattle linings are usually a form of revetment, but may include a step or steps. There may also be a need for a step even if there is no revetment, and occasionally the steps may be part of the revetment. The long timbers in Pit 1622 could have been derived from this kind of structure. If they were ever set vertically they would have been very tall. Also, the one which has its end intact is trimmed to be blunt, suggesting that it was never inserted vertically. Pit 1942 has two parallel timbers which are almost certainly *in situ*. These 'steps' in waterholes seem to work by trapping loose gravel behind them. Especially where the horizontal timbers are quite heavy, they often appear to be re-used and this is the case with the structure in Pit 1942. Pit 660 is another pit with clear signs of a revetment. The roundwood stakes, together with one made from a timber off-cut, were set vertically in the base of the pit. They are reasonably substantial, between 95 and 121mm diameter with well fashioned points which would have helped insertion into the gravel. No evidence for a horizontal element was recorded.

The material from Pit 1942 is particularly interesting. Timber EE is very fragmentary and impossible to reconstruct, which is unfortunate as it is extremely important. Its importance lies in the fact that it is not oak - it is almost certainly willow or poplar – and is hewn. This is quite different to the norm for most 'domestic' wood working. From the Late Bronze Age onwards oak planks were routinely produced by radial splitting from small trunks or overgrown coppice. Timber WW from the same pit is quarter split and squared with probable tow hole but it was badly broken on excavation (Fig 28). The species is probably alder (*Alnus glutinosa*). The timbers WW and EE were horizontal and parallel, 1 m apart but not in the base of the pit. They were held in place by pegs (BB and CC) driven well into gravel. The timbers survived flat, rather than on edge, which suggests that they were to function as a step.

Pond 1907 contained some of the most important material from the site. Although prehistoric waterholes are relatively common, prehistoric ponds, and in particular, prehistoric ponds with waterlogged material, are much rarer. Timber RR, for example is jointed (mortise) and had some partial toolmarks. Timber JJ is a felled tree, and probably had a tow hole, although it was too damaged to reconstruct. There are quantities of possible stakes, but there is a problem in the analysis because so much was broken and there are so many ends missing. Some of the material may have been discarded from coppicing in the area, but because of the fragmentary nature of the material it has not been possible to do detailed analysis.

The 14 pieces of timber and timber debris are particularly unusual from a non-ritual site. Although extensive finds of timber have been made on sites such as Flag Fen there are very few finds from domestic and agricultural contexts. Very little of the timber from the site is derived from mature trees, for example, with most material derived from oak or ash trunks between 100 and 250mm. In particular, many of these trunks seem to be derived from multiple stemmed coppice stools which have become overgrown. Many of these pieces have been radially split, which is the preferred way of splitting smaller trunks (Taylor 2001, 203), eg half split oak timbers from 1829 with a diameter of 140 mm and 130 mm and the half split ash from 1907, VV, had a diameter of 145 mm. Most of the timber debris also appears to be radial, suggesting that it is possibly the debris from the splitting of these smallish trunks. There is virtually no debris from any other wood working activity which is strange given the number of sharpened stakes and other roundwood. In fact the overall quantity of wood working debris is low.

Artefacts

The bucket appears to be a classic two-piece carved vessel with an integral handle. Vessels such as these are very rare. The fact that it was found on an excavation, in a dateable context, is even rarer but to have the handle intact is almost unique. A good, early example of a similar vessel is the Stuntney bucket from the Isle of Ely. It is fragmentary and missing the rim and handle. (Earwood 1993, 288), but the method of construction is similar. The body is carved from a solid log, the bark and sapwood has been trimmed off to make a smooth surface. The interior has been hollowed out, with a heavy flange towards the base. A slot in the flange would accommodate a one piece base with a bevelled edge, which would have to be sprung into place from below. The slot on the vessel from Thorney is unique in retaining some kind of organic matter (not identified). It has always seemed likely that these vessels would need to be caulked in some way to make them water-tight but this is the first time potential evidence for how this might have been done has been found. These vessels were made over a long period from the Late Bronze Age until the Iron Age. A number of other vessels of this type have recently been excavated at Thorney, Peterborough and Cassington, near Oxford, but all of these are yet to be studied. The Thorney example is possibly the best preserved, and most complete.

The other identified artefact may have been some kind of maul or hammer, but no parallels have been found to date.

Species

It is interesting to note the different species occurring in the samples of charcoal and unworked waterlogged wood, when compared to worked material. The worked wood was almost entirely oak (*Quercus* sp.), ash (*Fraxinus excelsior*), alder (*Alnus glutinosa*), willow (*Salix* sp.) and poplar (*Populus* sp.), whereas the unworked material also contained honeysuckle (*Lonicera* sp.), privet (*Ligustrum* sp.), prunus (including blackthorn – *Prunus spinosa*), pomoideae (including hawthorn), birch (*Betula* sp.), beech (*Fagus sylvatica*), and elm (*Ulmus* sp.). All of these species are likely to have been in the hedges which would have fringed the fields. The pollen shows most of these species to be poorly represented, as is pine (*Pinus sylvestris*), lime (*Tilia* sp), and holly (*Ilex aquifolium*),

but hedges, especially if they enclose livestock fields, tend to produce less pollen. Several of these species, especially beech and holly would be more likely to have been growing on the slightly higher (drier) ground of Thorney Island. It is obvious that species selection was important with only a proportion of this material being selected for functional purposes.

Hedges

There is no wood in the assemblage that looks like hedge cuttings or prunings. There is, however, *Prunus* in the charcoal, and this would fit with recent finds relating to hedges in the area. There has been evidence for laid hedges running alongside droves and field boundaries for some time (Pryor 1980, plate 15; fig.128). Recent finds from a site in Fengate, Peterborough have produced direct evidence for laid hedges of blackthorn (*Prunus spinosa*) from the Bronze Age (but this is yet to be studied in depth).

Woodworking

There is evidence for various kinds of wood working from the site, including splitting, trimming, sapwood trimming, hewing, tree-felling and coppicing. The artefacts, whilst sophisticated are too well finished to produce data about how they were worked and what tools were used. Most of the material from the site is similar to that used in bodging and woodland work, eg Pit 1622, 1741 etc. It is possible that pollards and coppices were in the hedges or scattered around the landscape. A farm would require quantities of wattle hurdles and fencing. Indeed, the sheep races and sorting gates in the area would not work without hurdles. Coppice material is also needed for houses, including spars for thatching as well as hedge-laying. This probably reflects the proximity of a domestic site. This material is very similar to assemblages such as that from the Bronze Age/Iron Age phase of Yarnton in the Thames Valley (Hey in prep.).

The size, shape, reduction and joints on Timber R from Context 1906 in the Pond 1907, are very similar to those found at Flag Fen (Taylor 2001, figs 7.39 and 7.41). Most of these timbers in the make-up of the platform from Flag Fen have been interpreted as 'dumped' material from domestic contexts.

The hewn plank was not the only example of hewing from the site. Wood such as alder, willow or poplar does not naturally split to a flat surface and usually needs to be hewn. The bucket from Pit 1741 is carved from tree trunk of alder (*Alnus glutinosa*). The finish of the outside, and the integral, loop handle show how skilled the Bronze Age craftsman could be. Most of the woodworking from the site is more 'rough and ready' because of its context, but less easy to understand is the range of quality in the preservation from extremely good, like the bucket, to weathered and damaged. It may be that some of the damage is ancient, but it is also possible that some was caused by slowness of excavation or dry packing for storage.

Colour plate 1: Pit 1741 quarter-sectioned

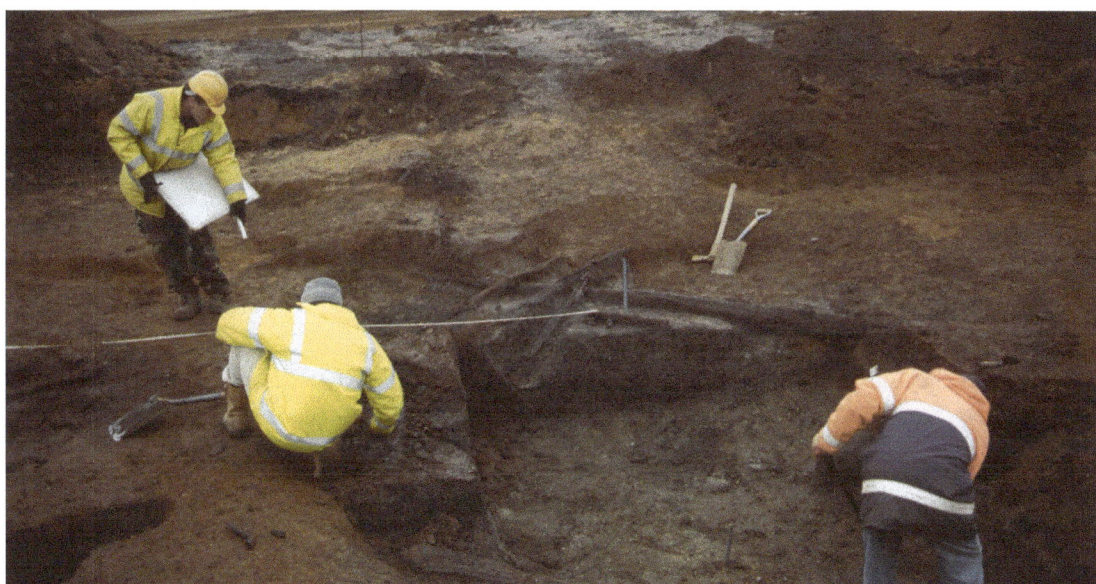

Colour plate 2: Pond 1907 under excavation. Associated pit 1942 is to the left

Colour plate 3: Pond 1829 with associated pit 1912 behind it

Colour plates 4-8
Wooden tub or bucket from
Pit 1741 following conservation
(courtesy York Archaeological
Trust Conservation Laboratories)

Chapter 4: **Environmental Evidence**

by N P Branch, I Poole, B Silva, S Elias, C P Green, A Vaughan-Williams and I Valcarcel

Introduction

Sampling of a range of pits, ponds and ditches on the site (sixty-five bulk samples, five monolith samples and thirty-two spot samples) for environmental archaeological analysis aimed to:

1. Reconstruct the changing nature of the landscape (biophysical environment)

2. Reconstruct the impact of human groups on the natural environment, especially in terms of farming practices, ie pastoral and/or arable agriculture

3. Elucidate the nature of the economy and diet of the local inhabitants

In order to achieve these aims, we employed the following objectives and associated methods:

1. To reconstruct feature-specific formation processes, both natural (both pedological and sedimentological) and anthropogenic (eg dump deposits), by analysing the pedo-sedimentary sequences captured in the monolith samples (<78>, <79>, <70> and<69>, and <72>; features 1829, 1907, 1714 and 1741 respectively)

2. To reconstruct the broad vegetation history by the pollen-stratigraphic analysis of two monolith samples (<78> and <79>) from the sedimentary fills of the ponds (features 1829 and 1907)

3. To reconstruct changes in local environmental conditions by analysing waterlogged plant macro-remains (seeds and wood) and insects in the bulk samples, and by undertaking measurements of the total phosphate content of the spot samples

4. To reconstruct the nature of human activities, especially those relating to the cultivation and processing of cereals, and the exploitation of other plant resources, eg grassland, by analysing waterlogged and charred plant macroremains (seeds, charcoal and waterlogged wood) in the bulk samples

Geological Context

The site is on the Fen margin between the Rivers Nene to the south and Welland to the north. This is a topographically featureless landscape at a level between 2m and 3m OD drained almost entirely through artificial channels. The underlying bedrock is the Oxford Clay but this is masked everywhere by superficial deposits. Peat is widely present but was formerly much more extensive and is now patchily preserved. It rests on a variety of sandy and gravelly deposits, representing terrace deposits of the Welland and the Nene and also including the March Gravels, possibly re-worked marine beach deposits. At the site, small patches of peat rest on sandy gravel, which incorporates well-rounded flint pebbles and may be a remnant of the March Gravel, or March Gravel reworked from an outcrop mapped immediately to the south of Thorney, into a low terrace deposit of the River Nene.

Methods

Field investigations and lithostratigraphic descriptions

Monolith samples, bulk samples and spot samples were recovered from a range of features for environmental archaeological analysis. The lithostratigraphy of the monolith samples (<69>, <70>, <72>, <78> and <79>) was described in the laboratory using standard procedures for recording unconsolidated sediment, noting the physical properties (colour), composition (gravel, sand, clay, silt and organic matter), unit boundaries and inclusions (eg artefacts) (see Tables 4.1 to 4.5 and Fig 35).

Pollen analysis

Eight sub-samples were extracted from monolith sample <78>, and eight sub-samples from monolith sample <79>, for pollen analysis. The pollen was extracted as follows:

1. Sampling a standard volume of sediment (1ml)

2. Deflocculation of the sample in 1% Sodium pyrophosphate

3. Sieving of the sample to remove coarse mineral and organic fractions (>125μ)

4. Removal of finer minerogenic fraction using Sodium polytungstate (specific gravity of 2.0g/cm3)

5. Mounting of the sample in glycerol jelly

Each stage of the procedure was preceded and followed by thorough sample cleaning in filtered distilled water. Quality control is maintained by periodic checking of residues, and assembling sample batches from various

55

depths to test for systematic laboratory effects. Pollen grains and spores were identified using the Royal Holloway (University of London) pollen type collection and the following sources of keys and photographs: Moore *et al* (1991), Reille (1992). Plant nomenclature follows the Flora Europaea as summarised in Stace (1997). For each sample, maximum pollen counts of 300 pollen grains and spores were attempted, although in several samples the pollen preservation and concentration was very poor, which prevented high counts being attained. The pollen diagram was produced using TILIA and TILIA*GRAPH (Grimm 1991, 1991-1993). The pollen results are presented as a percentage of total pollen (including aquatics and spores because these form a minor component of the pollen assemblage) (see Figs 34 & 35).

Plant macrofossil analysis

Sixty-six bulk samples were processed by either flotation (to recover charred plant remains) or wet sieving (to recover waterlogged plant remains) using 300 micron and 1mm mesh sieves and subject to an assessment of the archaeobotanical remains, noting the concentration, preservation and main taxa. Following the assessment, twenty-one bulk samples were selected for analysis of waterlogged and charred plant macrofossils. Identifications were made under a low power zoom-stereo microscope. Identifications were made with reference to the modern seed reference collection at Royal Holloway University London, and Berggren (1981) and Anderberg (1994). Plant nomenclature follows Stace (1997) (see Appendix 2, Tables 4.6, 4.7a and 4.7b).

Insect analysis

Three bulk samples were processed for the insect analysis. Samples were processed by paraffin flotation following the methodology of Atkinson *et al* (1987):

1. Wash bulk peat samples through a 5mm mesh using hot water to remove larger wood fragments
2. Wash remaining fraction onto a 300 micron mesh
3. Wash twice with hot water to remove the fine fraction, and two cold water washes to remove the possibility of a thermal gradient forming during the subsequent flotation
4. Drain well and mix with paraffin in a large bowl for 5 minutes
5. Decant excess paraffin back into the stock bottle through an 80 micron mesh
6. Add cold water to the organic fraction, mixing thoroughly
7. Leave to stand for 15 minutes
8. Decant the oil overlying the bulk material onto a 300 micron mesh and wash gently with detergent and hot water
9. Rinse with distilled water, dehydrate in 95% ethanol, and transfer to a sealed container for storage in 95% ethanol

Flots were scanned using a low power binocular microscope (x10) to record the concentration and state of preservation of insect taxa, and to record beetle (Coleoptera) and bug (Hemiptera) taxa (see Table 4.8).

Waterlogged wood analysis

Four samples were analysed using standard techniques (Gale and Cutler 2000) and examined using an Olympus BX41 microscope. The waterlogged wood samples were studied by transmitted light with magnifications up to x400. Material was identified from three planes of section (whenever possible) and compared, when necessary, with samples in the wood slide collection housed in the Utrecht University branch of the National Herbarium of the Netherlands and relevant literature (eg Schweingruber 1990). When a genus is represented by a single species in the native British flora it is named as the most likely origin of the wood although it must be noted that wood anatomy alone is often not enough to secure identification to individual species. Classification follows that of Tutin *et al* (1964-1980) (see Tables 4.9 and 4.10).

Charcoal analysis

Ten samples were analysed, with >100 pieces of wood per sample ranging from less than 2mm diameter to greater or equal to 4mm in diameter. The charcoal was examined using reflected light with magnifications of up to x400. Wherever possible a random selection of 100 pieces of charcoal ranging from >2mm diameter in transversal section were studied to ensure a statistically representative selection from the samples. This was undertaken for seven samples. However, when the number of unidentifiable pieces was greater or equal to 50% on reaching 50 pieces, the analysis was truncated. This was the case for the three samples, namely sample <12> (context 175), sample <25> (context 600) and sample <67> (context 1688), which contained many wood fragments <2mm in diameter the larger material was selected (ie. non-random) to ensure the greatest chance of identification. When a genus is represented by a single species in the native British flora it is named as the most likely origin of the wood although it must be noted that wood anatomy alone is often not enough to secure identification to individual species. Classification follows that of Tutin *et al* (1964-1980) (see Tables 4.11 and 4.12).

Phosphate analysis

Phosphorus occurs in nature almost entirely as Phosphate - both the organic and inorganic forms are of major significance in plant-soil studies and in phosphorus cycling in the natural system (Allen 1974, Cavanagh *et al* 1988). It strongly binds with iron, aluminium and calcium cations in soils causing negligible horizontal or vertical movement, and no gaseous escape, and is thus extremely stable. For this reason, the most important changes in the condition of this element are from human activities, which make phosphorus extremely mobile as an output of an economic system through tasks such as disposal of waste products or manuring (Bethell and Maté 1989). Phosphate analysis of soil and sediments in archaeological features and contexts may therefore provide a more detailed understanding of past human activities (Balaam and Porter 1982). Thirty-two samples were analysed for Total Phosphate. The Total Phosphate extraction method was based on techniques outlined in the following publications: Allen 1974, Leonardi 1999. The method is as follows (all glassware is acid rinsed in 10% Hydrochloric acid for 24 hours and the water used is de-ionised using Millipore®, type GS, 0.22μm):

1. All soil samples are air dried (30°C) for one week. They are then gently disaggregated, sieved (<2mm), grinded and sieved (<500μm) again

2. 3ml of 38% Hydrogen Peroxide (H2O2) and 3ml of concentrated Sulphuric Acid (H2SO4) is then added to 0.2g of each sample. Once the reaction has subsided the samples are heated for 2 hours

3. The samples (including solution) are filtered (filter paper 542) into 50ml volumetric flasks and made up to volume

4. The extracts are then diluted for measurement using the Molybdenum Blue method (see below)

The samples were measured using the Molybdenum Blue method in a segmented flow analyser (Skalar Sansplus system®) measuring ranges of 0-100ppm and 100-1000ppm at a wavelength of 880nm.

This colourimetry technique is based upon the formation of phosphoantimonyl-molybdenum complex when othophosphate reacts with molybdenum and antimony. Reduction of this complex with Ascorbic acid will produce a characteristic molybdenum blue colour, the intensity of which gives an indication of the phosphate content (Leonardi 1999) (see Table 4.13).

Lithostratigraphic Descriptions
C P Green

Ponds 1829 and 1907 (Tables 4.1 and 4.2)

Monolith samples <78> (feature 1829) and <79> (feature 1907) were both taken from the lower parts of sequences interpreted, based on field evidence, as pond infills (Fig 35). The upper part of feature 1829, context 1849, is a very compact stony horizon, possibly artificial in origin or reflecting a period as a surface horizon subject to trampling. The lower part of the sequence is much less compact and less stony (context 1886). Charcoal particles are present throughout the sequence. The upper 300m of feature 1907, contexts 1901 and 1902, is a chaotic mixture of clayey sand, plant remains, and wood fragments with particles of charcoal. The lower part of the sequence passes from a sandy clayey silt with charcoal (contexts 1903/1904) down into slightly disturbed gravelly sand which probably represents the March Gravels which are the Quaternary geological deposits underlying the site (context 1905).

Depth (m)	Context Number	Description
0.00-0.25	1849	10YR5/4 dark greyish brown and 7.5YR4/4 dark brown - patchy with colours becoming duller downward; very poorly sorted clayey silt with numerous clasts of sub-angular and well-rounded flint of all sizes up to 30mm becoming less stony downward; unstructured compact; plant remains common including well-preserved leaf fragments; charcoal; no acid reaction; well-marked transition to:
0.25-0.50	1886	10YR4/4 dark yellowish brown and 2.5Y4/2 dark greyish brown; very poorly sorted clayey/silty medium to coarse sand with clasts up to 15mm; unstructured, less compact than overlying; common plant remains; charcoal; no acid reaction.

Table 4.1 Lithostratigraphic sequence from monolith sample <78>, Pond 1829

Depth (m)	Context Number	Description
0.00-0.05	1901	5YR4/4 reddish brown; poorly sorted sandy silty clay with clasts up to 25mm; unstructured; several fragments of wood (up to 100mm) in remnants of a compact clayey matrix; no acid reaction; sharp contact with:
0.05-0.30	1902	Black; poorly sorted gritty sandy silty clay with clasts up to 25mm; chaotic mixture of clayey sand and plant debris; abundant plant remains; wood fragments up to 60x15mm; scattered mollusc shell; charcoal; no acid reaction; well-marked transition to:
0.30-0.43	1903/ 1904	10YR3/3 dark brown; moderately sorted sandy clayey silt; unstructured; abundant plant remains; wood fragments up to 15mm; charcoal; no acid reaction; well-marked transition to:
0.43-0.48	1905	10YR5/4 yellowish brown; well sorted medium sand with clasts up to 25mm; unstructured; scattered plant remains; wood fragments (up to 5mm); no acid reaction.

Table 4.2 Lithostratigraphic sequence from monolith sample <79>, Pond 1907

Pit 1714 (Tables 4.3 and 4.4; Fig 30)

Samples <69> and <70> represent the infill of pit 1714. The upper part of the sequence is organic-rich (contexts 1697, 1698, 1699, 1700) with little sign of soil development but between 0.30m and 0.33m from the top of the sample (context 1701) a thin sandy horizon is present in which evidence of soil formation is more common. Evidence of soil formation extends downward into the underlying, more peaty horizon (contexts 1702 and 1703). This in turn overlies a clayey context (1704) and a dark organic silt (1705) that probably includes the disturbed upper part of the underlying March Gravels (redeposited as context 1706).

Pit 1741 (Table 4.5; Fig 31)

Sample <72> is taken from the lower part of the infill of a pit (not in illustrated section). The upper part of the sequence is rather chaotic peaty sand with inclusions of silt and fragments of wood (context 1816). This context rests on a thick (0.22m) layer of silt in which evidence of soil forming processes is preserved (context 1730) and which passes down gravelly sand, probably representing the disturbed upper part of the underlying March Gravels (context 1817).

In summary, these sequences indicate the episodic infill of shallow depressions created in the surface of the late Quaternary sands and gravels. The presence of buried horizons incorporating evidence of soil forming processes and of surface compaction suggests that in some cases there were lengthy interruptions of the infill process, allowing incipient soil formation (eg contexts 1701 and 1730). There is, however, very little pedo-sedimentary evidence of local occupation or land-use, although charcoal was present in the pond deposits.

Depth (m)	Context Number	Description
0.00-0.12	1697	Black; gritty peat (broken up in tray)
0.12-0.21	1698/1699	10YR3/2 very dark greyish brown; poorly sorted gritty peaty silt with clasts up to 15mm; unstructured; occasional root channels and root remains; abundant plant debris; no acid reaction; gradual transition to:
0.21-0.30	1700	10YR3/2 very dark greyish brown; poorly sorted clayey/silty peaty sand with clasts up to 15mm; unstructured; occasional root channels and root remains; common plant remains; no acid reaction; well-marked transition to:
0.30-0.33	1701	10YR3/1 very dark grey; well sorted slightly sandy silt with scattered granules (up to 5mm); unstructured; root channels with iron-stained margins; roots common; scattered plant remains; no acid reaction; gradual transition to:
0.33-0.50	1702/1703	10YR3/4 dark yellowish brown; moderately sorted peaty silt with patchily distributed sand grains and clasts up to 20mm; unstructured; root channels with iron-stained margins; scattered root remains; common plant remains; no acid reaction.

Table 4.3: Lithostratigraphic sequence from monolith sample <69>, upper monolith sample in Pit 1714

Depth (m)	Context Number	Description
0.00-0.31	1704	10YR3/4 dark greyish brown; very poorly sorted gritty and peaty silty clay with clasts up to 20mm; unstructured; abundant plant remains; a few whole molluscan shells (gastropods); no acid reaction; well-marked transition to:
0.31-0.50	1705	10YR5/4 yellowish brown; moderately sorted clayey medium sand with inclusions of plant-rich silt; unstructured; scattered plant remains in clayey sand; no acid reaction.

Table 4.4: Lithostratigraphic sequence from monolith sample <70>, lower monolith sample in Pit 1714

Depth (m)	Context Number	Description
0.00-0.25	1816	10YR3/2 very dark greyish brown; sandy peat/peaty sand with inclusions of bluish grey clay; unstructured; abundant plant remains; wood fragments up to 80x30mm; no acid reaction; well-marked transition to:
0.25-0.47	1730	2.5Y3/2 very dark greyish brown; moderately sorted silt with scattered sand grains and clasts up to 20mm; unstructured; root channels with clay coatings; scattered root remains; common plant remains; wood fragments up to 40x15mm; no acid reaction; well-marked transition to:
0.47-0.50	1817	10YR4/2 dark greyish brown; well sorted very slightly silty medium sand with clasts up to 20mm; unstructured; scattered plant remains; no acid reaction.

Table 4.5 Lithostratigraphic sequence from monolith sample <72>, Pit 1741

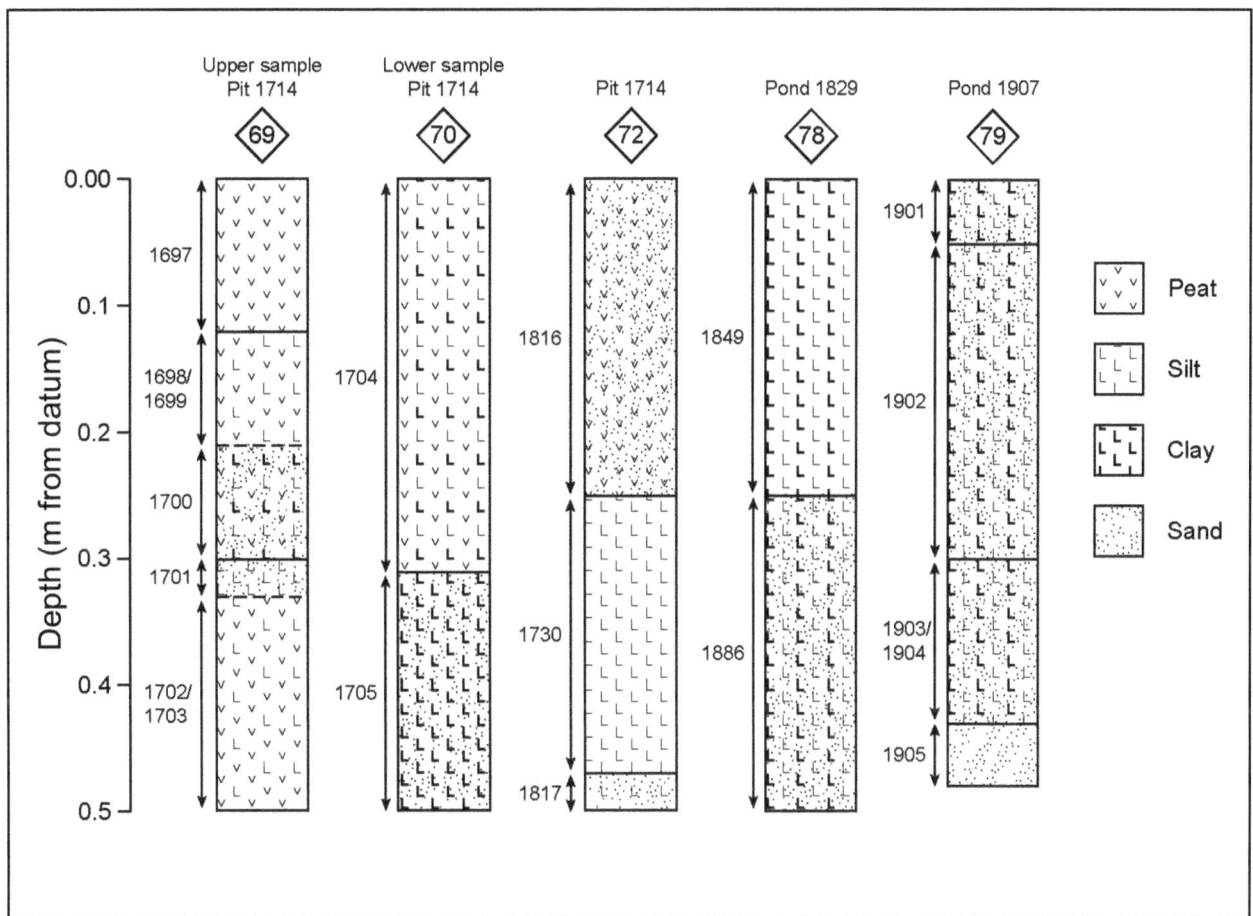

Fig 35. Lithostratigraphy of monolith samples 69, 70, 72, 78 and 79

Pollen Analysis
by N Branch and B Silva

Pond 1829 [Phase 8] (Fig 36)

The pollen analysis of contexts 1886 and 1849 (monolith sample <78>) indicates that non-arboreal taxa dominate the assemblage. These include Poaceae (grass family; *c* 45%), *Plantago lanceolata* (ribwort plantain; *c* 15%) and Lactuceae (eg *Taraxacum officinale*, dandelion (daisy family); *c* 5%). A diverse range of other herbaceous pollen taxa are also present, such as *Anthemis* (eg *Anthemis cotula*, stinking mayweed), *Chenopodium* type (eg *Chenopodium album*, fat hen; *Atriplex hastata*, orache), *Ranunculus* type (eg *Ranunculus repens*, creeping buttercup), *Rumex acetosella* (dock), *Trifolium* type (clover) and *Urtica* (eg *Urtica dioica*, common nettle). Tree pollen taxa are poorly represented, but include *Alnus glutinosa* (alder; *c* 6%), *Betula* (eg *Betula pendula*, silver birch), *Fraxinus excelsior* (ash; *c* 2%), *Pinus sylvestris* (pine), *Quercus* (oak; *c* 9%) and *Tilia* (lime). Shrub taxa are represented by *Ilex aquifolium* (holly), *Hedera helix* (ivy), *Corylus* type (eg *Corylus avellana*, hazel; *c* 10%), *Salix* (eg *Salix alba*, white willow; *c* 5%) and *Sambucus nigra* (elder). Aquatic and spore taxa are also poorly represented, but include *Nuphar lutea* (white waterlily), *Potamogeton* (pondweed), *Typha latifolia* (reedmace) and *Sparganium* type (eg *Sparganium erectum*, branched bur-reed). Finally, cereal pollen occurs throughout the sequence with values between 1-3%.

The pollen-stratigraphic record indicates that the pond was colonised by free-floating aquatic vegetation, such as waterlily and pondweed, in the deepest areas, and by aquatics with a preference for shallow water on the margins of the feature, such as reedmace and bur-reed. This pond edge habitat was also probably colonised by alder and willow, forming an isolated stand rather than dense woodland. On dryland, the pollen assemblage indicates the presence of open woodland with birch, ash, oak, lime and possibly pine. Forming the woodland understorey, or occurring in isolated communities, shrubs such as hazel, holly, ivy and elder were also present. The diverse assemblage of herbaceous pollen taxa indicates, however, that grassland and arable fields dominated the dryland vegetation cover. The former consisted of tall herb communities (eg *Centaurea nigra*, black knapweed; docks and sorrels), suggesting meadowland, as well as short turf grassland, suggesting pasture (eg clover). The relatively high values of cereal pollen, and associated taxa commonly found as weeds of arable fields (eg ribwort plantain), indicate localised cultivation.

Pond 1907 [Phase 6] (Fig 37)

The pollen analysis of contexts 1905, 1904, 1903, 1902 and 1901 (monolith sample <79>) indicates that non-arboreal taxa dominate the assemblage. These include Poaceae (grass family; *c* 50% decreasing to *c* 30%), *Plantago lanceolata* (ribwort plantain; *c* 18% decreasing to <5%) and Lactuceae (eg *Taraxacum officinale*, dandelion (daisy family); *c* 10% decreasing to <5%). A diverse range of other herbaceous pollen taxa is also present, such as Apiaceae (eg *Apium* (carrot family), marshwort), *Chenopodium* type, Cyperaceae (sedge family), *Plantago media/major* (eg hoary plantain; *c* 5% declining to *c* 1%), *Polygonum aviculare* (knotgrass; *c* 4%), *Ranunculus* type and *Trifolium* type. Tree pollen taxa are poorly represented, but include *Alnus glutinosa* (*c* 5%), *Betula*, *Fraxinus excelsior* (*c* 3%), *Pinus sylvestris* (pine; *c* 2%) and *Quercus* (*c* 7%). Shrub taxa are represented by *Solanum dulcamara* (bittersweet; *c* 2%), *Ilex aquifolium* (holly), *Corylus* type (eg *Corylus avellana*, hazel; *c* 8% declining to <5%), *Salix* (eg *Salix alba*, white willow; increasing to *c* 20%) and *Sambucus nigra*. Aquatic and spore taxa are also poorly represented, but include *Nuphar lutea* (white water lily, *c* 5%) and *Potamogeton* (pondweed). Finally, cereal pollen occurs throughout the sequence with values of approximately 1%.

The pollen-stratigraphic analysis of Pond 1907 provides a broadly similar record to Pond 1829 with overwhelming evidence for presence of dryland grassland and cultivated fields, especially in the lowermost part of the sequence. Aquatic pollen taxa confirm the presence of an open water body, with the deepest parts colonised by waterlily and pondweed, and the margins colonised by alder and willow. The latter, in particular, increases in abundance throughout the sequence suggesting a natural succession from reed, grass and sedge swamp to willow and alder carr woodland. On dryland, the woodland cover was open in character, and included oak, birch, ash and possibly pines. These trees probably colonised the drier margins of the pond, and the edges of ditches and fields, either as isolated trees or in small thickets. Supporting this interpretation is evidence for the presence of bittersweet, a woody climber that is characteristic of wet woods, such as alder or willow, forming carr or within woodland occupying riverbanks and hedgerows near wet ditches.

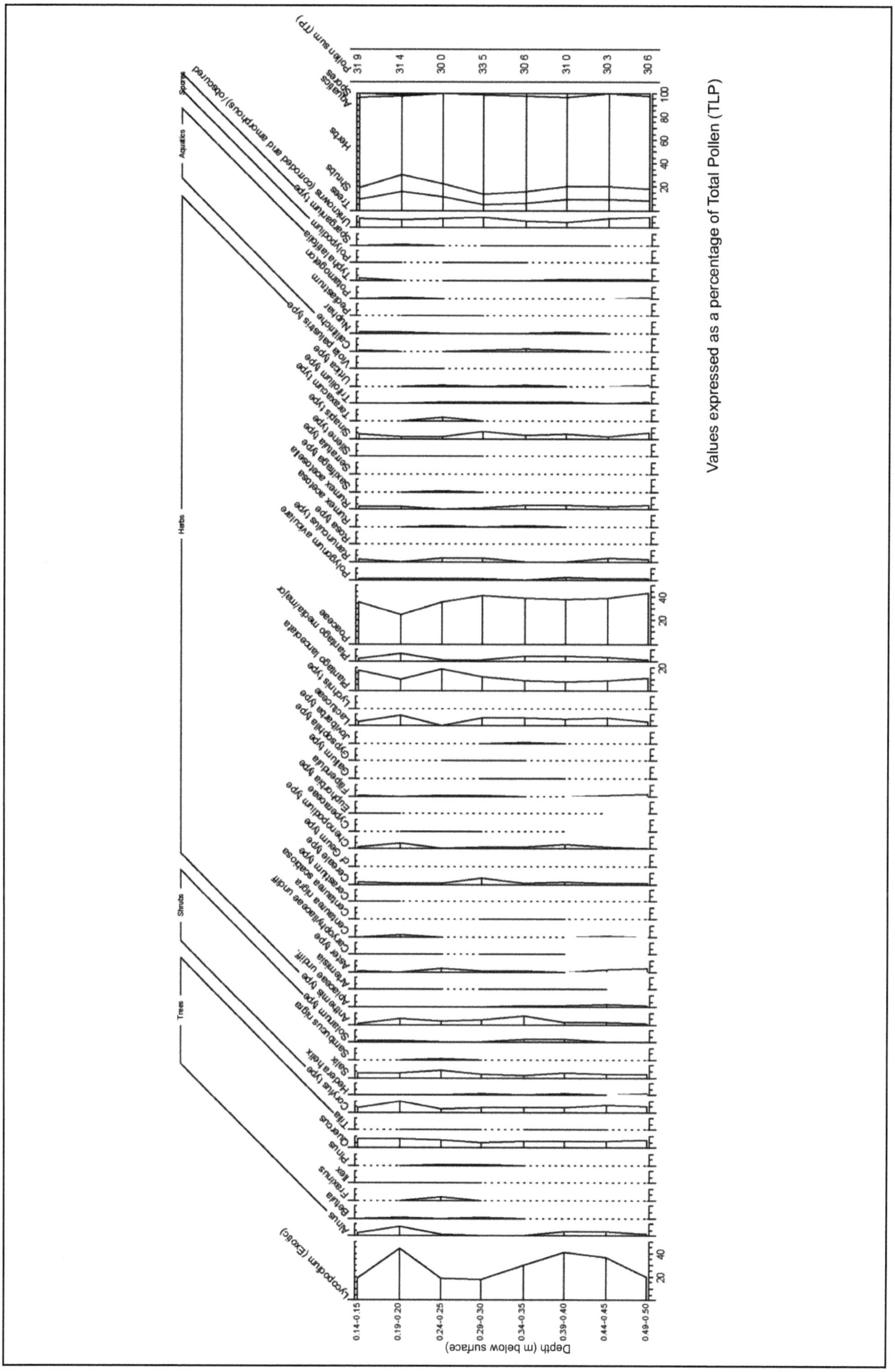

Fig 36. Percentage pollen diagram for monolith sample 78, Pond 1829

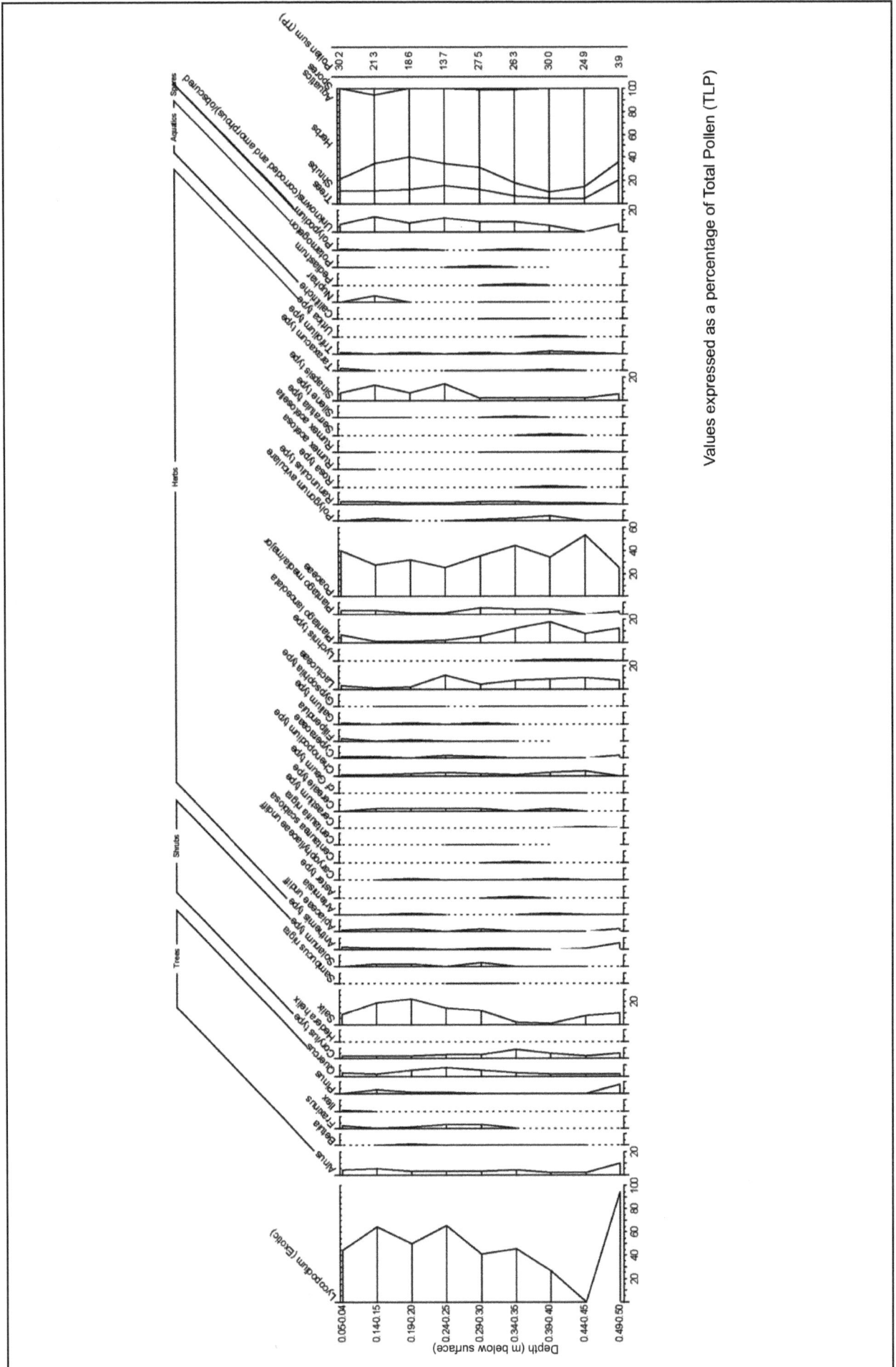

Fig 37. Percentage pollen diagram for monolith sample 79, Pond 1907

Plant Macrofossil Analysis

by A Vaughan-Williams

Pond 1907 (Appendix 2: Tables 4.6 and 4.7a)

Context 1902 (sample <81>) from the pond contained an assemblage dominated by waterlogged seeds of *Stellaria media* (common chickweed; n=198). The remainder of the assemblage consisted mainly of seeds of Cyperaceae (sedge family; n=4) and *Potentilla* sp (cinquefoil; n=5), and *Polygonum persicaria* (redshank; n=1), *Polygonum* sp. (knotgrass; n=6), *Centaurea* sp (knapweed; n=1) and *Ranunculus repens* (creeping buttercup; n=4). The preservation of the seeds by waterlogged conditions clearly confirms the presence of a standing body of water in the pond. Surprisingly however, aquatic taxa were absent from the plant macrofossil assemblage, with only marginal, wet ground taxa being represented, namely sedge and cinquefoil. This suggests that the feature may not have contained a permanent body of standing water. Their absence is unlikely to reflect the lack of suitable conditions for preservation due to the high concentration of other seeds, such as common chickweed, as well as redshank, knotgrass, knapweed and creeping buttercup. Today, chickweed is a common weed found in various locations including disturbed ground, vegetable gardens and arable fields, hence it could reflect either/both an arable field or/and the presence of a settlement, with the concentration reflecting the prolific presence of this plant near to the pond. Together with the other plants represented, the evidence suggests a mosaic of damp ground, tall grassland (eg meadow) and cultivated fields.

Pits (Tables 4.6, 4.7a and 4.7b)

The thirteen pits analysed produced mainly waterlogged seeds, the most common/abundant taxa being *Stellaria media* (n=30 in pit 660; n=160 in pit 1608; n=24 in pit 1622), *Chenopodium album* (fat hen; n=12 in pit 1608; n=25 in sample <62> pit 1622; n=31 in sample <61> pit 1622), *Atriplex* (orache; n=10 in pit 1608; n=19 in pit 1622; n=10 in pit 1659), *Rubus* (bramble; n=17 in pit 20; n=57 in pit 660; n=55/53 in pit 660; n=120 in pit 1622; n=15 in pit 1659; n=18 in pit 1714), and *Solanum dulcamara* (bittersweet; n=11/88 in pit 1622). These taxa indicate the presence of grassland, probably tall herb communities forming meadow or waste ground, and shrubland with bramble and hazel (*Corylus avellana*; pits 660, 1659 and 1860), which were invaded by woody climbers such as bittersweet. The presence of frequent bramble (blackberry) seeds may also indicate that the pits were used for the disposal of cess. Charred grains of *Hordeum* (barley; n=2) and *Triticum* (wheat; n=11) were present in pit 72, context 70, indicating the consumption of these cereals by the local population. Together with the diverse range of seeds from weeds of cultivated fields, the evidence indicates that the cereals were cultivated locally.

Ditches (Tables 4.6, 4.7a and 4.7b)

Seven ditch samples were analysed, and contained both waterlogged and charred seeds. These were from Ditch 2041 Cut 593 (sample <25> context 600), Ditch 2016 Cut 1060 (sample <41> context 1058), Ditch 2005 Cut 173 (sample <15> context 171), Ditch 2037 Cut 1544 (sample <46> context 1543), Ditch 2031 Cut 1651 (sample <59> context 1653), Ditch 2027 Cut 1696 (sample <67> context 1688), and Ditch 2029 Cut 1925 (sample <77> context 1923). Dominating the plant assemblages are *Chenopodium album* (fat hen; n=16 in Ditch 2016 Cut 1060), *Stellaria media* (common chickweed; n=40 in Ditch 2031 Cut 1651), *Sambucus nigra* (elder; n=44 in Ditch 2041 Cut 593) and *Rubus* (bramble; n=100 in Ditch 2016 Cut 1060). Other seeds included orache (*Atriplex* sp.), woundwort (*Stachys* sp.) and lady's bedstraw (*Galium verum*). These taxa indicate the presence of grassland and shrubland, perhaps bordering agricultural fields. Supporting this interpretation is evidence for the cultivation/consumption of cereals and possibly pulses, eg charred grains of hulled barley (*Hordeum*; n=1) and grass seeds (Poaceae) were present in Ditch 2037 (1544), and charred seeds of vetches (*Vicia* sp.) and the pea family (*Fabaceae* sp.), and occasional charred weed seeds, were present in ditches 2037 (1544) and 2029 (1925). Although the pulses may have been cultivated, they may also have grown as weeds of arable fields. These taxa probably became charred accidentally during food preparation or cooking, or deliberately following their use as fuel (see Hillman 1981, 1984). They were probably discarded into the ditch as a waste product following cleaning of the domestic hearth.

Insect Analysis
by S Elias

Pond 1907 (Table 4.8)

These assemblages are dominated by swamp-dwelling species in a variety of families. The presence of alder is indicated by the leaf beetle, *Chrysomela aenea*, that feeds exclusively on the leaves of *Alnus glutinosa*. This species of alder is commonly found in alder carr environments. Damp woodland habitats are indicated by the ground beetle, *Badister sordis*, and the rove beetle, *Anthobium atrocephalum*. The proximity of the site to the margin of a stream or river is suggested by the presence of several riverbank beetle inhabitants, including the ground beetles, *Dyschirius luedersi* and *Amara lunicollis*. Dung inhabiting beetles suggest the presence of large animals near the site. These include two species of rove beetles, *Anotylus sculpturatus* and *Tachinus signatus*. Both of these beetles prey on maggots and other small insects attracted to animal dung. The dryland vegetation was included deciduous woodland, and we can be certain that *Tilia* (lime) was growing nearby, because of the presence of the bark beetle, *Ernoporus caucasicus*, which attacks the stems and shoots of this tree. In addition to the above, Pond 1907 indicated the nearby presence of agricultural fields, as suggested by the presence of the ground beetle, *Trechus quadristriatus*, and by *Helophorus nubilus*. The latter species is a member of an aquatic beetle family, but this particular species inhabits dry habitats, such as meadows and agricultural fields, and the larva of this beetle attacks wheat stems. The dung beetle, *Aphodius distinctus*, suggests the likely presence of horses or cattle.

Pit 1741 (Table 4.8)

The insect assemblage from Pit 1741 provided good evidence of alder carr, with the presence of the ground beetle, *Pterostichus minor*, that inhabits this kind of environment, as well as the leaf beetle, *Plagiodera versicolora*, that feeds on alder leaves. Swamp environments with shallow water and abundant, reedy vegetation are documented by the presence of the water beetles, *Limnebius papposus* and *Ochthebius minimus*, as well as the short-winged mould beetle, *Rybaxis laminata*. The dryland near to the pit included deciduous woodland. This is indicated by the presence of the weevil, *Rhuncolus punctatulatus*. However, there were also dry to damp meadows nearby, as suggested by the presence of the ground beetle, *Lebia cruxminor*.

Waterlogged Wood Analysis
by I Poole

Pit 20 (Tables 4.9 and 4.10)

The majority of the material (up to 61%) in Pit 20 had anatomical characters consistent with *Alnus* (alder; n=9+?2). Minor amounts of the *Salix/Populus* type (willow/poplar; n=4) were also identified. Four specimens had undergone too much disintegration to enable anatomical identification beyond dicotyledonous angiosperm. The material was from wood of unknown diameter, and thus probably stems. No roundwood was recorded which may have provided evidence for coppicing practised at this time.

Pit 1741 (Tables 4.9 and 4.10)

This pit contained material with anatomical consistency with *Salix/Populus* type (willow / poplar; n=2+?3) along with a possible *Prunus* (n=?1). The material was from wood of small diameter, and thus twigs. No roundwood was recorded which may have provided evidence for coppicing practised at this time.

Pit 1860 (Tables 4.9 and 4.10)

Only *Alnus* (alder n=1) could be identified. One specimen had undergone too much disintegration to enable anatomical identification beyond dicotyledonous angiosperm. The second was waterlogged charcoal and was again not identifiable beyond dicotyledonous angiosperm. The material was from wood of unknown diameter, and thus probably stems with one piece of roundwood recorded. From analysis of the growth rings no evidence could be obtained to indicate that silviculture was taking place.

Pit 1942 (Tables 4.9 and 4.10)

The material with identifiable anatomy was consistent with *Lonicera/Ligustrum* type (honeysuckle/privet; n=2+?3). The remainder (n=7) was unidentifiable beyond dicotyledonous angiosperm. The material was from wood of unknown diameter, and thus probably stems. No roundwood was recorded which may have provided evidence for coppicing practised at this time.

Charcoal Analysis
by I Poole

Ditch 137 (Tables 4.11 and 4.12)

This feature contained a mix of charcoal greater or equal to 4mm in size. The material is relatively poorly preserved and somewhat friable. Only one taxon that could be identified, namely the *Quercus* type, accounting for up to 25% of the material. Twenty-five pieces could not be identified beyond dicotyledonous angiosperm due to lack of diagnostic anatomical characters. The majority of the material was from wood of unknown diameter, and thus probably stem material. No roundwood was recorded which may have provided evidence for coppicing practised at this time.

Pit 160 (Tables 4.11 and 4.12)

This feature contained charcoal less than *c* 4mm diameter. The material is relatively poorly preserved and somewhat friable. The majority of the material (50%) could not be identified beyond dicotyledonous angiosperm due to lack of diagnostic anatomical characters. From the remainder (the larger diameter fraction) the majority of the material was *Fraxinus* (ash; n=12+?6) with smaller amounts material with anatomical similarity to *Corylus* (n=2+?1), Pomoideae (n=1+?1), *Quercus* (n=1) and possible *Betula* (birch; n=?1). The majority of the material was from wood of unknown diameter, and thus probably stem material. No roundwood was recorded which may have provided evidence for coppicing practised at this time. This sample was truncated at 50 pieces due to the small size of the wood material, which hindered further identification.

Ditch 593 (Tables 4.11 and 4.12)

The material was relatively poorly preserved and somewhat friable, and only two taxa could be recognised, namely *Quercus* (oak; n=11+?7) and *Corylus* (n=?2). The thirty pieces that could not be identified due to lack of diagnostic anatomical characters had dicotyledonous angiosperm origins. The majority of the material was from wood of unknown diameter, and thus probably stem material. No roundwood was recorded which may have provided evidence for coppicing practised at this time. This sample was truncated at 50 pieces due to the poor preservation and size.

Ditch 1060 (Tables 4.11 and 4.12)

The majority of the material was unidentifiable (74%) and only two taxa could be recognised, namely *Quercus* (oak; n=4+?4) and *Prunus* (n=3+?2). The thirty-seven pieces that could not be identified due to lack of diagnostic anatomical characters had dicotyledonous angiosperm origins. The majority of the material was from wood of unknown diameter, and thus probably stem material. No roundwood was recorded which may have provided evidence for coppicing practised at this time. This sample was truncated at 50 pieces due to the poor preservation.

Pit 61 (Tables 4.11 and 4.12)

This feature contained a mix of charcoal greater or equal to 4mm in size. The material is relatively poorly preserved and somewhat friable, with one main taxon represented, namely the *Prunus* type, which accounts for up to 50% of the material studied. Four other taxa are present, namely *Quercus* (oak; n=4), *Alnus* (alder; n=2+?4). *Corylus* (hazel; n=2) and *Salix/Populus* (willow/poplar; n=1). Due to lack of diagnostic anatomical characters 37% could not be identified beyond dicotyledonous angiosperm. The majority of the material was from wood of unknown diameter, and thus probably stem material. No roundwood was recorded which may have provided evidence for coppicing practised at this time.

Pit 72 (Tables 4.11 and 4.12)

This feature consisted of a mix of charcoal greater or equal to 4mm in size. The material is reasonably preserved, although somewhat friable, with relatively good anatomical preservation facilitating identification. One main taxon is represented, namely the *Alnus*, or alder, type which accounts for up to 31% of the material studied. Two other taxa are relatively abundant, namely *Salix/Populus* (willow/poplar; n=18) and *Quercus* (oak; n=12). Also present are *Corylus* (hazel; n=3), *Fagus* (beech; n=3+?2), *Ulmus* (elm; n=1) and *Prunus* (n=1). Twenty-nine pieces could not be identified beyond dicotyledonous angiosperm due to lack of diagnostic anatomical characters. The majority of the material was from wood of unknown diameter, and thus probably stem, material. No round wood was recorded which may have provided evidence for coppicing practised at this time.

Ditch 2035 Cut 1547 (Tables 4.11 and 4.12)

This feature contained a mix of charcoal greater or equal to 4mm in size. The material is reasonably preserved, although somewhat friable, with relatively good anatomical preservation facilitating identification. One main taxon is represented, namely *Fraxinus*, or ash type, which accounts for up to 75% of the material studied. Other taxa include *Corylus* (hazel; n=9+?1), *Quercus* (oak; n=2), *Ulmus* (elm; n=1), *Betula* (birch; n=1) and possible *Alnus* (alder; n=?1). Nine pieces could not be identified beyond dicotyledonous angiosperm due to lack of diagnostic anatomical characters. The majority of the material was from wood of unknown diameter, and thus probably stems. One piece of hazel roundwood was recorded. Growth ring measurements of this piece of roundwood found a sharp decrease in growth ring width after the first year, which might suggest that coppicing was practised at this time.

Pit 1714 (Tables 4.11 and 4.12)

This feature consisted of a mix of charcoal greater or equal to 4mm in size. The material is reasonably preserved with relatively good anatomical preservation facilitating identification. One main taxon is represented, namely the *Salix/Populus*, or willow/poplar type, which accounts for up to 93% of the material studied. The remainder of the material could not be identified beyond dicotyledonous angiosperm due to lack of diagnostic anatomical characters. All material was from wood of unknown diameter, and thus probably stems. No roundwood was recorded and thus no evidence for woodland management or silviculture could be obtained.

Ditch 2026 Cut 1696 (Tables 4.11 and 4.12)

The material was relatively poorly preserved and somewhat friable. The majority of the material (86%) could not be identified beyond dicotyledonous angiosperm due to lack of diagnostic anatomical characters. From the remainder (the larger diameter fraction) the material was of the *Quercus* (oak; n=3+?4) type. The majority of the material was from wood of unknown diameter, and thus probably stems. No roundwood was recorded which may have provided evidence for coppicing practised at this time. This sample was truncated at 50 pieces due to the small size of the wood material which hindered further identification.

Ditch 2029 Cut 1925 (Tables 4.11 and 4.12)

This feature contained a mixture of charcoal greater or equal to 4mm in size, with the majority (60%) of the material studied not identifiable beyond dicotyledonous angiosperm (including two pieces of probable root wood <2mm in diameter) due to the absence of preserved anatomical characters. The taxa that could be identified had anatomical characters consistent with *Salix/Populus* (willow/poplar; n=8+?3), *Alnus* (alder; n=4+?2) and *Prunus* (n=1+?2). The majority of the material was from wood of unknown diameter, and thus probably stems. One piece each of *Prunus* and an unidentifiable angiosperm roundwood were recorded but in both cases, growth ring measurements could not provide any indication of possible silviculture. This sample was truncated at 50 specimens due to the poor preservation.

Phosphate Analysis
by I Valcarcel

Several features show enhanced total phosphate values by comparison with the control sample (Table 4.13; natural; 919mgP/kg). These are: Pit 1714, >1400mgP/kg; Pit 1577, 1698mgP/kg; Pit 660, >1000mgP/kg; Pit 193 (cut into Pit 160), 3069mgP/kg; Pit 160, 1698mgP/kg; Pit 72, 3475mgP/kg; Pit 61, 2397mgP/kg; Ditch 2032 Cut 1557, 1181mgP/kg; Ditch 2035 Cut 1547, 1511mgP/kg; Ditch 2041 Cut 593, 1036mgP/kg; Ditch 2014 Cut 137, 1290mgP/kg (Fig 44). These enhanced values may be due to the deposition of phosphate-rich faecal material (cess) or urine in the features, which could be animal and/or human in origin. However, while this interpretation may confidently be applied to the ditches on the edges of fields or settlement areas where human and animal activities would be locally intensive, it seems unlikely that the pits, which were probably used as waterholes, would have been deliberately contaminated with cess. Alternatively, the enhanced phosphate levels in the pits may be due to the localised drainage patterns with groundwater passing through phosphate-rich contaminated land before entering the pits.

66

Discussion

The environmental archaeological analysis at Thorney Bypass Borrow Pit aimed to (1) reconstruct the changing nature of the landscape (biophysical environment), (2) reconstruct the impact of human groups on the natural environment, especially in terms of farming practices, ie pastoral and/or arable agriculture, and (3) elucidate the nature of the economy and diet of the local inhabitants. In order to achieve these aims, a multi-proxy study was conducted on a variety of Bronze Age features.

The pollen and insect analyses of the sedimentary fills of ponds 1829 and 1907 revealed the presence of open water, with water lily and pondweed in the deepest areas, and reed-mace and bur-reed on the margins with alder and willow. There is also some evidence in Pond 1907 for natural, hydroseral succession from swamp to carr woodland, indicating the gradual infilling of the pond with organic sediment and the colonisation of more terrestrial plant taxa. In contrast, the plant macrofossil analysis of Pond 1907 only provided confirmation for the presence of damp ground, with sedges and cinquefoil, and not open water. This suggests that the presence of open water in the ponds may have been localised, indicating a mosaic of vegetation cover, or that the water level fluctuated episodically or perhaps on a seasonal basis. The pollen, plant macrofossil and insect data indicate that the surrounding dry land consisted of a mosaic of open woodland and grassland, with the former dominated by birch, ash, oak and lime trees, and with an understorey of hazel, holly, ivy, elder and bittersweet. These trees and shrubs would have colonised the margins of the ponds, formed hedgerows, as well as lining the edges of ditches and fields. The grassland comprised three broad plant communities: meadow with tall herbs, pasture with short herbs, and cultivated land with cereals. The insect remains in particular provide direct evidence for the presence of large domesticated animals (eg cattle or horses), and the cultivation of wheat. This reconstruction, based upon the evidence from the ponds, is broadly consistent with the national picture, which suggests that the vegetation cover during the Bronze Age was a mosaic of woodland, shrubland and grassland, with intensification of agricultural activities resulting in substantial reductions in a range of tree taxa, especially elm and lime (Branch *et al* 2005). Whilst the clearance of these and other trees was a prerequisite for the creation of suitable land for pastoral and arable activities, the branches and leaves of both elm and lime are undoubtedly highly nutritious and would probably have been used for animal fodder.

The pits and ditches provide broad support for the environmental archaeological data from the ponds. The insect and plant macrofossil evidence, supplemented by the geochemical data, indicates standing water, surrounded by meadow and pastureland, and shrubland with hazel and bramble, as well as the local cultivation of barley and wheat, and possibly vetches. These features have also provided further evidence for the nature of the surrounding vegetation cover, indicating the presence of a range of tree and shrub taxa, including alder and willow, oak, ash, birch, hazel, elm and beech. The presence of beech is particularly interesting because pollen-stratigraphic evidence suggests that beech woodland was not common in the British Isles until after *c* 500 BC (Branch *et al* 2005). The presence of these tree taxa in pits and ditches indicates that local economic activities included the exploitation of a wide variety of trees for fuel wood and possibly construction, rather than the collection or management of specific taxa. A similar picture of arable fields and grassland has been obtained from neighbouring areas. For example, at Ashville Trading Estate (Oxfordshire), two ring ditches used for cremations contained weed seeds such as chickweed, fat hen, sedges, grasses, and clover and ribwort plantain (Jones 1978). Whilst West Row Fen in Suffolk (Martin and Murphy 1988) and Little Waltham, Chelmsford (Peglar and Wilson 1978) contained similar, diverse plant assemblages indicating grassland and arable fields containing emmer wheat.

Conclusions

The environmental archaeological analysis indicates that the Bronze Age features studied contained standing water that was colonised by aquatic and marginal aquatic vegetation. Woodland dominated by willow and alder fringed the open water bodies forming carr, whilst on dry land a mosaic of open woodland, shrubland and grassland was present. The evidence suggests that the woodland consisted of a range of tree and shrub taxa, including lime, elm, oak, beech, hazel and ash, which would have fringed the settlement, fields, ditches and pits. The Bronze Age inhabitants exploited many of these taxa for fuel wood, with only equivocal evidence for woodland management. The multi-proxy data indicates that meadow, pasture and arable land existed at the site during the Bronze Age, providing suitable grazing land and fodder for domesticated animals, and cereals (wheat and barley) and possibly legumes. This mixed agricultural economy undoubtedly has an impact on the local environment, which is suggested by the open character of the landscape.

Chapter 5: **Non-Wood Finds**

Prehistoric Pottery

by Andy Chapman

A total of 70 sherds, weighing 915g, of prehistoric hand-built pottery was recovered, with an average sherd weight of 13g. Only one feature, Pit 160, produced a small assemblage of diagnostic pottery, while two further contexts, 1658, Pit 1659, and 1937 Pit 1912 each produced large sherds from single vessels. Another 12 contexts each produced between one and five small plain body sherds (Table 5.1).

Fabrics

Three fabric types were identified:

Fabric 1: A soft, poorly fired, fabric containing small pellets of grog. The sherds typically have pale brown to near white external surfaces, with a grey core and inner surfaces

Fabric 2: A hard fabric containing sparse to moderate crushed shell. The sherds typically have oxidised surfaces and a grey core, and on some the inner surface is also grey

Fabric 3: Soft, with voids from leached inclusions, probably of shell. This is most probably the same as Fabric 2 in origin but leached through deposition under different soil conditions

The assemblage is dominated by the shelly fabric (Fabric 2), which makes up 59% of the total by weight, with the sherds with leached inclusions (Fabric 3) contributing a further 30%, the majority of this coming from a single vessel. The grogged fabric (1) forms only 11% of the total by weight.

Forms, decoration and date

The assemblage is dominated by small plain body sherds, often considerably eroded, that offer no diagnostic potential.

The only significant group is from Pit 160. It contained rim sherds from three similar vessels, all in the shelly fabric, 6-8mm thick, but with thickened rims with a marked internal bevel, and rim diameters of around 250-300mm (Fig 38, 1-3). They are distinguished by variations in the rim decoration. There are two rim sherds from a vessel with fingertip impressions on the bevel, paired fingernail incisions along the rounded outer edge of the rim and fingertip impressions on the external surface below the rim (1). There is a single rim sherd with fingernail incisions along the outer, flattened edge of the rim (2), and another single rim sherd has a simple chevron design of twisted cord impressions along the bevel (3).

Context	Feature	Fabric	Sherds	Weight (g)	Site phase
60	Pit 61	1	3	22	?
68	Pit 72	1	1	3	?
175	Pit 160. Middle fill of main pit	2	2	97	?
197	Pit 160. Lowest fill of main pit	2	4	180	?
526	Ditch 2040 Cut 522. Lower edge fill	2	1	13	6-7
1011	Ditch 2019 terminal, Cut 1013 Possible recut or upper fill	1	1	10	?
1505	Ditch 2036 Cut 1507. Main fill	1	5	5	1-2
1543	Ditch 2037 terminal Cut 1544	3	5	15	1-2
1564	Ditch 2038 Cut 1567	2	1	4	1-2
1565	Ditch 2038 Cut 1567. Beneath 1564	2	1	1	1-2
1572	Pit 1577. Upper fill	1	1	14	?
1573	Pit 1577. Beneath 1572	1	2	43	?
1658	Pit 1659. Shallow pit with peaty fill	3	36	263	?
1734	Pit 1741. Thin layer within upper part of fill	2	4	38	?
1863	Ditch 2027 Cut 1864. Lower fill	2	1	7	6-7
1937	Pit 1912. Basal fill (same as 1911)	2	2	200	8-9

Table 5.1 Contexts containing pottery

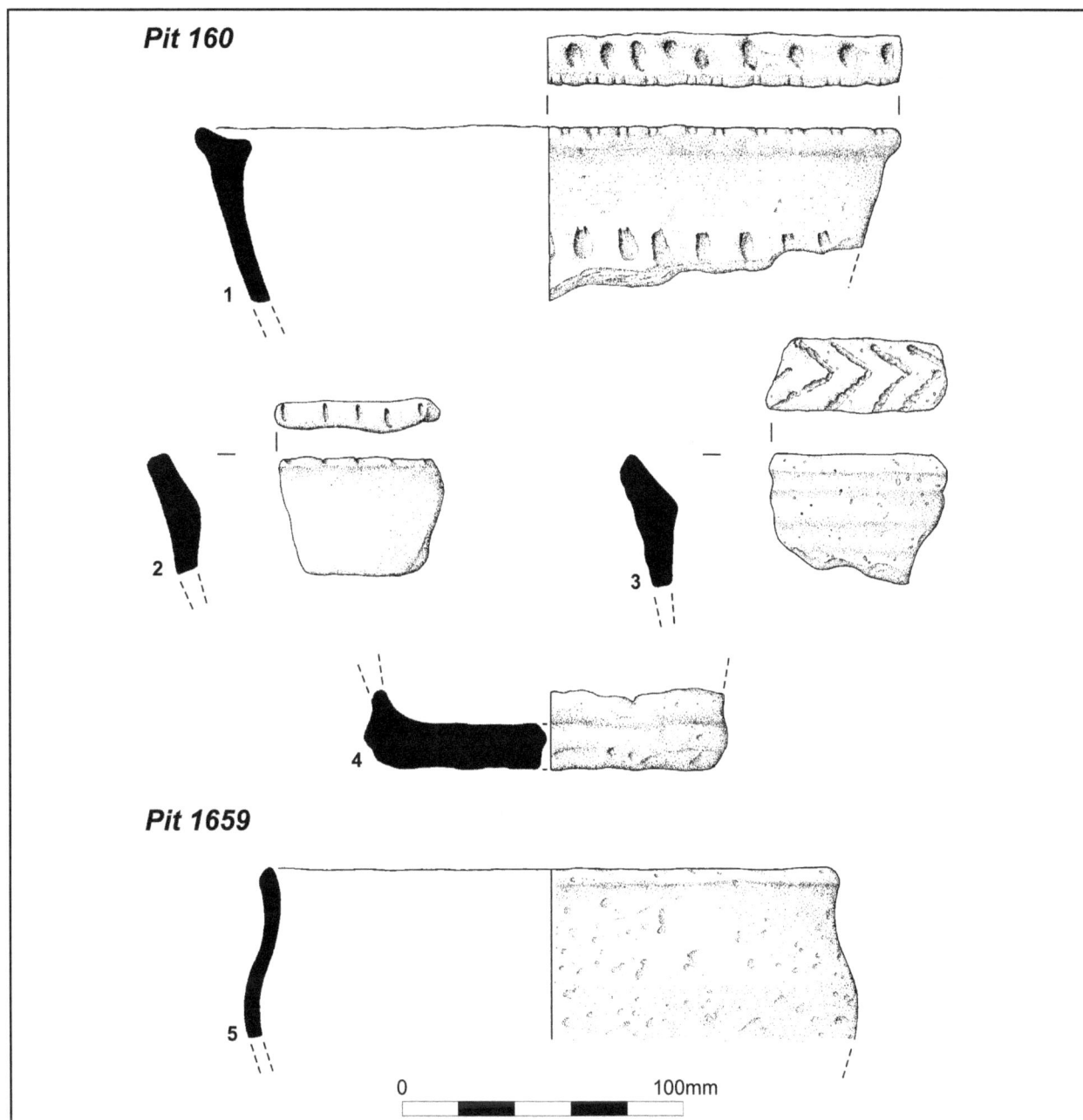

Fig 38. Prehistoric pottery from pits 160 and 1659

From the same pit there is also part of a simple flat base, 120mm in diameter and 17mm thick, in the same shelly fabric (Fig 38, 4).

Bevelled rims first appear in Late Neolithic impressed wares, and are common on a wide range of 2nd millennium vessel forms, such as food vessels, collared urns, food vessel urns, cordoned urns, accessory vessels and Deverel-Rimbury urns (Gibson & Woods 1997, 106-107 & 164-165). Given the survival of only the rims, it is difficult to ascribe these sherds to a specific vessel form. However, they seem most likely to belong within the Food Vessel urn tradition, which would place them at the end of the 3rd and into the first half of the 2nd millennium, during the Early Bronze Age (Gibson & Woods 1997, 164-165). Radiocarbon dating on associated wood has given a date at the very end of the 3rd millennium BC, and therefore quite early in the currency of Food Vessels (Chapter 7: Fig 41).

The only other vessel from the site with an identifiable form is a bowl from Pit 1659. This appears to have been deposited as an intact or partial vessel, but is in a soft fabric, 8mm thick, with voids from leached inclusions. It had fragmented into numerous small sherds, although part of the rim is intact. The vessel is a plain, slack shouldered bowl, 200mm in diameter, with a simple rounded rim (Fig 38, 5). It is difficult to place this bowl form within a single tradition, but a Middle to Late Bronze Age/Early Iron Age date would seem most appropriate.

The only other significant quantity of pottery comprises two large body sherds of thick-walled shelly ware from context 1937 Pit 1912. These are from a large plain jar form that cannot be attributed to any specific date.

Catalogue of illustrated pottery *(Fig 38)*

1   Bevelled rim of open bowl form, Fabric 2, light brown external surface, brown to grey internal surface, fingertip and fingernail decoration on rim and neck. Context 197, Pit 160

2   Bevelled rim of open bowl form, fabric 2, light brown external surface, light grey internal surface, fingernail decoration on rim. Context 197, Pit 160

3   Bevelled rim of open bowl form, fabric 2, light brown surface, impressed cord decoration on rim. Context 197, Pit 160

4   Flat base, fabric 2, light brown external surface, dark grey core and internal surface. Context 197, Pit 160

5   Rim and upper body of slack-shouldered bowl, Fabric 3, grey-brown external surface and grey internal surface. Fills 1658 & 1660, pit 1659

Fired Clay
by Pat Chapman

This very small assemblage of 17 fragments of fired clay, weighing 157g, comprises small, amorphous lumps. Only one fragment, from context 70, Pit 72, has any feature, a wattle impression 10mm in diameter.

The eleven fragments from contexts 70, 168 and 1617 are slightly soft and sandy with a few flint and shell up to 4mm and reddish orange in colour. The five from context 1545 are soft and reddish with occasional flint up to 2mm, with one piece blackened. Only the fragment, from context 1011 Ditch 1013, is different, being hard and slightly sandy, pink with a few fine flint and shell and one cockle shell 20mm wide at the rim.

The fragment with the wattle impression indicates some sort of structural use, but otherwise these fragments are just random debris.

Flint
by Andrew Mudd

A total of five worked flints were recovered from all features and are listed below (Table 5.3).

The only item of intrinsic interest is a concave or 'horned' scraper from Pit 1942 (associated with Pond 1907). The finished artefact is triangular in shape, made from a natural tablet of chert about 50 mm across and 10 mm thick, with one side or corner worked to a steeply retouched concave curve about 30 mm in width (Fig 39). It would have fitted comfortably between thumb and forefinger and it could possibly have been used for whittling wood.

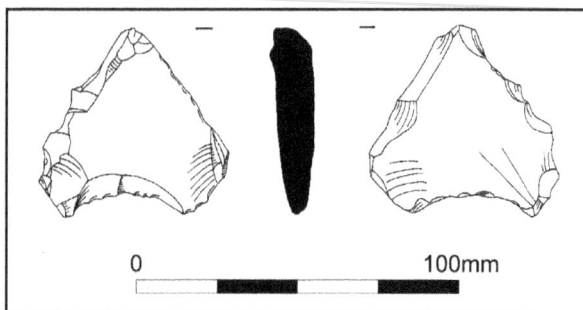

Fig 39. Flint scraper

Context/feature	No.	Weight (g)
70 / pit 72	1	40
168 / ditch 170	1	10
1011 /ditch 1013	1	30
1545 / ditch 1547	5	30
1617 / ditch 1621	9	47
total	17	157

Table 5.2 Quantity of fired clay

Plate 12: Perforated cockle shells and whelk shell from terminal 1696, Ditch 2027

Context	Feature	Description	Date
70	Pit 72	Thin tertiary flake made from dark translucent flint. Possible use-wear on one edge	Unphased EBA/MBA?
70	Pit 72	Thin primary flake from broken gravel flint	Unphased EBA/MBA?
659	Pit 660	Thin, sharp broken flake fragment from reddish brown flint	Unphased MBA/LBA
1061	Cut 1080 Ditch 2016	Thick tertiary flake from opaque cherty flint. Possible use-wear on end and one edge.	Phase 2 recut MBA?
1942	Pit 1942	Thick natural tablet of chert, probably originally rectangular, with one corner reduced to form a triangular concave scraper.	Phase 6 MBA?

Table 5.3 Flint contexts

Context	Feature	No.	Weight (g)
21	Pit 20	2	37
644	Pit 660	1	46
1546	Ditch 2035	1	45

Table 5.4 Burnt flint contexts

Note On Unworked Stones
by Steve Critchley and Andrew Mudd

Twenty-three pieces (3.14 kg) of unworked natural stone were collected from the site for identification as possible exotic items, or because they appeared to be burnt. Three were crazed and fractured flint pebbles (Table 5.4). Most of the other pieces were quartz arenite pebbles and cobbles, almost certainly derived from the March gravels. A number exhibited reddening caused by post-depositional iron staining (rather than burning).

There were three pieces of igneous rock, probably collected as erratics from the Anglian till. From Pit 160 (fill 197) were several broken fragments (443 g) of weathered diorite. While none of the pieces exhibited a worked or utilised surface, it is possible that it had been collected and used for its abrasive properties.

A large broken cobble of dolerite (660 g) came from Ditch 2025 (fill 1546) and another cobble (166 g), possibly of basalt, came from Pit 1860 (fill 1858).

While all these pieces may have been collected locally, they would seem to have been deliberately selected over the more commonly occurring angular flints and limestones, presumably because of their size and roundedness (eg for use as post-packing), and possibly for durability or abrasiveness in other cases (eg for rubbing and grinding) although there were no extant surfaces to confirm this.

Perforated Sea Shells
by Andrew Mudd

A collection of eight perforated shells were recovered from 1695, the lower fill of terminal cut 1696 of Ditch 2027. Seven were cockle shells, six of these being complete and one just a fragment, and there was one whelk

(Plate 12). It is likely that they were deposited together a group, probably as a necklace or other ornament. The object would seem to have been deliberately discarded or deposited, rather than casually lost.

The perforations are not of uniform size and shape and it appears that they were not neatly done, although it is possible that the damage was post manufacture.

The common cockle (*Cerastoderma edule*) is an intertidal species and the whelk (*Buccinum undatum*) is an intertidal or subtidal species. Both would have been collected from the coast rather than locally.

Bronze Palstave-adze
by Stuart Needham

The palstave-adze (Fig 40) came from the edge of an irregular hollow in the corner of a land plot in Plot 11 which appeared more like a tree root hole than a boundary ditch (Pit 130, Group 2003; Fig 11).

The object was studied prior to conservation; soil still adhered in places, particularly in the haft-slot ends. Some soft soil was carefully removed to reveal critical features. Where soil in the haft-slot meets the flanges and stop, there is a thin dark grey layer in places; this is probably due to iron enrichment at the soil/bronze interface. There is a large lumpy extrusion on one face, which seems to have a high metallic content. However, it is very amorphous in form and unlikely to conceal an extension of the object (such as a loop). It is presumed to be incidental material which has become heavily corrosion impregnated. The overall surface of the object is rough textured due to corrosion. In colour, it is mainly mid-green, with orangey-brown staining from soil.

Overall length 114.7mm; length of haft slots 54mm; width of extant edge 29.2mm; width of stop 23.5mm; breadth of stop *c* 16.5mm; height of stop 6.5mm; breadth of butt 16 mm; thickness of edge bevel 9.5mm; depth of edge bevel 16mm. Weight (including soil) 124g.

This is an unusual variant of the palstave family, the blade and cutting edge being set transverse to the septum, adze-fashion. The faces of the blade therefore run into what would normally be the sides of the haft end; this may be referred to as the face on this variant; the sides therefore bear the haft slots.

The faces of the Thorney Borrow Pit example are almost flat with just a slight contraction in profile from the haft end to the blade. There is, however, a fairly marked edge bevel, some 16mm above the cutting edge. This is associated with pronounced expansion of the blade tips, one of which is missing due to corrosion chipping. The blade is otherwise almost parallel-sided, but at the top expands a little close to the stops. The stops are flush with the crest of the flanges. Despite corrosion damage, the flanges were almost certainly near triangular in shape. The blade section has strong body angles, the faces and sides being only slightly bowed. The cross section of the haft end has a flat septum with sharp angles at the junction with steep flange insides. The haft-slot end is square, but a slight beading runs along the inner edge of the stop. It is possible this is the result of deformation from hammering of the top edge of the stop. The butt is somewhat corrosion damaged, but is roughly arched and is 1.5mm thick. Part of the cutting edge beside the intact tip is fairly sharp, but most has suffered chipping due to corrosion.

Comparanda

This object type with slender blade and cutting edge transverse to the septum is extremely rare anywhere. Rowlands only listed five from southern Britain describing them as 'transverse flanged chisels' (Rowlands 1976, 44-5, 350-4). A few others occur in Scotland, where Coles described them as 'flanged chisels' although at the same time acknowledging that the blade is set adze-fashion (Coles 1963-4, 116-7 fig. 14.1-2, 146). In cataloguing the three examples from Lincolnshire, Davey applied the term 'adze palstaves' (1973, 64). Rowlands correctly linked this adze-like form to similarly slender bladed palstaves in which the cutting edge and septum were in line; these are generally known as palstave-chisels. For consistency palstave-adze is therefore the preferable term for the type under consideration here. Palstave-chisels are likewise known only in small numbers. These two specialized forms are though readily distinguished from palstaves by their very slender blades.

In addition to the examples listed by the above authors, another has been published from Martin Mere, Lancashire (Davey & Forster 1975, no 61), while two have since been acquired by the British Museum (accession nos 1992 9-2 1-2; Needham 1993) reputedly from Knowle Hill, Lichfield, Staffordshire, a provenance now regarded as somewhat dubious. Notwithstanding this uncertainty, it is noteworthy that several examples come from the Midlands, between Warwickshire/Lancashire and Lincolnshire and southwards to the Upper Thames valley at Pusey, Oxfordshire (formerly Berkshire; Rowlands 1976, 350 no 1095). The Thorney Borrow Pit example fits neatly within this distribution. A rare example from more southerly counties in fact comes from off-shore – a new find from the seabed scatter known as Salcombe B, just off the Devon coast (Parham *et al* 2006). This is the only potentially datable context for the type; if the Salcombe example is contemporary with the great majority of bronzes in that scatter, as seems likely, it would belong

to the Penard metalworking tradition, *c* 1300 - 1125 BC. Palstave-adzes would not, however, need to be confined to this phase.

Palstave-adzes are also known in Ireland and north-west France, but are similarly rare in those lands (Evans 1881, 104-5; Briard & Verron 1976, 79); indeed, some of the French examples discussed by Briard and Verron have broader, chunkier blades and are dated in the Menez-Tosta hoard (Finistère) to Bronze Final III equivalent to the Ewart phase in Britain, *c* 1000 – 800 BC.

Function and hafting

The asymmetric profile often taken to be characteristic of the adze does not appear to be present on this group of 'palstave-adzes'. One must therefore consider the possibility that the reorientation of the blade merely implies that for these particular implements the haft was slotted on the perpendicular axis to normal. In this way, the cutting edge could still have been parallel to the handle as for any axe. If this were an acceptable and practical alternative for mounting the bronze head in the haft it seems strange that it was almost universally avoided for the flanged axes, palstaves and winged axes of many different phases of the Bronze Age. It may be that cutting the slot in the haft transverse to the normal alignment gave rise to a much greater risk of the head of the haft shearing off when put under stress. With the standard alignment, the two sides of the split part of the haft not only share the impact of blows but also transfer it bilaterally to the elbow, the junction with the main shaft.

Another possibility to be dealt with is that these lighter-weight cutting tools were not mounted in elbow hafts at all, but instead in simple handles as with a modern chisel. This might be the case for the palstave-chisels, but does not provide an obvious explanation for the rotated blade/septum relationship of the palstave-adzes, unless this was just a peculiarity adopted by one particular metalworking tradition. It should be noted that the technology involved in producing the adze variant was more problematical than that for palstaves and palstave-chisels. Using the standard bivalve casting methods of the period, the cutting edge would have had to be set perpendicular to the plane of the junction between the mould valves. This would preclude natural venting along the whole of the thin cutting edge through the valve junction and thus increase the risk of gas bubbles becoming trapped in the matrix during casting unless other vents were pierced through the valves themselves. Casting the object instead, unconventionally, from the blade end would mitigate this problem, but would instead necessitate more post-cast working to thin and prepare the cutting edge. A way around some of these problems would be to use cire-perdue instead bivalve casting technology, although venting would still be an issue. However, evidence for cire-perdue in the British Bronze Age is rare and, where it does occur, tends to date to the Late Bronze Age (Bowman & Needham in press).

Certainty is not possible, but the above discussion

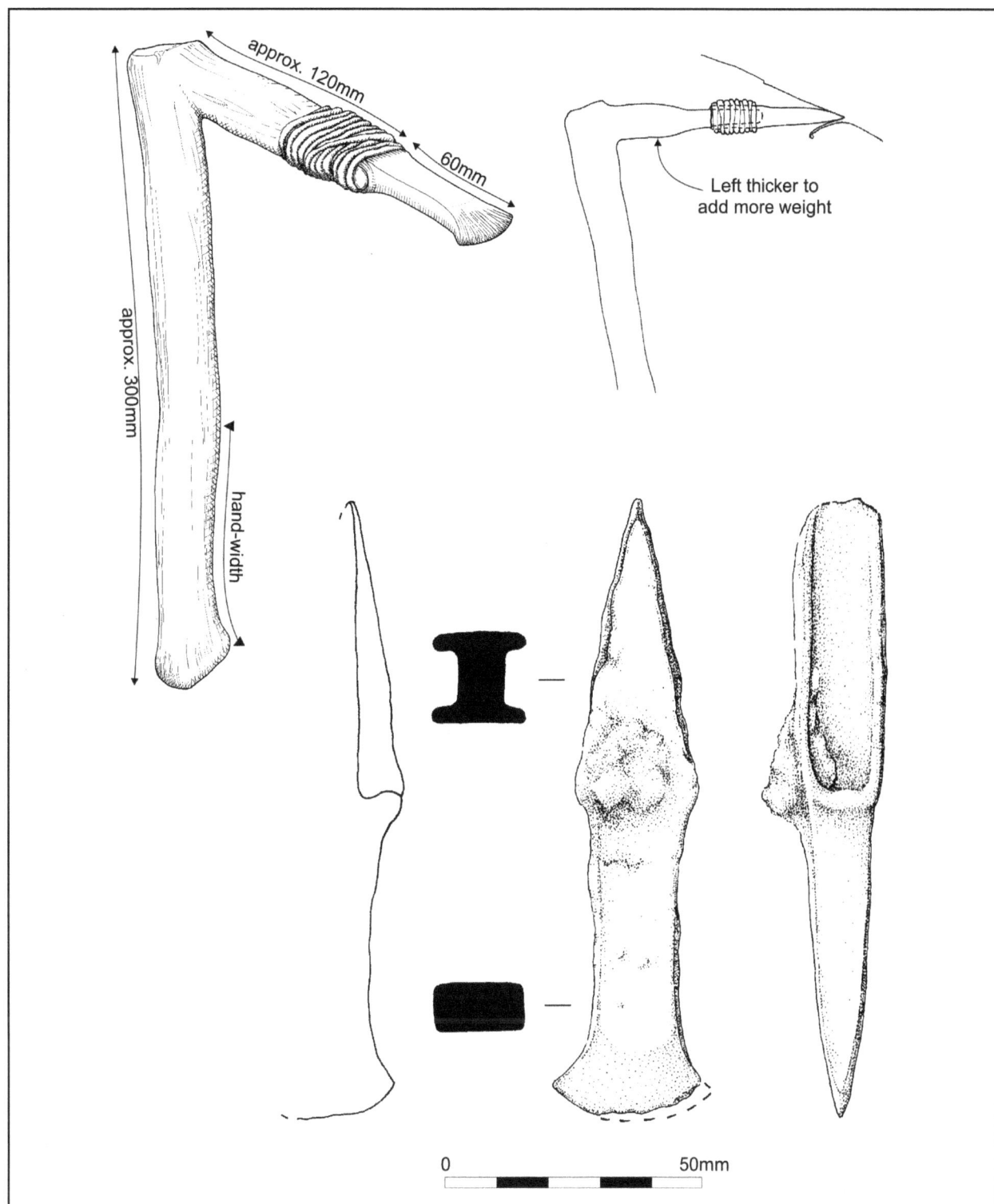

Fig 40. Bronze palstave-adze and suggestion for hafting (after S Needham)

suggests that the palstave-adze was a specialized tool type adapted from the everyday tool of the Middle Bronze Age – the palstave – with the specific intention of creating an adze-oriented blade in an elbow haft. The lack of an asymmetric profile would not have prevented its use as an adze although it may have altered its effectiveness and led to greater risk of biting deeper than wanted into the timber being trimmed. Only experimental work could clarify these questions of functionality. The fact that known palstave-adzes in Britain tend to have parallel-sided blades supporting narrow cutting edges suggests

that they were intended for more controlled woodworking than axes which would, for example, be adequate for initial shaping of large timbers and creating the point on stakes. Palstave-adzes mounted in an elbow haft would have been used with a swinging action, but in skilled hands would be capable of the more precise planing of timber. These tools would not have the degree of control of a handled chisel but would do many trimming jobs much more quickly. One can envisage their use for the finer dressing of squared timbers and planks as well as the cutting of large grooves, rebates and other linear features.

73

Chapter 6:   Animal Bones

by Karen Deighton

Method

Animal bones recovered by hand from a range of Bronze Age features were analysed using standard zooarchaeological methods (Davis 1987, Grant 1982, Grigson 1982, Rackham 1994, Schmid 1972, Silver 1969, von den Driesch 1976, Watson 1979).

The material has been treated as two assemblages, one dating to the Early Bronze Age (Pit 160) and the other to the Middle to Late Bronze Age (other contexts) although both assemblages are quite small (285 identifiable fragments).

Results

Preservation

Canid gnawing was moderate. Fragmentation was high with only 9.3% of bones whole, largely the result of old breaks as only one fresh break was noted. Abrasion of the bone surfaces was heavy. The frequency of cut marks was low at only 3.46%. Only three examples of burning were noted which suggests possibly that this was not a preferred method of disposal.

Skeleton

An almost complete sheep skeleton came from context 95, Ditch 2008 (Plate 2). Only small bones such as phalanges are missing due to preservation and recovery bias (Payne 1985). Epiphyses are fused, skull sutures are visible and toothware suggests an age of 8-10 years. The fact the remains were articulated could suggest a deliberate burial. No evidence of butchery was noted, although this could have been obscured by heavy surface abrasion.

Skulls

Three partial cattle skulls were noted, all from the later assemblage.

Context 1733 (Pit 1741)

A frontal bone with horn cores and attached occipital condyle was recovered. No evidence of butchery was noted. The animal appeared to be fairly small. Cattle leg bones and ribs and deer antler tines were recovered from the same context.

Context 1902 (Pond 1907)

A frontal bone with horn cores and occipital condyle was recovered. No evidence of butchery was observed. Again the animal appeared to be fairly small. The context also contained a cattle scapula and metatarsal. It is uncertain whether these were all from the same animal.

Context 1907 (Pond 1907)

The skull remains consisted of maxilla fragments with teeth. Unfortunately, aging from maxilla teeth is unreliable. Cattle leg bones were present in the same context, although it is uncertain if these were from the same animal.

Ageing

Five *Bos* neonatal bone elements were noted, along with two "young" *Sus* bones. Eight *Sus* mandibles were available for ageing, all from the Early Bronze Age pit. These suggested animals of 6 to 22 months and a single adult.

Sexing

One female *Sus* tusk was noted.

Pathologies

No pathologies were noted.

Common name	Cattle	Sheep/goat	Pig	Deer	L.ungulate	S.ungulate	Indet. bird	Total
Species	*Bos*	*Ovicaprid*	*Sus*	*Cervid*	*Large hooved*	*Small hooved*	*Avis*	
Pit 160								
Number	31	3	46	2	12	12		106
%	29.2	2.8	43.4	1.9	11.3	11.3		100
MBA-LBA features								
Number	101	20	30	7	16	3	2	179
%	56.4	11.2	16.8	3.9	8.9	1.7	1.1	100

Table 6.1 Quantity of animal bones by species

Discussion

The high frequency of fragmentation could suggest trampling or heavy handed butchery techniques, although it is unclear if the material is chopped. The charred articulation could suggest roasting on bone was taking place although evidence is slight.

The assemblage is dominated by the three major domesticates (cattle, sheep/goat, pig) which is expected for both periods, although the prevalence of pigs over sheep is a little unusual for the period, especially as pig bones are generally the least well preserved of the major domesticates (Stallibras 1985). This factor could be related to environmental conditions (ie heavily wooded or waterlogged?).The fact that deer bone as well as antler was present suggests hunting was practised, although the low percentage indicates that wild resources were not relied upon. The presence of evidence for canid gnawing could suggest the presence of dogs at site although no identifiable dog bones were recovered.

Temporal comparisons are tentative due to the small sizes of the assemblages. A similar range of species is seen for both the Early and Middle-Late Bronze Age phases, with the exception of the bird bones in the later period. Pig dominates in the earlier period and cattle in the later, which could relate to an earlier dominance of woodland which later became opened up.

It would be unwise to attempt any reconstruction of the age or sex structure of the animal population of the site with so little suitable data. However, the low number of neonates present could suggest stock rearing took place off site or could be a function of preservation and recovery bias as the material was recovered by hand. The age at death of the pigs suggests that these were slaughtered as the meat yield reached an optimum.

For cattle it appears that the more robust bone elements (radius, metatarsal) are the most abundant. The relatively small number of identifiable bones per element per species renders any attempt at bodypart analysis of questionable value.

This small assemblage provides information on the species of animals exploited at the site, but little else. Tentative comparisons with contemporary sites in the region suggest similar results in terms of species composition.

Chapter 7:   **Radiocarbon Dating**

Four samples of wood were selected for radiocarbon dating. Two were from Pit 160 which contained decorated pottery and other cultural material in the middle fill and some unfeatured sherds in the lowest fill (Chapman, Chapter 5 & Fig 38; Fig 5 contexts 175 and 197). The other two were from *in situ* stakes in Ponds 1907 and 1829. The results are shown in Fig 41 and Table 7.1.

Discussion

Pit 160

There is no reason to doubt the validity of these dates (SUERC 13970 and 13969), and their consistency supports the confidence which can be placed in them. Both samples were of small roundwood and would not have been of any great age when they found their way into the pit, so it can be assumed that they provide a good approximation of the date of the pit and the associated finds. In view of the radiocarbon dating from the ponds (below), which is consistently Middle Bronze Age, it seems probable that this pit is one of the earliest features on the site.

The pit was not of unusual form, although it was slightly shallower than most and there was no evidence that it had been lined. It was probably used as a waterhole. The preserved woodworking detritus gives some indication of coppicing and woodland clearance or management at this time.

Ponds 1907 and 1829

The dating from the constructions in the ponds confirms that they were in use in the Middle Bronze Age. The dating is consistent with the observed construction sequence (Pond 1907 – Phase 7, Pond 1829 – Phase 8). It is interesting to note that the dates are almost inseparable suggesting that Pond 1829 might not have replaced 1907, but rather both may have been concurrent use. Both ponds are relatively late in the construction sequence of the field system so it seems likely that the use of the ponds, and perhaps the field system itself, would not have extended much (if at all) into the first millennium BC.

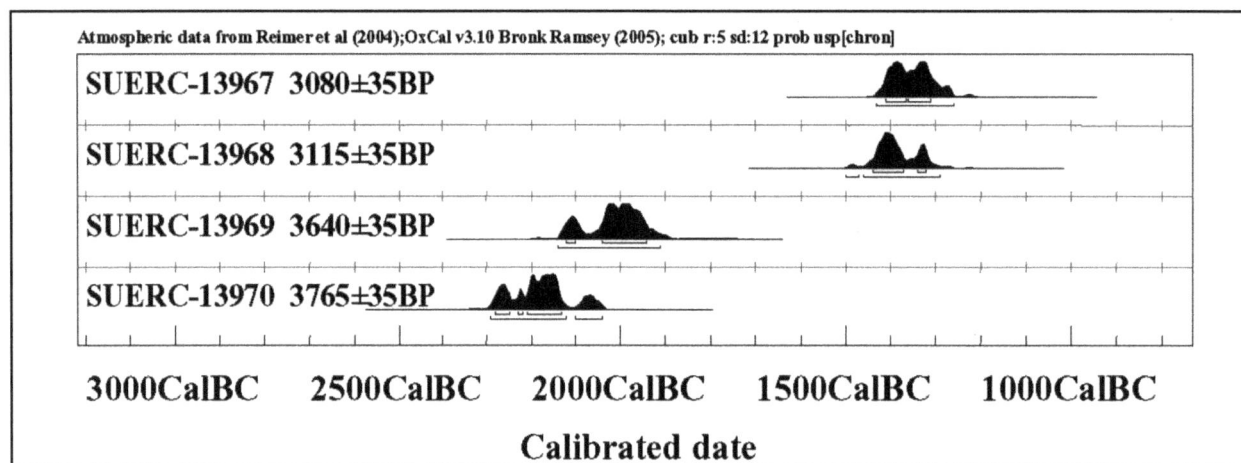

Fig 41. Radiocarbon dates

Laboratory Number	Context Number	Context Type	Material	Radiocarbon Age (BP)	d¹³C per thousand	Calibrated date range 95% confidence
SUERC-13970 (GU-15230)	197	Lowest fill of Pit 160	wood, twigs, species unk.	3765 +/- 35	-26.9	2290-2120 calBC (82.9%) & 2100-2040 calBC (12.5%)
SUERC-13969 (GU-15229)	175	Middle fill of Pit 160	roundwood, species unk.	3640 +/- 35	-27.8	2140-1910 calBC
SUERC-13968 (GU-15228)	1906 XX	in situ at base of pond 1907	wooden stake, species ash	3115 +/- 35	-28.7	1500-1470 calBC (1.3%) & 1460-1290 calBC (94.1%)
SUERC-13967 (GU-15227)	1886 AE	in situ at base of pond 1829	wooden stake, species oak	3080 +/- 35	-27.0	1430-1260 calBC

Table 7.1 Radiocarbon dates (calibration using OxCal v.3.10)

Chapter 8: **Discussion**

Dating

The limited amount of pottery (915 g) and other finds from the features on the site, together with two radiocarbon dates from the ponds, indicate a general date for the field system in the Middle Bronze Age. The evidence is very sparse and there is little dating from most of the site, particularly the ditches where the pottery comprised entirely unfeatured body sherds of unspecific date (Chapman, Chapter 5). The only featured pottery came from Pit 160 (Plot 11) which yielded bevelled rim sherds dated by two radiocarbon determinations to the very end of the 3rd millennium BC. The pit was an isolated one, not obviously associated with any of the boundary ditches. It is possible that it was related to tree clearance and may therefore have pre-dated the main occupation on the site and the layout of the fields, but the relatively high quantity of material from the feature (particularly animal bones – see below) does suggest that it was within or close to an area of occupation.

The main pattern of ditches and associated pits are dated to the Middle Bronze by two radiocarbon dates from *in situ* wooden stakes in Ponds 1907 and 1829. The dates came out broadly to 1500-1290 BC (Pond 1907) and 1430-1260 BC (Pond 1829) which are firmly within the Middle Bronze Age. It can be noted that both ponds are tied into the field system's construction sequence (Figs 4a-4g) and are relatively late in that sequence (Phases 7 and 8 respectively) so the initial laying out of the field system may have been rather earlier. While the sequence in which the system was constructed has been outlined, it seems likely the usage of ponds and ditches was, or at least mostly, contemporaneous across the site. The broadly Middle Bronze Age usage for the site therefore seems confirmed. However, the dating of the field system's demise, as well as its initiation, cannot be inferred with any precision on current evidence.

A plain bowl from the small pit 1659 (Plot 8) is probably later Bronze Age (or even Early Iron Age). Although this pit was unphased, its peaty fill was characteristic of the upper fills of a number of the larger pits and ditches and it is thought to be relatively late for that reason. The other pottery from the site would not be out of place in Middle or Late Bronze Age context, and there is no reason to suppose that there are any pits and ditches of a substantially different date. There is, for instance, no later Iron Age or Roman pottery from the site.

While it is possible that some of the pits are of a different date to the boundary ditches (Pit 160 is a case in point), this is not considered to be generally the case because a number of the pits (and the ponds) can be put into a stratigraphic sequence with the ditches.

The other finds are not closely datable either, although the bronze palstave-adze, from a root hole or other natural feature associated with Ditch 2002 and Pit Group 2003 (Plot 11, Phases 1-3) is broadly Middle Bronze Age on stylistic grounds (Needham, Chapter 3).

The site dating is supported by the general site context, including, in particular, the more extensive pattern of pits and field boundary ditches from Pode Hole Quarry to the south (Phoenix Consulting 2005) for which a Middle Bronze Age date (conventionally *c* 1600-1200 BC) is more securely advanced through the pottery (2758 g from Extraction Area 7 – Morris 2005) and radiocarbon dating (Daniel, pers comm). Furthermore, Tower's Fen can be seen to conform to a wider pattern of Bronze Age land use, which in the Thorney area below *c* 2.5 m OD, occupies a period of fen-edge stability between imprecisely recorded marine incursions in the early and late 2nd millennium BC (French 2003). The occupation can be seen to have taken advantage of a window of opportunity between episodes or greater wetness which probably rendered the land unsuitable for agriculture, or settlement of any form.

Early Bronze Age Occupation

One pit (Pit 160) near the southern edge of the site was dated by two radiocarbon determinations to the Early Bronze Age. It may have been used as a waterhole although it was slightly shallower than the Middle Bronze Age features interpreted as waterholes and did not show the characteristic sequence of dark organic silts overlain by edge collapse. It may not have been lined. The waterlogged wood included woodworking debris, but possibly not stakes.

The pit was unusual in the relatively large amount of material within it, including 4,500 g of animal bone and some pottery from the lowest fill (197). This context also contained pieces of diorite which may have been fragments of quern or other utilised stone. Material also came from the middle fill 175. It is noteworthy that this pit contained more evidence of human occupation than was associated with the later field system. The evidence is insufficient to determine the nature of this occupation, although it may well have been related to farming activities rather than something more temporary such as woodland clearance. There is evidence woodland management from the pit but no indication that this took place within a landscape bounded by ditches.

The two radiocarbon dates (from the lowest and middle fills) are very similar and do not suggest that the pit was in use for a long time. The upper fills have the appearance of deliberate levelling with gravelly sediment. Later a narrower pit or posthole (193) was cut into the top infilled pit. This event is undated but it seems likely that it was intended to mark the position of the pit. It can be speculated that this was connected with the main ditch alignment in Pode Hole Quarry to the south (Fig 2), although this location may just be coincidental.

Character Of The Middle Bronze Age Occupation

The site shows part of a rectangular pattern of fields or plots demarcated by ditches, together with a scatter of pits, some of which are directly associated with the ditches in the sense of showing a physical relationship with them. Other pits are discrete, in the northern part of the site perhaps tending to occupy the edges of the plots, while in the southern part they appear more scattered. The plots include a double ditched enclosure (Plot 3) with two exceptionally large pits, interpreted as ponds, on two sides.

While the field pattern can be described as co-axial, orientated on roughly perpendicular axes, the fields are not standardised and the rectangular pattern is often open-ended or incomplete. Some of the boundaries are composed of short lengths of ditch, sometimes irregular in plan and slightly misaligned with respect to neighbouring ones. It must be suspected that some of this pattern has been lost to recent ploughing. The aerial photographic plot (reproduced in Figure 2) shows several lengths of ditch not recorded in the excavations. In particular, there is a broad cropmark feature appearing to continue the northern alignment of Ditch 2008. Targeted evaluation trenches also failed to reveal this feature (Coates and Cherrington 2004, Trs 14 & 15). It seems likely that the cropmarks were caused by the remnants of the ditch fill in the modern soil.

The field pattern is essentially a simple one, without a great density of features, realignments or reconfigurations. The analysis of the relationships between features and their patterning indicates distinct construction episodes to the field pattern (see Chapter 2). There seems to have been a progression of ditch cutting from east to west, and possibly also from north to south, although this is more conjectural. There is therefore good evidence for development through a process of 'field accretion' rather than the subdivision of larger units, although this process must have taken place within a wider landscape framework of ordered space which acted to maintain boundary alignments.

The sub-division of the land into fields and enclosures is commonly found in the fen edge region from the Middle Bronze Age onwards. The 'classic' site is Fengate, although numerous other sites have since been investigated, including large areas at Maxey and Welland Bank (south Lincolnshire), Borough Fen (north Cambridgeshire), Barleycroft Farm/Over (Needingworth), Colne Fen (Earith) and Pode Hole (Thorney). It has been argued that the land divisions at Fengate and the surrounding area were used to apportion grazing in a system which saw the fen itself used for summer pasture and the drier fen-edge for overwintering and stock management (Pryor 1998). There is, however, no need to seek a unitary explanation for all the fen-edge land divisions. Analysis even at a superficial level shows a variety of forms, and even where originally intended to control livestock, fields may have had different uses over time.

There is no firm indication of settlement associated with the ditches and pits although there are several lines of evidence suggesting that there was occupation on the site. No house sites or structures of any sort were identified, but this may be due to ground truncation or the particular methods of construction used. The sporadic occurrence of pottery, animal bone, fired clay, burnt stone, charred grain and wood charcoal do, however, suggest that occupation took place on or very close to the site. The range of evidence is similar to that from Pode Hole Quarry to the south. Evans has drawn attention to the shortage of material culture from the Bronze Age Holme field system at Colne Fen with the suggestion that low artefact counts are typical of fen-edge settlements in the 2nd millennium BC generally (Evans & Patten 2003).

The pottery distribution (Fig 42) shows small groups, perhaps particularly in Plot 11 (Pits 72 and 61) and the eastern side of Plot 1 (Ditches 2038, 2039, 2036 and Pit 1577). Perhaps tellingly, charred cereals grains came from Pit 72 (SS4) and Ditch 2037 (SS46) in these areas (Table 4.7b; Fig 43). It is unclear how phosphate levels should be interpreted, but it can be noted that enhanced phosphate levels came from similar areas, although there is more of a concentration in the north-east corner of the double-ditched enclosure (Fig 44: Plot 3, Pit 1714 and Ditch 2035).

It is possible that animal bones should be considered the most useful indicator of occupation because food debris is likely to be present on occupation sites regardless of the level of material culture of its inhabitants, assuming that it was not disposed of a long way from where food was consumed. The animal bone distribution is in fact not dissimilar to the pottery distribution, although more widespread (Fig 45). The largest single group of animal bones came from the Early Bronze Age pit 160 (over 5000 g) and large amounts (over 1000 g) from each of Pit 1741 (Plot 8), Pond 1907 (Plot 3) and Pit 660 (Plot 4).

It can also be noted that, with the possible exception of the quantity of animal bones, there is no particular indication that the double-ditched enclosure (Plot 3) was a focus of settlement.

Purpose Of The Ditches

The ditches defining the various plots of land would undoubtedly have been associated with hedges. The waterlogged wood from the pits shows abundant evidence that coppicing was practised, much of it oak and ash from overgrown coppices (Taylor, Chapter 4). Alder, willow, poplar, honeysuckle, privet, birch, beech and elm were also present while the charcoal included likely hedgerow species such as *Prunus* (plum/cherry/blackthorn) and hazel. It is suggested that the general shortage of pollen found from these species could relate to their use as

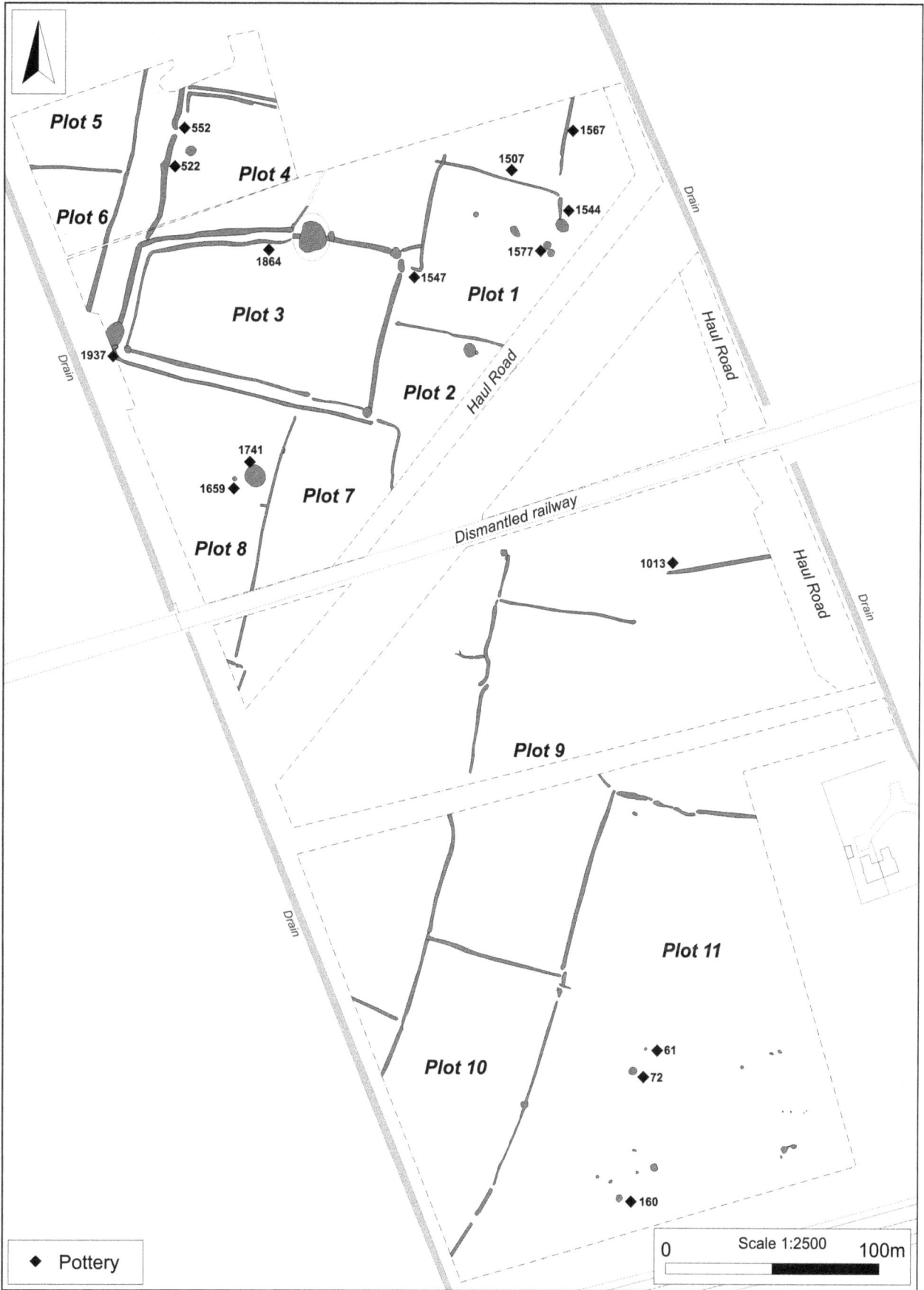

Fig 42. Finds distribution: pottery

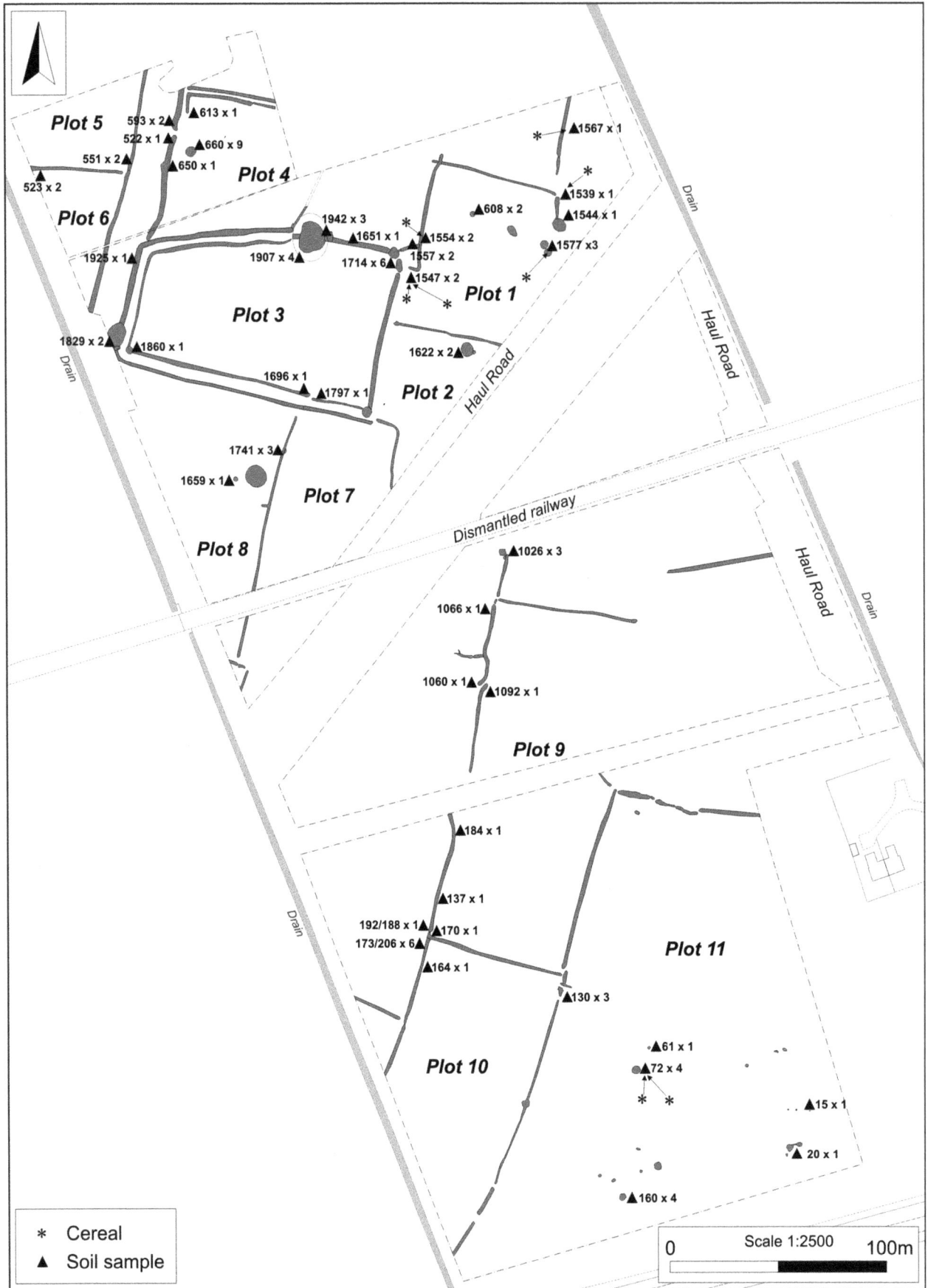

Fig 43. Finds distribution: cereals

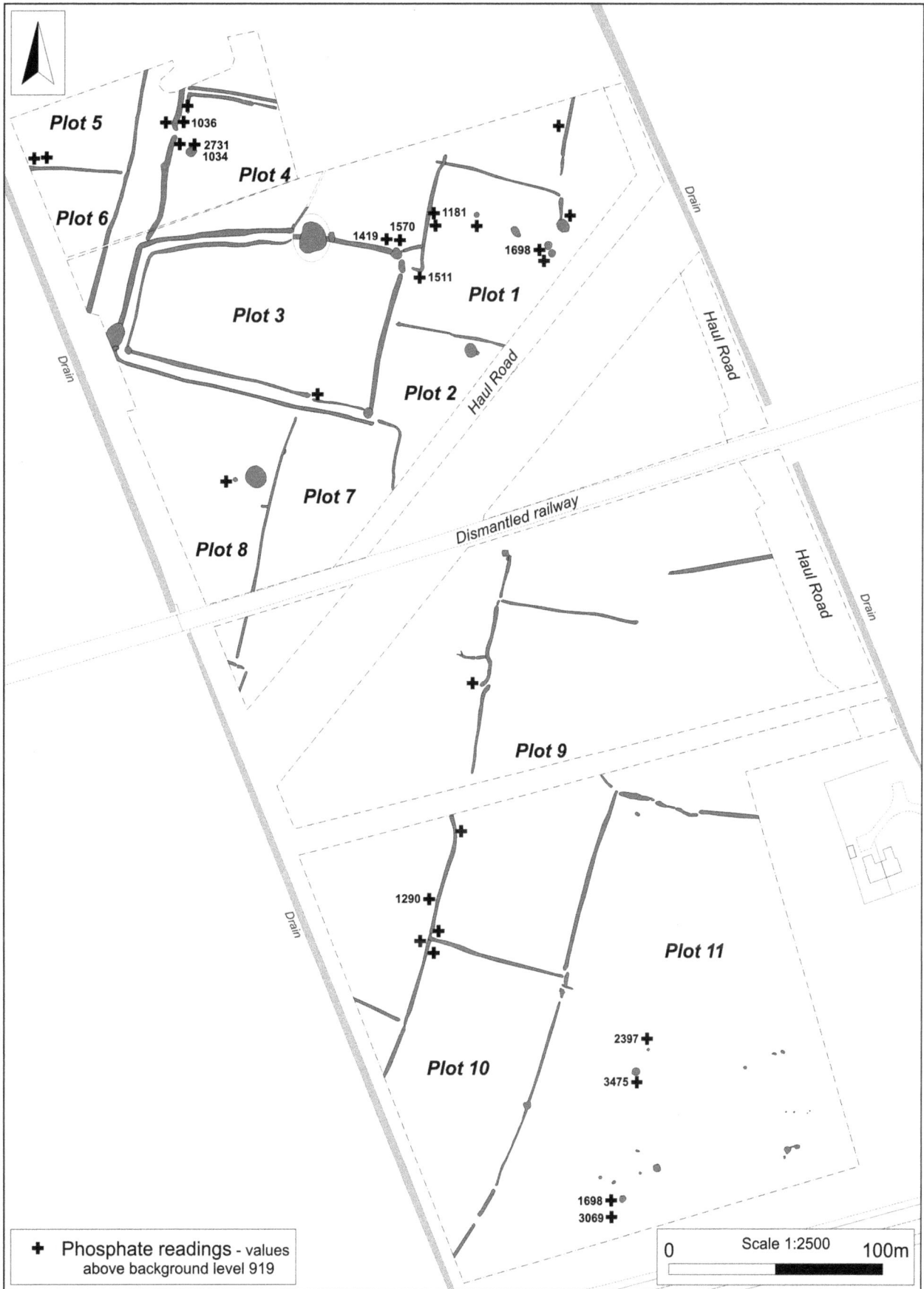

Fig 44. Finds distribution: phosphates

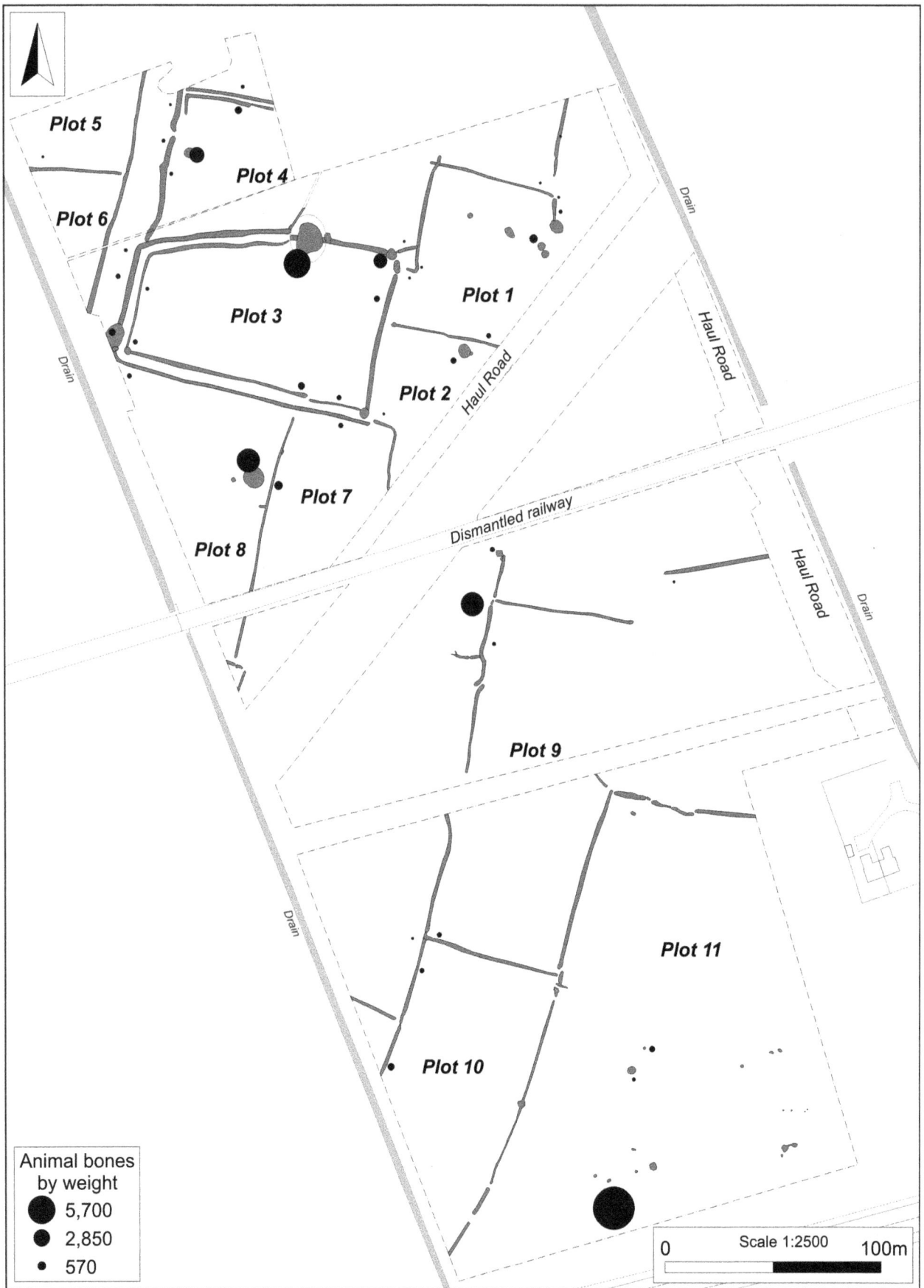

Fig 45. Finds distribution: animal bones

hedging since in this situation they would be liable to browsing by livestock (Taylor, Chapter 4).

Patterns of ditch infilling and recutting indicate the positions of banks in some instances – for instance between the ditches of the double-ditched enclosure (Fig 5). This may indicate that the gap between the ditches, which is just 2.5-3.0 m on the northern side and possibly occupied by upcast from two ditches surmounted by a hedgerow, would not have been used as a routeway.

The boundary ditches were frequently not linked to one another but stopped short leaving narrow gaps, often at the corners of the plots and sometimes elsewhere. Plot 4 had a clear entrance on its western side 2.5 m wide providing access to and from a droveway. This may have been around the standard width needed for general access, intended for domestic animals and farm equipment as well as people. People on their own could have used much narrower gaps, but taking into account the presence of banks and hedges, as well as the ditches themselves, it is often not clear that the narrower gaps would have provided points of access. The possibility has been raised (Chapter 2) that there was no formal access between the bank on the eastern side of Ditch 2033 and Ditch 2034 and there are several other instances of gaps in ditches perhaps not indicating points access.

The ditches would also have helped drain the various plots but this does not seem to have been their primary purpose since they are not connected into a unified drainage system to channel water off site.

The division of the land by ditches, banks and hedges would have been important in controlling grazing and the movements of livestock, but perhaps would have been more important in a mixed farming regime than in purely pastoral one because of the need to keep livestock away from growing crops. The dominance of non-arboreal pollen, including grass, herbaceous vegetation and cereals, from Ponds 1907 and 1829, give a clear indication of dry grassland and cultivated fields in the area (Chapter 5).

Another possible function of the ditches might have been as property boundaries. The subject of landownership is immensely problematic from archaeological evidence and recognition of separate landholdings is highly speculative. At the large scale it is sometimes possible to discern regularities to landscape divisions which may have demarcated individual landholdings. At Perry Oaks (Heathrow Terminal 5, Middlesex) it has been suggested that Bronze Age landholdings associated with individual settlements were defined by ditched droveways running parallel at intervals of 100-200 m (Framework Archaeology 2006, fig. 3.15). A similar pattern may be evident at Flag Fen, with droveways at intervals of approximately 100 m or slightly less forming the axes of the Bronze Age field system (Pryor 2001, 408). At a smaller scale, with a very fragmentary picture, the recognition of this sort of pattern is made more difficult. Nevertheless it is possible that the process of dividing the land here, which seems to have been undertaken in

a piecemeal fashion, rather than as some kind of overall plan, and in tandem with settlement, rather than preceding it, was carried out by several different family or other social groups. There are, for instance, some suggestions of a lack of interconnectedness between Plot 3 and surrounding plots. Plot 3 had an eastern boundary (2033) dug from inside the plot, with the bank thrown up outside, an arrangement in north-eastern corner suggesting the need to block an entrance here, and a blocked gap on the southern boundary (2028). The only access seems to have been on the northern side by Pond 1907, but this may not have provided a link to Plot 4 which had an entrance on the western side to a (more public?) droveway and another pond (1829), but no access to Plots 5 and 6 beyond. It is possible that this reflects the operations of different landowners or farming units.

Nature And Purpose Of The Pits

There were about 18 large pits distributed more or less evenly around the site and two exceptionally wide features interpreted as ponds, on the margins of Plot 3, the double-ditched enclosure. There were also several smaller pits. The large pits and ponds were generally 1.0-1.5 m deep, reaching the watertable, and they tended to contain waterlogged organic material in their bases. Nine of the large pits are interpreted as waterholes. These were of a fairly regular size, 3.0-4.0 m across. Another pit may have been exclusively a tree-clearance pit (although any or all of the large pits could have started with the digging out of a tree root), and one pit may have held a post. The interpretation of the other pits is unclear, although drainage sumps is one possibility.

Ponds

Two features, 1907 and 1829, were interpreted as ponds because of their exceptional breadth (about 7 m across at the base), although at about 1.5 m they were no deeper than many of the other pits. Both had asymmetrical cross profiles with a gently sloping 'access ramp' on one side and steeper sides elsewhere. There is no doubt that they held water during their use since they yielded abundant waterlogged organic remains including pollen indicating an aquatic environment.

Worked timbers in both ponds indicates that they probably contained structures, but very little survived *in situ* and the evidence is slender. Pond 1829 had four *in situ* wooden stakes in its base driven 500 mm or so into the gravel. The most likely interpretation is that they were the remains of a stake revetment at the steepest (ie eastern) edge of the pond. The other stakes must have been removed (or had broken off at a deeper level below the gravel surface without trace). At least five were found lying *ex situ*. These were incomplete, but the longest was 1.68 m in length, indicating that the 'revetment' would have lined the pit to most of its depth. There was no indication of wattlework in this, or any of the other features, nor is there any indication that the stakes might have formed a continuous 'wall', so it is not clear how the revetment would have been completed. It is possible that the wattle lining was entirely removed in every case, but it may be more plausible to suggest that the pits and ponds were lined with timber planking, or other odd pieces of wood, wedged behind the uprights. These would have been easy to remove or dislodge once the uprights had gone.

Pond 1907 contained only two stakes *in situ*, but it seems likely that these were the remnants of a similar revetment to the one in 1829. There were at least four removed pieces which could have been stakes, including three in a line overlying a 3.7 m length of worked timber across the southern side of the pond. The size of this timber suggests that it was more or less *in situ*, and it would appear to have formed part of a lining to the pond on the shallower southern side.

In all probability the ponds were constructed as water sources and their use by cattle seems their most likely function. The access ramps would have been suitable for animals in small numbers, and this would have been more convenient than drawing water by hand to fill a trough. The positions of the accesses show that Pond 1907 would have been entered from Plot 3 – the double-ditched enclosure, and Pond 1829 from the droveway.

Waterholes

A number of the pits are likely to have been dug specifically as waterholes. Each pond was associated with a smaller pit, dug to a similar depth within the pond cavity. It is likely that these pits would have fulfilled a different role to that of the ponds, perhaps specifically as sources of water for human use.

Pit 1942 (next to Pond 1907) contained two *in situ* planks which could have been used as staging/duckboards to collect water from. Pit 1912 (next to Pond 1829) was a similar size to 1942.

Pit 660, not far from the entrance to Plot 4, was probably kept clean during its use as there was little accumulation of basal silts before the sides of the pit collapsed, presumably after the withdrawal of the lining. A single stake point came from the lowest fill. There seems to have been some attempt to halt the slumping of the pit sides with a revetment of closely spaced stakes which partly survived. Following the demise of this lining there was an inwash of silts and gravels. The overwhelming majority of the finds from this pit came from these middle fills (646, 644) suggesting either that occupation took place or continued nearby after the waterhole had ceased to function, or that it was used as a rubbish pit following the abandonment of the occupation here. The finds comprised over 1000 g of animal bones (Fig 43).

Pit 1741, towards the corner of Plot 8, showed a similar sequence of clean lower organic fills (1728, 1729) overlain by sandier deposits containing more material. The incomplete bucket from the base of 1730 may have been lost during the process of water collection, but it lacked an attached rope as well as base, so it perhaps represents

an object discarded at the end of its usefulness. A number of the other wooden pieces from this fill may have been stakes withdrawn from the pit lining. The gravelly layer immediately above (1733) yielded over 2000 g of animal bones and a few sherds of pottery came from 1734. Again this material appears to reflect occupation nearby or an episode of clearance following abandonment.

Pit 1622 at the northern edge of Plot 2 was probably also a waterhole. A number of the timber pieces in the base could have been withdrawn stakes, although the forked branch lacks any obvious interpretation. Other finds were few, but the occasional fragments of animal bone came from the middle fills above deposits of gravelly slumped material.

Pit 1026, at the northern end of Ditch 2020, also had a sequence of fills which suggests that the pit sides had collapsed. The lowest fill contained a single split timber stake as well as some animal bone, but above this was a jumble of oak which appeared to be off-cuts from woodworking (Taylor, Chapter 4). It is not clear whether this was related to the use of the pit at all, or whether it was material dumped when the feature went out of use. After the pit had been filled it was recut centrally by a probable posthole whose purpose remains obscure.

Pit 1714, in the north-east corner of Plot 3, was probably dug as a waterhole as it was one of the deepest features on the site (1.85 m). There was no indication of a lining and little identifiable organic material from it. Pit 1860 in the south-west corner of Plot 3, was shallower than 1714, but appeared to have dug as a waterhole and was probably lined. It may indeed have replaced 1714 as a water source since it was dug in a later phase. It had a clean lower silting overlain by edge-collapsed gravel. The middle and upper fills contained a small amount of animal bone.

Posthole

Pit 1577, on the eastern side or Plot 1, was smaller than pits interpreted as waterholes, and a consideration of its fills suggests that it may have held a post about 300 mm wide and 3 m long. It may be significant that it aligned quite precisely with boundary Ditch 2038 and it may therefore have been a boundary marker. It is worth noting that this alignment is continued southward by the main axis of land division (Ditch segments 2020, 2016 etc) marked by Pit 1026 at the northern end which had a possible posthole (1029) cut into it after it had gone out of use. It does not seem that the two postholes were contemporaneous, but there is the suggestion that boundaries may have been marked out by more than ditches and hedges.

Tree removal pit

Pit 20, which was a relatively isolated feature in the south-eastern corner of the site, may have been dug to remove a tree. The preserved rootwood at the base of the pit, may however, have been a coincidence and have pre- or post-dated the pit considerably, so the evidence is certainly not conclusive. The pit was distinguished by the unusual depth of clean gravel over the primary organic material suggesting that it had very unstable sides. This might be expected if the purpose of the pit were limited to extracting a tree rather than needing to be left open as a water source or for another purpose. The Holme beach timber circle ('Seahenge') shows that Bronze Age people might have wanted to remove trees in their entirety for reasons not primarily connected with land clearance.

Other pits

Two pits, 61 and 72, were located 60 m or so north of the Early Bronze Age pit 160 (Plot 11). They both contained some sherds of pottery, charcoal and animal bones, while 72 also contained fired clay and charred cereal grains. It seems therefore that they were closely associated with occupation although their date and functions are not known.

Pits 1659, 1774 and 1776, near waterhole 1741, were no more than shallow scoops. Pit 1659 was probably of a relatively late phase and contained some pottery but the others were without finds.

Pit 1608 (Plot 1), about 1.8 m across and nearly 1.0 m deep is of unknown function. It contained no datable finds and it possibly did not relate to the main occupation here. Its position toward the centre of Plot 1 is somewhat anomalous for the Bronze Age occupation.

Pit 1674 in the south-eastern corner of Plot 3 is too shallow to have been a waterhole and was probably dug as a drainage sump.

Feature 130, near the northern terminal of Ditch 2002, was an irregular pit which may have been a root hole. It did, however, contain, on its margin, the complete head of a bronze palstave-adze. Its presence is probably best explained as a dedicatory deposit connected with farming or land allotment rituals. Alternatively it may have been lost during coppicing or hedge maintenance, although this seems less probable since the tool is likely to have been quite valuable and not relinquished easily. Despite assertions that there is no real evidence for ritual deposition of metalwork in Bronze Age East Anglia, generalised mapping of bronze distributions adopted by Pendleton (2001) fails to take account of possible ritual deposits within or at the margins of domestic life, so that a distinction between 'wetland' (ritual) and 'dryland' (non-ritual) finds is in all probability a misleading standpoint to be trying to discredit. Boundary locations, at a number of scales, may have been the significant factor behind deposits of a ritual nature.

Land Allotment, Farming And Settlement

The site at Tower's Fen has many characteristics in common with Bronze Age fields and farming settlements both from the Fen-edge region and elsewhere in lowland southern England. The extent and implications of these

prehistoric landscapes has only become apparent in the last 15 years or so, particularly as a consequence of developer-funded archaeology (Yates 2001, Pryor 2001, 418-20). The site is shown in Figure 2 in relation to the excavation at Pode Hole Quarry (Phoenix Consulting forthcoming) and the surrounding cropmarks (Palmer 2004). On the basis of the excavations it seems safe to assume that the cropmark fields and enclosures are also of a broadly Middle to Late Bronze Age date (rather than Roman as originally expected). The same may also be true of the scheduled earthworks at Pode Hole Farm whose alignment is similar. The fields and enclosures form an agricultural landscape similar in pattern and scale to others in the lower Welland, Nene and Ouse valleys, such as those at Eye Quarry, 3 km to the south-west (Patten 2004), Fengate (Pryor 2001), Welland Bank, Borough Fen (Pryor 1999), Barleycroft Farm/Over (Evans and Knight 2000), West Deeping (Pryor 2001) and Colne Fen, Earith (Regan *et al* 2004; Evans and Patten 2003).

There is reasonably good evidence that the Tower's Fen field system developed piecemeal, albeit with reference to an axial NNE-SSW 'template' (Figs 4a-g), but there is no clear indication when or why the process started. It has been argued, for example in the Flag Fen basin (Pryor 2001, 407) and Barleycroft (Evans and Knight 2000) that earlier Bronze Age barrows and ring-ditches acted as landscape references or boundary markers for later sub-division using ditches and hedges. This development is not obvious from Tower's Fen, although a wider examination of the landscape may reveal evidence that the disposition of fields was in some way conditioned by later Neolithic/earlier Bronze Age traditions of land use. It is possible, however, that the ground was unsuitable for anything other than quite transient activity much before the Middle Bronze Age, and this may be a factor behind the piecemeal nature of land enclosure found here. There is certainly no evidence that droveways formed the primary elements of the division (cf Fengate, Perry Oaks) and indeed the only droveway at Tower's Fen is relatively late in the sequence. This suggests that a model which sees access for stock to summer grazing through allotted land as the prime motive for land division is not appropriate in this case.

The taking in of land for agriculture would have started with the clearance of the natural vegetation, although there is no direct indication as to when this took place. At least one of the pits on the site seems to have been dug purely to remove a tree, but there was no indication of its date and no reason to suppose that it belonged to a specific 'phase' of clearance pre-dating the creation of the fields. Pit 160, was the earliest dated feature and two radiocarbon determinations place it at the end of the 3rd millennium BC. The pit was certainly associated with occupation but it is not clear whether this was contemporary with the setting out of the fields, or somewhat earlier.

It is possible that clearance started with assarting, creating fields in a selective manner. It is difficult to know how this might be recognised archaeologically since ditches would not initially have been needed. Had they been added at the completion of the field, they might be recognisable as concave or otherwise irregular in plan. None of the Tower's Fen ditches give a good indication of this, but there are some irregular and intermittent ditches that suggest that they were laid out taking account of existing vegetation (or possibly other obstacles). They include Ditches 2009-2012, 2016 and 2014, all of which were probably relatively early features. The later ditches would be expected to be straighter with lines of sight becoming clearer over time. A notable example of this pattern has been demonstrated at Perry Oaks, Heathrow, where the north-south droveway boundaries, forming the primary elements of land division, are considerably more irregular than the later east-west subdivisions (Framework Archaeology 2006, 101). It is possible that this pattern of landscape development could be recognised more widely.

There is ample evidence that the Tower's Fen fields were bounded by hedgerows and the woody detritus showed a wide range of tree species, some coppiced. It is not known whether the hedgerows were deliberately planted or developed through natural colonisation of the field margins and ditch banks. It seems, however, that ditches on their own would not have been sufficient to control livestock, so it is likely that fences or hedges would have been employed as part of the overall design. It is interesting to note that much of the wood recovered in the excavations (overwhelmingly from the waterholes rather than the boundary ditches) was from mature coppiced trees (Taylor, Chapter 3). This may indicate the presence of nearby managed woodland, but it may rather suggest that the hedgerows were old ones, predating the waterholes (or at least their latest phases of use) by an appreciable period. While the time difference cannot be inferred reliably it is possible that the inception of the field system was several decades or conceivably centuries earlier than the dating obtainable from the fills of the pits.

There is also clear evidence from pollen and cereal grains that at least some of the fields were cultivated. The weed component in the plant assemblages also suggests the presence of arable land but at the same time evidence for meadow and pasture. The rove beetles in the insect assemblages are a clear indication of larger domesticates (cattle and horses). The presence of deer and pigs is shown in the animal bone assemblage. The inhabitants therefore engaged in a mixed agricultural economy within a landscape of woodland, scrub, grassland and arable fields.

As has been noted in relation to not dissimilar evidence from Perry Oaks, this kind of agricultural regime is somewhat at variance with recent models which have argued that bounded landscapes of droveways, fields and waterholes were related to intensive stock-rearing (Pryor 2001, 418-20; Yates 2001). It is possible that specialised stock-rearing was more localised than has often been suggested. At Flag Fen, for example, the pollen sequence shows cereal pollen throughout, and that "... it is likely that a mixed arable and pastoral agriculture was being practised throughout the period represented by these peats, that is, the Bronze Age ..." (Scaife 2001, 366-368). With now widespread evidence for bounded landscapes from the Middle Bronze Age onward, the challenge for future research is to characterise the agricultural regimes at a sub-regional level from a close appraisal of the evidence.

It has been suggested from the pottery, animal bones and charred grain that there was settlement among the enclosures at Tower's Fen. No structures as such were identified and the evidence is admittedly meagre, but it is in keeping with settlement evidence from similar sites. The excavations at Fengate (Pryor 2001), Holme (Evans and Patten 2003), Barleycroft (Evans and Knight 1997), and Perry Oaks (Framework Archaeology 2006) indicate that this type of settlement comprised individual or small groups of post- or wattle-built houses set at the edges or in the corners of fields – mostly in the same sort of locations as the waterholes. The evidence of structures is often minimal. Among the three 'probable' and three 'possible' settlements identified at Perry Oaks, for instance, there were no convincing building plans at all. Settlement 4 was only identified as such by its insect assemblage which included synanthropic beetles and insects dependent upon stinging nettles (Framework Archaeology 2006, 126). The nature of this type of settlement, dispersed among fields and with a low level of material culture, is one which is enigmatic but may relate to more temporary, task-specific inhabitation rather than a permanent home base. It contrasts with the larger nucleated settlement type, identified for instance at Welland Bank and possibly at Tower Works, Fengate, where round and rectangular structures are associated with dark earth and considerable quantities of domestic refuse (Pryor 2001, 411-2). So far there has been little opportunity to examine the relationship between these differing settlement types other than note the contrast.

There was no strong indication of non-domestic or ritual land use at Tower's Fen, although the bronze adze and collection of perforated shells, both from boundary contexts, were probably deliberately placed items rather than casual losses. Unusual placed deposits were not present in any of the waterholes or ponds although they are sometimes found in these contexts elsewhere (for instance, a wooden axe haft and 'beaters', and complete pottery vessels from Perry Oaks – Framework Archaeology 2006, 142). It is possible that almost any of the animal bone and pottery could have been deposited as part of ritual activity, but there was no indication of this. Waterholes are so characteristic of the later 2nd millennium BC in southern England, and rare earlier and subsequently, it is tempting and not unreasonable to see them as fulfilling some of the functions of the funerary/ceremonial monuments of the 3rd-4th millennium BC as arenas for the resolution of tensions and integration of communities through participation in ritual actions.

Bibliography

Allen, S E, (ed) 1974 *Chemical Analysis of Ecological Material,* Oxford: Blackwell Science

Allen, S J, 2006 *Report on the conservation of a prehistoric hollowed wooden vessel for Northamptonshire Archaeology,* York Archaeological Trust Conservation Laboratories, Report **2006/12**

Anderberg, A-L, 1994 *Atlas of Seeds: Part 4, Swedish Museum of Natural History,* Risbergs Trycheri AB, Uddevalla: Sweden

Atkinson, T C, Briffa, K R, and Coope, G R, 1987 Seasonal temperatures in Britain during the past 22,000 years, reconstructed using beetle remains, *Nature,* **325,** 587-592

Baker, J, and Brothwell, D, 1980 *Animal Diseases in Archaeology,* London, Academic Press

Balaam, N D, and Porter, H M, 1982 The Phosphate Surveys, in N D Balaam *et al* (eds), 215-219

Balaam, N D, Smith, K, and Wainwright, G J, (eds) 1982 The Shaugh Moor Project: fourth report – environment, context and conclusion, *Proceedings of the Prehistoric Society,* **48**

Bengtsson, L, and Enell, M, 1986 Chemical analysis, in B E Berglund (ed), 423-454

Berggren, G, 1981 *Atlas of Seeds: Part 3,* Swedish Museum of Natural History, Berlings, Arlöv: Sweden

Berglund, B E, (ed) 1986 *Handbook of Holocene Palaeoecology and Palaeohydrology,* Wiley: Chichester

Bethell, P, and Maté, I, 1989 The Use of Phosphate Analysis in Archaeology: A Critique, in J Henderson (ed)

Binford, L, 1978 *Nunamuit ethnoarchaeology*

Binford, L, 1981 *Bones: Ancient man and modern myths,* New York: Academy Press

Boessneck, J, 1969 Osteological differences between sheep and goat, in D Brothwell and E Higgs (eds), 331-358

Bowman, S, and Needham, S, in press The Dunaverney and Little Thetford flesh-hooks: history, technology and their position within the later Bronze Age Atlantic zone feasting complex, *Antiquaries Journal*

Brain, C K, 1981 *The Hunters or the Hunted?* Chicago: University of Chicago Press

Briard, J, and Verron, G, 1976 *Typologie des Objets de l'Age du Bronze en France, Fascicule IV: Haches (2), Herminettes,* Paris: Société Préhistorique Française, Commission du Bronze

Brothwell, D, and Higgs, E, (eds) 1969 *Science in archaeology,* London: Thames and Hudson

Brück, J, (ed) 2001 *Bronze Age Landscapes: Tradition and Transformation,* Oxbow Books

Bull, G, and Payne, S, 1982 Tooth eruption and epiphyseal fusion in pigs & wild boar, in B Wilson *et al* (eds), 55-77

Cavanagh, S, Hirst, S, and Litton, C D, 1988 Soil phosphate, site boundaries, and change point analysis, *Journal of Field Archaeology,* **15,** 67-83

Clason, A, (ed) 1975 *Archaeozoological Studies,* Amsterdam: N.Holland Publishing Co

Coates, G, and Cherrington, R, 2004 *Archaeological Evaluation at Thorney Borrow Pit, Pode Hole, Peterborough,* Phoenix Consulting, **PC/245/a**

Coates, G, and Richmond, A, 2004a *An Archaeological Contribution to an Environmental Impact Assessment, Thorney Borrow Pit, Pode Hole, Peterborough,* Phoenix Consulting, **PC/245/a**

Coates, G, and Richmond, A, 2004b *Specifications for an Archaeological Strip, Map & Sample Exercise: Thorney By-pass Borrow Pit, Tower's Fen, Pode Hole, Peterborough,* Phoenix Consulting, **PC/245d**

Cohen, A, and Serjeantson, D, 1996 *A manual for the identification of bird bones from archaeological sites,* Archetype Publications Ltd

Coles, J M, 1963-4 Scottish Middle Bronze Age metalwork, *Proceedings of the Society of Antiquaries of Scotland,* **97,** 82-156

Cutler, R, and Ellis, P, 2000 *A Bronze Age barrow and Romano-British features at Pode Hole Farm, Cambridgeshire,* Birmingham University Field Archaeology Unit, Report **439.01**

Davis, S J M, 1987 *Animals in Archaeology,* London Batsford

Davey, P J, 1973 Bronze Age metalwork from Lincolnshire, *Archaeologia,* **104,** 51-127

Davey, P J, and Forster, E, 1975 *Bronze Age metalwork from Lancashire and Cheshire,* University of Liverpool, Dept of Archaeology Work Notes, **1**

Dawson, M, (ed) 2000 *Prehistoric, Roman and post-Roman landscapes of the Great Ouse Valley,* Council British Archaeology Research Report, **119**

Drury, P J, 1978 *Excavations at Little Waltham 1970-71,* Council British Archaeology Research Report, **26,** Chelmsford Excavation Committee

Earwood, C, 1993 *Domestic Wooden Artefacts,* Exeter

Evans, C, and Knight, M, 2000 A Fenland delta: Later prehistoric land-use in the lower Ouse reaches, in M Dawson (ed), 89-106

Evans, C, and Patten, R, 2003 *Excavations at Colne Fen, Earith: the Holme Fieldsystem 2002,* Cambridge Archaeology Unit, Report **527**

Evans, J, 1881 *The Ancient Bronze Implements, Weapons and Ornaments of Great Britain and Ireland,* London: Longmans, Green & Co

Fieller, N R J, Gilbertson, D D, and Ralph, N G A, (eds) 1985 *Palaolobiological investigations,* British Archaeology Reports, International Series, **266**, Oxford

Forestry Commission 1956 Utilisation of hazel coppice, *Bulletin,* **27**, 33

Framework Archaeology 2006 *Landscape Evolution in the Middle Thames Valley: Heathrow Terminal 5 Excavations Volume 1,* Perry Oaks, Framework Archaeology Monog, **1**

French, C A I, 1991 *Proposed Mineral Extraction between Eye and Thorney, Cambridgeshire,* The Archaeological Statement

French, C A I, 2003 *Geoarchaeology in Action: Studies in Soil Micromorphology and Landscape Evolution,* Routledge

Gale, R, and Cutler, D, 2000 *Plants in Archaeology,* Westbury and RBG Kew: London

Gibson, A, and Woods, A, 1997 *Prehistoric Pottery for the Archaeologist,* Leicester University Press, second edition

Grant, A, 1982 The use of tooth wear as a guide to the age of domestic ungulates, in B Wilson *et al* (eds), 91-108

Grigson, C, 1982 Sex and age determination of some bones and teeth of domestic cattle: a review of the literature, in B Wilson (eds), 7-23

Grimm, E C, 1991 *TILIA and TILIA*GRAPH software package,* Springfield IL: Illinois State Museum

Hall, D, 1987 *The Fenland Project 2. Cambridgeshire Survey, Peterborough to March,* East Anglian Archaeol Report, **35**

Hall, D, and Coles, J, 1994 *Fenland Survey ; an essay in landscape and persistence,* English Heritage Archaeol, Report, **1**

Halstead, P, 1985 A study of mandibular teeth from Romano-British contexts at Maxey, in F Pryor and C A I French, 219-24

Henderson, J, (ed) 1989 *Scientific Analysis in Archaeology*

Hesse, B, and Wapnish, P, 1985 *Animal bone archaeology,* Washington D.C. Taraxacum

Hey, G, in prep *Yarnton: Neolithic and Bronze Age settlement and landscapes. Results of excavations 1989-1998,* Thames Valley Landscapes Monog, Oxford

Hillman, G, 1981 Reconstructing crop husbandry practises from charred remains of crops, in R Mercer (ed), 123-62

Hillman, G, 1984 Interpretation of archaeological plant remains: the application of ethnographic models from Turkey, in W Van Zeist and W A Casparie (eds), 1-44

Jones, A, 1996 *Excavations at Pode Hole Farm 1996,* Birmingham University Field Archaeology Unit Report

Jones, M, 1978 The plant remains, in M Parrington (ed), 93-110

Klein, R G, and Cruz-Uribe, K, 1984 *The Analysis of animal bones from Archaeological Sites,* Chicago: University of Chicago Press

Leonardi, G, 1999 Soil phosphorus analysis as an integrative tool for recognising buried ancient ploughsoils, *Journal of Archaeol, Science,* **26**, 343-352

Lyman, R, 1992 Anatomical considerations of utility curves in archaeozoology, *Journal of Archaeol Science,* **19**, 7-22

Lyman, R L, 1994 Quantitative units and terminology in zooarchaeology, *American Antiquity,* **59**, 36-71

Lyman, R L, 1994 *Vertebrate taphonomy,* Cambridge University Press

Martin, E, and Murphy, P, 1988 West Row Fen, Suffolk: a Bronze Age fen-edge settlement site, *Antiquity,* **62**, 353-8

Mercer, R, (ed) 1981 *Farming practice in British prehistory,* Edinburgh University Press

Moore, P D, Webb, J A, and Collinson, M E, 1991 *Pollen Analysis,* Blackwell: Oxford, second edition

Morris, E L, 2005 Appendix B: Prehistoric Ceramics Assessment, in Phoenix Consulting

Needham, S P, 1993 A Bronze Age goldworking anvil from Lichfield, Staffordshire, *Antiquaries Journal,* **73**, 125-132

Noddle, B, 1984 Exact chronology of epiphyseal closure in domestic mammals of the past, *Circaea,* **2**, 21-27

Palmer, R, 1996 *Pode Hole Farm Aerial Photographic Assessment,* Air Photo Services Report **R94**

Palmer, R, 2004 *Great Tower's Fen, Pode Hole - Aerial Photographic Assessment,* Air Photo Services Report **2004.19**

Parham, D, Needham, S, and Palmer, M, 2006 Questioning the wrecks of time, *British Archaeology* (November-December), 43-7

Parrington, M, (ed) 1978 *The excavation of an Iron Age Settlement, Bronze Age ring-ditches and Roman features at Ashville Trading Estate, Abingdon (Oxfordshire) 1974-6,* Oxford Archaeol Unit Report, **1**, Council British Archaeology Research Report, **28**

Payne, S, 1973 Kill off patterns in sheep and goats: the mandibles from Asvan Kale, *Anatolian Studies*, **23**, 281-303

Payne, S, 1975 Partial recovery and sample bias, in A Clason (eds), 7-17

Payne, S, and Munson, P, 1985 Ruby and how many squirrels? in N R J Fieller *et al* (eds), 31-40

Peglar, S M, and Wilson, D G, 1978 Appendix II The abandoned river channel, in P J Drury, 146-8

Pendleton, C, 2001 Firstly, let's get rid of ritual, in J Brück (ed), 170-8

Phoenix Consulting 2004 *Thorney By-pass Borrow Pit, Tower's Fen, Pode Hole, Peterborough,* Unpublished report

Phoenix Consulting 2005 *Pode Hole Quarry (Extraction Area 7), Archaeological Watching Brief and Excavation,* Phoenix Consulting Ltd for Aggregate Industries UK Ltd, January 2005

Pryor, F, 1974 *Excavation at Fengate, Peterborough, England,* The First Report, Royal Ontario Museum Monog **3**

Pryor, F, 1980 *Excavation at Fengate, Peterborough, England,* The Third Report, Royal Ontario Museum Monog, **6**, Northamptonshire Archaeol Soc Monog, **1**

Pryor, F, 1998 *Etton – Excavations at a Neolithic causewayed enclosure near Maxey, Cambs 1982-7,* English Heritage

Pryor, F, 1999 *Farmers in Prehistoric Britain*, Tempus

Pryor, F, 2001 *The Flag Fen Basin: Archaeology and Environment of a Fenland Landscape,* English Heritage Archaeological Reports

Pryor, F, and French, C A I, 1985 *The Fenland Project No.1: Archaeology and Environment in the Lower Welland Valley*, East Anglian Archaeol, **27**

Rackham, J, 1994 *Animal Bones,* London: BM Press

Regan, R, Evans, C, and Webley, L, 2004 *The Camp Ground Excavations, Colne Fen, Earith:* Assessment Report, Cambridge Archaeology Unit, Report, **654**

Reille, M, 1992 *Pollen et Spores d'Europe et d'Afrique du Nord,* Laboratoire de Botanique Historique et Palynologie: Marseille

Reitz, E J, and Wing, E S, 1999 *Zooarchaeology,* Cambridge University Press

Richmond, A, 2004 *Specifications for an archaeological strip, map and sample exercise: Thorney By-pass Borrow Pit, Tower's Fen, Pode Hole, Peterborough,* Phoenix Consulting Unpublished Report

Rowlands, M J, 1976 *The Production and Distribution of Metalwork in the Middle Bronze Age in Southern England,* British Archaeological Reports, British Series, **31** (2 vols) Oxford

Scaife, R, 2001 Flag Fen: the vegetation and environment, in F Pryor, 366-8

Schmid, E, 1972 *Atlas of Animal bones*, London: Elsevier

Schweingruber, F H, 1990 *Mikroskopische Holzanatomie. Anatomie microscopique du bois, Microscopic wood anatomy,* Swiss Federal Institute of Forestry Research

Silver, I, 1969 The ageing of domestic animals, in D Brothwell and E Higgs (eds), 283-302

Stace, C, 1997 *New Flora of the British Isles,* Cambridge University Press: Cambridge, second edition

Stallibras, S M, 1985 Some effects of preservation biases on interpretations of animal bones, in N R J Fieller, 65-73

Taylor, M, 1998 Wood and Bark from the Enclosure Ditch, in F Pryor

Taylor, M, 2001 The Wood, in F Pryor, 167-228

Tutin, T G, Heywood, V H, *et al* 1964-1980 *Flora Europaea,* 1-5, Cambridge: University Press

Van de Noort, R, Ellis, S, Taylor, M, and Weir, D, 1995 Preservation of archaeological sites, in R Van de Noort and S Ellis, 1995

Van de Noort, R, and Ellis, S, 1995 *Wetland Heritage of Holderness – an archaeological survey,* Humber Wetlands Project

Van Zeist, W, and Casparie, W A, (eds) 1984 *Plants and ancient man: studies in palaeoethnobotany, Proceedings of the Sixth Symposium of the International Work Group for Palaeoethnobotany,* 6th International Work Group for Palaeoethnobotany Symposium (1983), Balkema: Rotterdam

Von den Driech, A, 1976 *Guide to the measurement of Animal Bones from Archaeological sites,* Harvard University

Watson, J P N, 1979 The estimation of the relative frequencies of mammalian species: Khirokitia 1972, *Journal of Archaol, Science,* **6**, 127-37

Wilson, B, Grigson, C, and Payne, S, (eds) 1982 *Ageing and sexing animal bones from archaeological sites,* British Archaeology Reports British Series, **109**, 55-77 Oxford

Yates, D, 2001 Bronze Age agricultural intensification in the Thames Valley and Estuary, in J Brück (ed)

Appendix 1: Wood Catalogue

Maisie Taylor

Pit 160

Context 175 - Roundwood, 1 end/2 directions (felling scars) - 1 end missing, L.310mm D.100/85mm

Context 197 - (Bag 1) 20 pieces v. small twigs, general detritus, too small for analysis

14 pieces v. gnarled bark (Typical thickness 15-25mm), 2 stones

24 pieces roundwood, diameter 15mm down, probably too dry for analysis

(Bag 2) fragment very weathered coppice, 1 bone, fragments of bark

(Bag 3) 27 fragments roundwood, gnarled bark and weathered woodchips

(Bag 4) 2 fragments roundwood, 20 woodchips, mostly radial but very soft and weathered

Pit 1622

Context 1685 - Roundwood, forked, trimmed 1 end/2 direction (felled), 1 fork trimmed 1 direction other fork missing L.2370mm D.95mm

Context 1686 - Roundwood, trimmed 1 end/bluntly (too heavily mineralized for id) L.1090+ D.61/55mm (Possibly P and M and S but too decayed for any analysis)

Context 1622 - Timber Q, roundwood (20 frags. oak (*Quercus* sp.) and ash (*Fraxinus excelsior*) + 3 sampled for id, but all very weathered

Context 1663 - (i) Roundwood, both ends missing L.1470+mm D.92/81mm

(ii) Wood too dried out for analysis

Context 1646 - Timber, oak (*Quercus* sp.), radial split, partially squared, both ends decayed and missing L.910+ 50 x 29mm

Pit 1741

Context 1730 - Timber D – 1 piece of 2-piece vessel, carved from tree trunk of alder (*Alnus glutinosa*) with an integral, carved loop handle. 'Diameter' (external) 140/262mm H.358mm (269mm exc.loop handle), Th.10-17mm

A Roundwood both ends missing L.630+mm D.54/51mm

C Timber, thin radial split, hewn into oval dowel, probably important but both ends missing L.615+mm 59 x 16mm

D Timber, thin radial split, both ends missing L.570+mm 50 x 40mm

E Roundwood,trimmed, 1 end/1 direction, 1 end missing L.525+mm D.34mm

F Roundwood, 1 end/4 directions, 1 end missing, L.560+m D.49/42mm

G Roundwood, oak (*Quercus* sp.), 1 end/ 1 direction and thinned an one side L.520mm D.150/130mm

Context 1733 - H Roundwood,?coppiced?, 1 end/2 directions, 1 end missing L.680+mm D.32mm

½ split tree L.3920mm W.260mm Th.130mm

Pit 660

Context 653 - (i) ?Artefact – ¼ split with burr – oak (*Quercus* sp.) - ?kind of maul or hammer

(ii) Roundwood, 1 end/all directions, 1 end decayed L.530+mm D.95mm

(iii) Roundwood, oak (*Quercus* sp.) 1 end/all directions, 1 end decayed L.160+mm D.121/110mm

(iv) Roundwood, 1 end/all directions, 1 end decayed and 1 side branch missing, ?coppiced L.460+ D.75/61mm

Context 659 - Timber debris, split, trimmed all directions (stake tip) L.40mm 25 x 20mm

Pit 1942

Timber BA	Roundwood debris, ½ split, ash (*Fraxinus excelsior*), trimmed 1 end/1 direction, 1 end missing L.515+ x 67 x 29mm
Timber BB	Roundwood, ?coppice?, ash (*Fraxinus excelsior*) trimmed 1 end/3 directions L.650mm D.84mm
Stake BB	Roundwood, ?coppice?, ash (*Fraxinus excelsior*) tip missing L.490+mm D.80mm
Timber BD	Roundwood debris, ½ split, 2 ends/bluntly, L.360 x 80 x 45mm
Timber CC	Timber, oak (*Quercus* sp.), ¼ split, trimmed tangentially L.370+ x 130 x 45mm
	Timber debris, oak (*Quercus* sp.), rough radial split L.435 x 80 x 45mm
	Timber, ¼ split, trimmed square L.370+mm 130 x 45mm
	Timber from end CC, radial, mineralised L.435mm 80 x 45mm
Timber DD	Roundwood, ash (*Fraxinus excelsior*), trimmed 1 end/3 directions (compensating for curve) L.570 D.70mm
Timber EE	Timber, hewn plank, very fragmentary L.1740 x 210 x 35-55mm
Timber WW	Timber, ¼ split and squared with probable tow hole but badly broken on excavation L.1190mm 190 x 55mm
Context 1653 -	(1651) Roundwood, badly compressed L.230 x 90 x 45mm

Pond 1907

Context 1906 -

Timber R	Timber, ¼ split, trimmed 1 end/all directions, mortice joint (broken), half lap joint, toolmarks - partial in joint (30:2.5) and on end (27:2),1 end degraded L.805+mm 135 x 81mm
Timber JJ	Roundwood (tree), trimmed 1 end/felling notch L.3900 D.200mm
Timber LL	Radial split and trimmed 1 end/2 directions L.1147mm 100 x 60mm
Timber SS	Roundwood, felled tree, oak (*Quercus* sp.), rotted in half L.520 x 250 x 160mm
Timber UU	Timber (?coppice), tapering split, toolmark L.1405mm 240 x 10mm
Timber VV	Timber or timber debris (Badly damaged on excavation), ash (*Fraxinus excelsior*), ½ split, tapering L.555mm 145 x 55mm
Timber XX	Roundwood debris, ash (*Fraxinus excelsior*), ½ split and trimmed 1 side/1 blow, L.460 x 70 x 40mm
	Timber debris, split and trimmed across the grain, ash (*Fraxinus excelsior*)
	[1901 & 7] Roundwood, ?coppice?, sample D.37mm

Pond 1829

Context 1848 - Hazel nut fragments

Context 1849 - Hazel nut fragments

Context 1886 - Hazel nut fragments

Timber AE,	timber, oak (*Quercus* sp.), ½ split, trimmed 1 end/all directions L.480 x 140 x 80mm
Timber AH,	roundwood, oak (*Quercus* sp.), ends missing, possible verticals L.410+mm D.16mm
Timber AK,	timber, oak (*Quercus* sp.), tangential split, trimmed square L.130 x 70 x 40mm
Timber AM,	timber, oak (*Quercus* sp.), radial split, trimmed square, badly broken L.1040+ x 80 x 50mm
Timber AP,	timber, ½ split, trimmed 1 end/all directions L.620 x 130 x 120mm
	(ii)Roundwood, 1 end/1 direction, 1 end missing L.450mm D.40/26mm
	Roundwood, ends missing L.410+ D.16mm
	Roundwood, trimmed 1 end/1 direction, 1 end missing L.450+ D.40/26mm

Pit 1026

Context 1037 (1035)

(i) Roundwood, trimmed both ends/1 direction L.321mm D.58/50mm

(ii) Timber, radial split, trimmed 1 end/2 directions L.503mm 66 x55mm

(iii) Timber, radial sp, squared, trimmed 1 end/1 dir, 1 end broken L.561+ 50 x 32mm

(iv) Timber debris, thin radial split, squared, 1 end missing L.290+mm 44 x 30mm

Context 1038 -

(i) Timber, oak (*Quercus* sp.), radially split, tangentially modified square, trimmed 1 end/2 directions L.503 x 66 x 55mm

ii) Timber, oak (*Quercus* sp.), radially split, tangentially modified square, trimmed 1 end/1 direction L.561+ x 50 x 32mm

(iii) Timber debris, oak (*Quercus* sp.), thin radial split, tangentially modified square, trimmed 1 end/1 direction L.290+ x 44 x 30mm

Context 1049 -

1. Timber, oak (*Quercus* sp.), ¼ split, squared, trimmed 1 end/2 directions, 1 end decayed L.823mm 124 x 98mm

2. Roundwood, oak (*Quercus* sp.)1 end/1 direction and torn, 1 end missing, possibly felled tree L.420+mm D.90/74mm

3. Not wood (peat)

Trench 2 - Roundwood, oak (*Quercus* sp.), trimmed 1 end/1 direction (felled tree) L.415 D.90/80mm

Context 564 -

Ditch 563 (labelled 664) Roundwood, possibly root, partially mineralised L.70mm D.20mm

Pond Samples

Pond sample 1 - Roundwood, fork, oak (*Quercus* sp.) L.sample D.45/33mm

Pond sample 2 - Roundwood, ?coppice? L.sample D.37mm

Pond sample 3 - Roundwood, ?coppice? L.sample D.23mm

Pond sample 4 - Roundwood, ?coppice? L.sample D.38mm

Pond sample 5 - Roundwood, ?coppice?, trimmed 1 end/1 direction L.sample D.18mm

Pond sample 6 - Roundwood, ?coppice? L.sample D.35mm

Pond sample 7 - Roundwood, ?coppice? L.sample D.17mm

Pond sample 9 - Roundwood, ?coppice? L.sample D.23mm

Pond sample 10 - Roundwood, ?coppice?, trimmed 1 end/3 directions, L.sample D.45mm

Pond sample 11 - Roundwood, ?coppice?, trimmed 1 end/3 directions, L.sample D.47mm

Pond sample 12 - Roundwood, ?coppice? L.sample D.38mm

Pond sample 13 - Roundwood, ?coppice? L.sample D.40mm

Pond sample 14 - Roundwood, ?coppice? L.sample D.22mm

Pond sample 15 - Roundwood, ?coppice? L.sample D.30mm

Pond sample 16 - Roundwood, ?coppice? L.sample D.42mm

Pond sample 17 - Roundwood, ?coppice? L.sample D.37mm

Pond sample 18 - Roundwood, ?coppice? L.sample D.22mm

Pond sample 19 - Roundwood ?coppice? L.sample D.22mm

Pond sample 20 - Roundwood L.sample D.45mm

Pond sample 21 - Roundwood L.sample D.47mm

Pond sample 22 - Roundwood, ?coppice? L.sample D.40mm

Pond sample 23 - Roundwood, ?coppice? L.sample D.36mm

Pond sample 24 - Roundwood, ?coppice? L.sample D.10mm

Pond sample 25 - Roundwood, ?coppice? L.sample D.16mm

Pond sample - Roundwood, forked, ?coppice? but too damaged D.45mm

Timber debris, split and trimmed across the grain L.165mm 70 x 50mm

Appendix 2: **Environmental Evidence: Tables 4.6 - 4.13**

N P Branch, I Poole, B Silva, S Elias C P Green, A Vaughan-Williams and I Valcarcel

Feature	Context Number	Sample Number	Area	Waterlogged Remains	Charred Remains	Insects	Waterlogged wood	Charcoal	Main Taxa
Pond 1907	1902	<81>	5	High		Yes	A3		Stellaria media
Pond 1907	1948	<83>	5		Low	Yes			Rosa sp., Rumex sp., Chenopodium album, Stellaria media
Pit 1942	1951	<84>	5						
Pit 1942	1947	<82>	5	High			A3		
Pit 1942	1946	<80>	5						
Pit 1860	1858	<76>	5	Medium			A2		
Pit 1741	1816	<75>	5		Low		A3		Ranunculus repens, Rubus sp., Polygonum hydropiper
Pit 1741	1731	<74>	5			Yes	A3		
Pit 1741	1730	<73>	5		Low		A3		Ranunculus sp.
Pit 1714	1705	<65>	5	Low					
Pit 1714	1700	<64>	5		Low				
Pit 1714	1699	<63>	5	Low				A3	
Pit 1659	1658	<60>	5	Low					
Pit 1622	1638	<61>	5	Medium					Rubus sp. Chenopodium sp.
Pit 1622	1631	<62>	5	Low			O1		Rubus sp.
Pit 1608	1610	<58>	5	Low					Chenopodium album, Atriplex sp. Stellaria media, Rubus sp., Solanum dulcamara
Pit 1608	1605	<57>	5		Medium		A2		Rubus sp, Atriplex sp., Chenopodium album, Polygonum hydropiper, Solanum sp., Stellaria media
Pit 1577	1574	<56>	5				O1	O2	Hordeum sp.
Pit 1577	1573	<55>	5					O1	

Table 4.6: Plant macrofossil assessment for all bulk samples, (A=abundant; F=frequent; O=occasional; 1=unidentifiable; 2=identifiable?; 3=identifiable)

Feature	Context Number	Sample Number	Area	Waterlogged Remains	Charred Remains	Insects	Waterlogged wood	Charcoal	Main Taxa
Pit 1029	1030	<40>	4						
Pit 1026	1036	<45>	4		Low			O1	
Pit 1026	1033	<43>	4		Low				Sambucus nigra, Rubus sp.
Pit 660	659	<30>	3		Low			O1	Rubus sp.
Pit 660	657	<32>	3	Medium					Rubus sp., Stellaria media
Pit 660	654	<34>	3	Medium					Rubus sp.
Pit 660	652	<31>	3		Low			O1	Polygonum sp., Chenopodium album, Urtica dioica, Stellaria media
Pit 660	648	<35>	3	Medium			A2/3		
Pit 650	644	<33>	3					O1	
Pit 650	641	<36>	3						
Pit 193	176	<13>	1					A3	
Pit 187	186	<17>	1						
Pit 160	175	<12>	1					A3	
Pit 72	71	<7>	1	Medium			O3	A3	Atriplex sp.
Pit 72	70	<4>	1	Medium	Low			A3	
Pit 72	69	<6>	1					A3	
Pit 72	68	<5>	1		Low			O1	Triticum sp. grain, Poaceae sp.
Pit 61	60	<2>	1		Low		A2	A3	Galium sp., Fabaceae sp.
Pit 20	97	<8>	1	Medium			F2/3	O1	
Ditch 2029 [1925]	1923	<77>	5	Low	Low			O1	
Ditch 2028 [1797]	1795	<71>	5		Low		O1		
Ditch 2026 [1696]	1688	<67>	5	Low				O1	

Table 4.6: Plant macrofossil assessment for all bulk samples, (A=abundant; F=frequent; O=occasional; 1=unidentifiable; 2=identifiable?; 3=identifiable)

Feature	Context Number	Sample Number	Area	Waterlogged Remains	Charred Remains	Insects	Waterlogged wood	Charcoal	Main Taxa
Ditch 2031 [1651]	1653	<59>	5	Medium					
Ditch 2038 [1567]	1564	<52>	5				O1	O2	Hordeum sp.
Ditch 2032 [1557]	1556	<50>	5					F3	
Ditch 2032 [1557]	1555	<49>	5	Low			O1		Triticum aestivum; Triticum sp.
Ditch 2035 [1554]	1558	<48>	5					O2	
Ditch 2035 [1554]	1552	<47>	5		Low			F2	Atriplex sp., Galium / Asperula sp., Chenopodium album
Ditch 2035 [1547]	1546	<51>	5	Low	Low			A3	Hordeum sp. grain, Polygonum sp.; Artiplex sp., Rubus sp.
Ditch 2035 [1547]	1545	<53>	5		Low				Artiplex sp Cereale indet
Ditch 2037 [1544]	1543	<46>	5	Low	Low		O2		
Ditch 2015 [1092]	1090	<42>	4	*			O1		
Ditch 2016 [1060]	1058	<41>	4	Low	Low			O1	Rubus sp.
Ditch 2043 [613]	612	<23>	3				O1		
Ditch 2041 [593]	601	<24>	3					O1	
Ditch 2041 [593]	600	<25>	3	Low				O1	
Ditch 2045 [551]	550	<27>	3						

Table 4.6: Plant macrofossil assessment for all bulk samples, (A=abundant; F=frequent; O=occasional; 1=unidentifiable; 2=identifiable?; 3=identifiable)

Feature	Context Number	Sample Number	Area	Waterlogged Remains	Charred Remains	Insects	Waterlogged wood	Charcoal	Main Taxa
Ditch 2045 [551]	549	<22>	3				O1		
Ditch 2047 [523]	525	<29>	3				O1		
Ditch 2047 [523]	524	<28>	3				O1		
Ditch 2040 [522]	526	<26>	3					O1	
Ditch 2014 [192]	190	<18>	1				O1	O1	
Ditch 2014 [184]	179	<14>	1					O1	
Ditch 2005 [173]	171	<15>	1	Low	Low				
Ditch 2014 [137]	136	<11>	1					A3	
Posthole 15	16	<1>	1					A3	

Table 4.6: Plant macrofossil assessment for all bulk samples, (A=abundant; F=frequent; O=occasional; 1=unidentifiable; 2=identifiable?; 3=identifiable)

Taxa	English Name	Ditch [173]	Ditch [593]	Ditch [1060]	Ditch [1544]	Ditch [1651]	Ditch [1696]	Ditch [1925]	Pit [20]	Pit [72]	Pit [660]	Pit [660]	Pit [660]	Pit [1608]	Pit [1622]	Pit [1622]	Pit [1659]	Pit [1714]	Pit [1860]	Pit [1942]	Pond [1907]
Context Number		(171)	(600)	(1058)	(1543)	(1653)	(1688)	(1923)	(97)	(70)	(648)	(654)	(657)	(1610)	(1631)	(1638)	(1658)	(1705)	(1858)	(1947)	(1902)
Sample Number		<15>	<25>	<41>	<46>	<59>	<67>	<77>	<8>	<4>	<35>	<34>	<32>	<58>	<62>	<61>	<60>	<65>	<76>	<82>	<81>
Sample vol. (l)		20	20	20	10	20	10	10	30	40	10	10	20	20	20	20	10	40	10	20	20
Ranunculus repens	Creeping buttercup												1					1			4
Fumaria sp.	Fumitories	1															1				
Urtica dioica	Common nettle														1		1		2		
Corylus avellana	Hazelnut										2										
Chenopodium album	Fat hen	1	2	16	1	4								12	25	31					
Atriplex sp.	Orache	1	1		1	5	2			2				10	19		10		4		
Stellaria media	Common chickweed					40							30	160	6	24			5		198
Polygonum sp.	Knotgrasses																1				
Polygonum persicaria	Redshank																				1
Polygonum Sect. *Avicularia*	Knotgrasses	1		1											4						6
Rumex sp.	Docks														6	6			1		

Table 4.7a: Plant macrofossil analysis (waterlogged remains)

Feature	Context Number	Sample Number	Sample vol. (l)	Viola sp.	Brassica / Sinapsis sp.	Brassicaceae indet.	Rubus sp.	Potentilla sp.	Vicia sp.	Euphorbia peplus	cf. Linum sp.	Apiaceae indet.	Apium sp.	Torilis japonica	Solanum dulcamara
English Name				Violet	Cabbage / mustard	Cabbage family	Bramble	Cinquefoil	Vetch	Petty spurge	Flax	Carrot family	Marshwort	Upright hedge-parsley	Bittersweet
Ditch [173]	(171)	<15>	20												
Ditch [593]	(600)	<25>	20												
Ditch [1060]	(1058)	<41>	20				100								
Ditch [1544]	(1543)	<46>	10												
Ditch [1651]	(1653)	<59>	20												
Ditch [1696]	(1688)	<67>	10				5								
Ditch [1925]	(1923)	<77>	10								1				
Pit [20]	(97)	<8>	30	1		1	17								
Pit [72]	(70)	<4>	40												
Pit [660]	(648)	<35>	10	1			57								
Pit [660]	(654)	<34>	10				55								
Pit [660]	(657)	<32>	20				53								2
Pit [1608]	(1610)	<58>	20				1								3
Pit [1622]	(1631)	<62>	20	3	2		120			1		1			11
Pit [1622]	(1638)	<61>	20										1	1	88
Pit [1659]	(1658)	<60>	10				15								
Pit [1714]	(1705)	<65>	40				18						1		1
Pit [1860]	(1858)	<76>	10				9								5
Pit [1942]	(1947)	<82>	20				4		1						
Pond [1907]	(1902)	<81>	20					5							
Taxa				Viola sp.	Brassica / Sinapsis sp.	Brassicaceae indet.	Rubus sp.	Potentilla sp.	Vicia sp.	Euphorbia peplus	cf. Linum sp.	Apiaceae indet.	Apium sp.	Torilis japonica	Solanum dulcamara

Table 4.7a: Plant macrofossil analysis (waterlogged remains)

98

Taxa	English Name	Pond [1907] (1902) <81> 20	Pit [1942] (1947) <82> 20	Pit [1860] (1858) <76> 10	Pit [1714] (1705) <65> 40	Pit [1659] (1658) <60> 10	Pit [1622] (1638) <61> 20	Pit [1622] (1631) <62> 20	Pit [1608] (1610) <58> 20	Pit [660] (657) <32> 20	Pit [660] (654) <34> 10	Pit [660] (648) <35> 10	Pit [72] (70) <4> 40	Pit [20] (97) <8> 30	Ditch [1925] (1923) <77> 10	Ditch [1696] (1688) <67> 10	Ditch [1651] (1653) <59> 20	Ditch [1544] (1543) <46> 10	Ditch [1060] (1058) <41> 20	Ditch [593] (600) <25> 20	Ditch [173] (171) <15> 20
Stachys arvensis	Field woundwort			5																	
Stachys sp.	Woundwort																		1		
Galeopsis sp.	Hempnettle						4														
Asperula arvensis	Blue woodruff																			1	
Galium verum	Lady's bedstraw																		1		
Sambucus nigra	Elder		1			7										2			2	44	
Centaurea sp.	Knapweed	1			1						1	1		2							
Lactuca cf. *sativa*	Garden lettuce	2			1		1			1											
Cyperaceae indet.	Sedges	4																			
	Nutlets										11				8						
	Buds		15									3									

Table 4.7a: Plant macrofossil analysis (waterlogged remains)

99

Genus	English Name		Pit [1714]	Pit [72]	Ditch [1925]	Ditch [1544]	Ditch [1060]	Ditch [593]	Ditch [173]
		Feature							
		Context Number	(1700)	(70)	(1923)	(1543)	(1058)	(600)	(171)
		Sample Number	<64>	<4>	<77>	<46>	<41>	<25>	<15>
		Sample vol. (l)	20	40	10	10	20	20	20
Atriplex sp.	Orache				1				
Rumex sp.	Docks					1			
Rosa sp.	Roses				4				
cf. *Lens* sp.	Lentil				6	1			
Fabaceae sp.	Pea family					3			
Geranium cf. columbinum	Long-stalked crane's-bill					1			
Anthriscus sp.	Chervils					1			
Stachys sp.	Woundwort				1				
Galium sp.	Bedstraw		1			1	6		1
Hordeum sp.	Hulled barley			2		1			
Triticum sp.	Wheat			11					
Hordeum / Triticum sp.	Barley / Wheat					2			
Poaceae sp.	Grass				1	3			

Table 4.7b: Plant macrofossil analysis (charred remains)

Feature	Pond [1907]	Pond [1907]	Pit [1741]
Context Number	(1902)	(1948)	(1731)
Sample Number	<81>	<83>	<74>
Area	5	5	5
Taxon			
COLEOPTERA			
Carabidae			
Carabus sp.		1	
Dyschirius luedersi Wagn.	1		
Dyschirius sp.			1
Trechus quadristriatus Schr.		1	
Bembidion aeneum Germ.		1	
Bembidion biguttatum (F.)	2		
Bembidion spp.	2		
Pterostichus minor (Gyll.)			1
Pterostichus spp.	2	1	
Amara lunicollis Schiodt.	1		
Agonum thoreyi Dej.	1		
Anisodactylus nemorivagus Duft.	1		
Badister meridionalis Puel.	1		
Badister sordis (Duft.)	1		
Lebia cruxminor (L.)			1
Genus indet.	2		
Dytiscidae			
Colymbetes striatus L.	1	1	
Hydroporus palustris (L.)	1		
Hydroporus sp.	1		
Agabus sp.	1		
Graphoderus sp.	1		
Rhantus exoletus (Forst.)	1		
Hydrophilidae			
Helophorus brevipalpus Bed.	2		
Helophorus nubilus Fab.		2	
Helophorus spp.		1	1
Cercyon marinus Thom.	1		
Cercyon sp.		1	
Hydrobius fuscipes (L.)	1		
Chaetarthria seminulum (Herbst.)	7		

Table 4.8: Insect analysis (in minimum number of individuals per sample)

Feature	Pond [1907]	Pond [1907]	Pit [1741]
Context Number	(1902)	(1948)	(1731)
Sample Number	<81>	<83>	<74>
Area	5	5	5
Taxon			
Hydraenidae			
Limnebius papposus Muls.		1	1
Ochthebius minimus (F.)	304	15	7
Leptinidae			
Catops sp.	2	1	
Staphylinidae			
Anthobium atrocephalum (Payk.)	1	2	
Bledius spp.			2
Stenus spp.	1		
Quedius spp.	2		1
Lathrobium sp.	3		
Anotylus sculpturatus Grav.	2		
Oxytelus sp.		1	
Platystethus cf. cornutus (Grav.)	2		
Tachinus signatus Dej.	1		
Tachinus sp.	2		
Aleocharinae		1	
Cordalia sp.			1
Pselaphidae			
Rybaxis cf. laminata (Mots.)			1
Scarabaeidae			
Aphodius distinctus (Müll.)		1	
Aphodius sp.	3	4	2
Dryopidae			
Helichus sp.	1		
Elateridae			
Athous haemorrhoidalis (Fab.)		1	
Anthicidae			
Anthicus spp.		2	
Corylophidae			
Corylophus cassidoides (Marsh).		1	
Chrysomelidae			
Donacia spp.	1	1	1

Table 4.8: Insect analysis (in minimum number of individuals per sample)

102

Feature	Pond [1907]	Pond [1907]	Pit [1741]
Context Number	(1902)	(1948)	(1731)
Sample Number	<81>	<83>	<74>
Area	5	5	5
Taxon			
Chrysomela aenea L.	1		
Plagiodera versicolora (Laich.)			1
Prasocuris phellandrii (L.)	1		
Altica sp.	1		
Curculionidae			
Apion sp.	1		
Sitona sp.	1	1	
Rhynchites spp.		1	
Rhynchaenus fagi (L.)	1		
Rhyncolus cf. punctatulatus Sch.		1	1
Bagous alismatis (Marsh.)	1		
Bagous sp.		1	
Rhynoncus bruchoides (Herbst)		1	
Genus indet.			
Scolytidae			
Ernoporus caucasicus (Lind.)	1		
TRICHOPTERA			
Limnephilidae			
Genus indet.	1		
HYMENOPTERA			
Formicidae			
Lasius sp.		2	
Formica sp.	1		

Table 4.8: Insect analysis (in minimum number of individuals per sample)

Family (subfamily)	Genus/species	Common Name	Comments
BETULACEAE	*Alnus*	alder	species cannot be differentiated
	Corylus avellana	hazel	only native of this genus
CAPRIFOLIACEAE/ OLEACEAE	*Lonicera* sp. *Ligustrum vulgare*	honeysuckle privet	often difficult to differentiate due to anatomical similarity
ROSACEAE (Pomoideae)	*Prunus* sp.	plum, cherry etc.	species cannot be differentiated
SALICACEAE	*Salix* sp. *Populus* sp.	willow poplar	often difficult to differentiate due to anatomical similarity

Table 4.9: Waterlogged wood analysis

Feature	Pit [1942]	Pit [1860]	Pit [1741]	Pit [20]
Context Number	(1947)	(1858)	(1730)	(97)
Sample Number	<82>	<76>	<73>	<8>
Area	5	5	5	1
Taxon				
Alnus		1 (rw)		9+?2(u)
Lonicera/Ligustrum	1+?1(u)			
Prunus			?1(tw)	
Salix sp./*Populus* sp.			2+?3(rw, tw)	2(u)
Corylus avellana				1
Unidentifiable	7†	2*†	0	4
Total	**9**	**3**	**6**	**18**

Table 4.10: Waterlogged wood analysis.
(Numbers refer to number of pieces of wood with anatomical consistency to the taxon indicated; When certain characters were missing or not located such that the identification is uncertain this can been identified by the preceding '?'; This unidentified section contains: one piece of bark * waterlogged charcoal †, round wood <20mm †, twig material tw, unknown maturity u)

Family (subfamily)	Genus/species	Common Name	Comments
BETULACEAE	*Alnus* sp.	alder	species cannot be differentiated
	Betula sp.	birch	species cannot be differentiated
	Carpinus betulus	hornbeam	only native of this genus
	Corylus avellana	hazel	only native of this genus
FAGACEAE	*Fagus sylvatica*	beech	only native of this genus
	Quercus sp.	oak	species cannot be differentiated
OLEACEAE	*Fraxinus excelsior*	ash	only native of this genus
ROSACEAE (Pomoideae)	*Cratagus* *Malus* sp. *Pyrus* sp. *Sorbus* sp.	hawthorn apple pear rowan & whitebeam	genera and species cannot be differentiated beyond subfamily on wood characters alone. Identifications most probably include *Sorbus* sp. and possibly *Crataegus* sp.
	Prunus sp.	plum, cherry etc.	species cannot be differentiated
SALICACEAE	*Salix* sp. *Populus* sp.	willow poplar	often difficult to differentiate due to anatomical similarity
ULMACEAE	*Ulmus* sp.	elm	species cannot be differentiated

Table 4.11: Charcoal analysis

Feature	Pit [1714]	Pit [160]	Pit [72]	Pit [61]	Ditch [1925]	Ditch [1696]	Ditch [1547]	Ditch [1060]	Ditch [593]	Ditch [137]
Context Number	(1699)	(175)	(70)	(60)	(1923)	(1688)	(1545)	(1058)	(600)	(136)
Sample Number	<63>	<12>	<4>	<2>	<77>	<67>	<53>	<41>	<25>	<11>
Area	5	1	1	1	5	5	5	4	3	1
Taxon										
Fagus sylvatica			3+?2(u)							
Quercus sp.		1(u)	12(u)	4(u)		3+?4(u)	2(u)	4+?4(u)	11+?7(u)	22+?3(u)
Corylus avellana		2+?1(u)	3(u)	2(u)			9+?1 (u, rw)		?2(u)	
Carpinus betulus			?1(u)							
Salix sp./ *Populus* sp.	64+?29(u)		18(u)	1(u)	8+?3					
Ulmus sp							1(u)			
Fraxinus sp.		12+?6(u)					71+?4(u)			
Pomoideae		1+?1(u)								
Alnus			31(u)	2+?4(u)	4+?2		?3			
Betula		?1(u)					1(u)			
Prunus			1(u)	44+?6(u)	1+?2 (u, rw)			3+?2(u)		
Unidentifiable	7(u)	25*(u)	29(u)	37(u)	30†(u)	43*(u)	9(u)	37*(u)	30*(u)	25(u)
Total	**100**	**50**	**100**	**100**	**50**	**50**	**100**	**50**	**50**	**50**

*Table 4.12: Charcoal analysis (Numbers refer to pieces of wood with anatomical consistency with the taxon indicated, when certain characters were missing or not located such that the identification is uncertain this can been identified by the preceding '?'; *this unidentified section is high because the material did not have large enough transverse diameter (c. 2mm) to enable identification, † includes pieces of root wood; rw, round wood <20mm; u, unknown maturity)*

105

Feature	Context Number	Sample Number	Area	Concentration of P(ppb)	Concentration of P minus blank effect (ppb)	Concentration of P (ppm)	Concentration (mg of P/Kg of air dry soil)
NATURAL	(0)	<3>		3707.448	3677.839	3.677839	919.45975
Pit [1714]	(1700)	<64>	5	6312.471	6282.862	6.282862	1570.7155
Pit [1714]	(1699)	<63>	5	5706.23	5676.621	5.676621	1419.15525
Pit [1659]	(1658)	<60>	5	3605.121	3575.512	3.575512	857.967
Pit [1608]	(1605)	<57>	5	3502.781	3473.172	3.473172	868.293
Pit [1577]	(1574)	<56>	5	3436.832	3407.223	3.407223	851.80575
Pit [1577]	(1573)	<55>	5	6822.286	6792.677	6.792677	1698.16925
Pit [650]	(644)	<33>	3	10955.906	10926.297	10.926297	2731.57425
Pit [650]	(641)	<36>	3	4167.761	4138.152	4.138152	1034.538
Pit [193]	(176)	<13>	1	12307.948	12278.339	12.278339	3069.58475
Pit [188]	(186)	<17>	1	2990.891	2961.282	2.961282	740.3205
Pit [160]	(175)	<12>	1	6822.286	6792.677	6.792677	1698.16925
Pit [72]	(69)	<6>	1	13930.703	13901.094	13.901094	3475.2735
Pit [61]	(60)	<2>	1	9620.563	9590.954	9.590954	2397.7385
Ditch 2028 [1797]	(1795)	<71>	5	1372.281	1342.672	1.342672	335.668
Ditch 2026 [1696]	(1693)	<68>	5	3400.429	3370.82	3.37082	842.705
Ditch 2038 [1567]	(1564)	<52>	5	3707.448	3677.839	3.677839	919.45975
Ditch 2032 [1557]	(1556)	<50>	5	4757.13	4727.521	4.727521	1181.88025
Ditch 2032 [1557]	(1555)	<49>	5	2643.479	2613.87	2.61387	653.4675
Ditch 2035 [1547]	(1545)	<53>	5	6074.982	6045.373	6.045373	1511.34325
Ditch 2037 [1544]	(1543)	<46>	5	3278.232	3248.623	3.248623	812.15575
Ditch 2016 [1060]	(1058)	<41>	4	2786.045	2756.436	2.756436	689.109
Ditch 2043 [613]	(612)	<23>	3	3707.448	3677.839	3.677839	919.45975
Ditch 2041 [593]	(601)	<24>	3	4176.501	4146.892	4.146892	1036.723
Ditch 2041 [593]	(600)	<25>	3	2219.997	2190.388	2.190388	547.597
Ditch 2045 [551]	(550)	<27>	3	2478.681	2449.072	2.449072	612.268
Ditch 2047 [523]	(525)	<29>	3	2222.457	2192.848	2.192848	548.212
Ditch 2047 [523]	(524)	<28>	3	1637.3	1607.691	1.607691	401.92275
Ditch 2014 [184]	(179)	<14>	1	2008.162	1978.553	1.978553	494.63825
Ditch 2005 [173]	(171)	<15>	1	1902.221	1872.612	1.872612	468.153
Ditch 2007 [170]	(190)	<18>	1	1690.292	1660.683	1.660683	415.17075
Ditch 2014 [137]	(136)	<11>	1	5189.754	5160.145	5.160145	1290.03625

Table 4.13: Phosphate analysis

www.ingramcontent.com/pod-product-compliance
Lightning Source LLC
Chambersburg PA
CBHW051302270326

41926CB00030B/4700